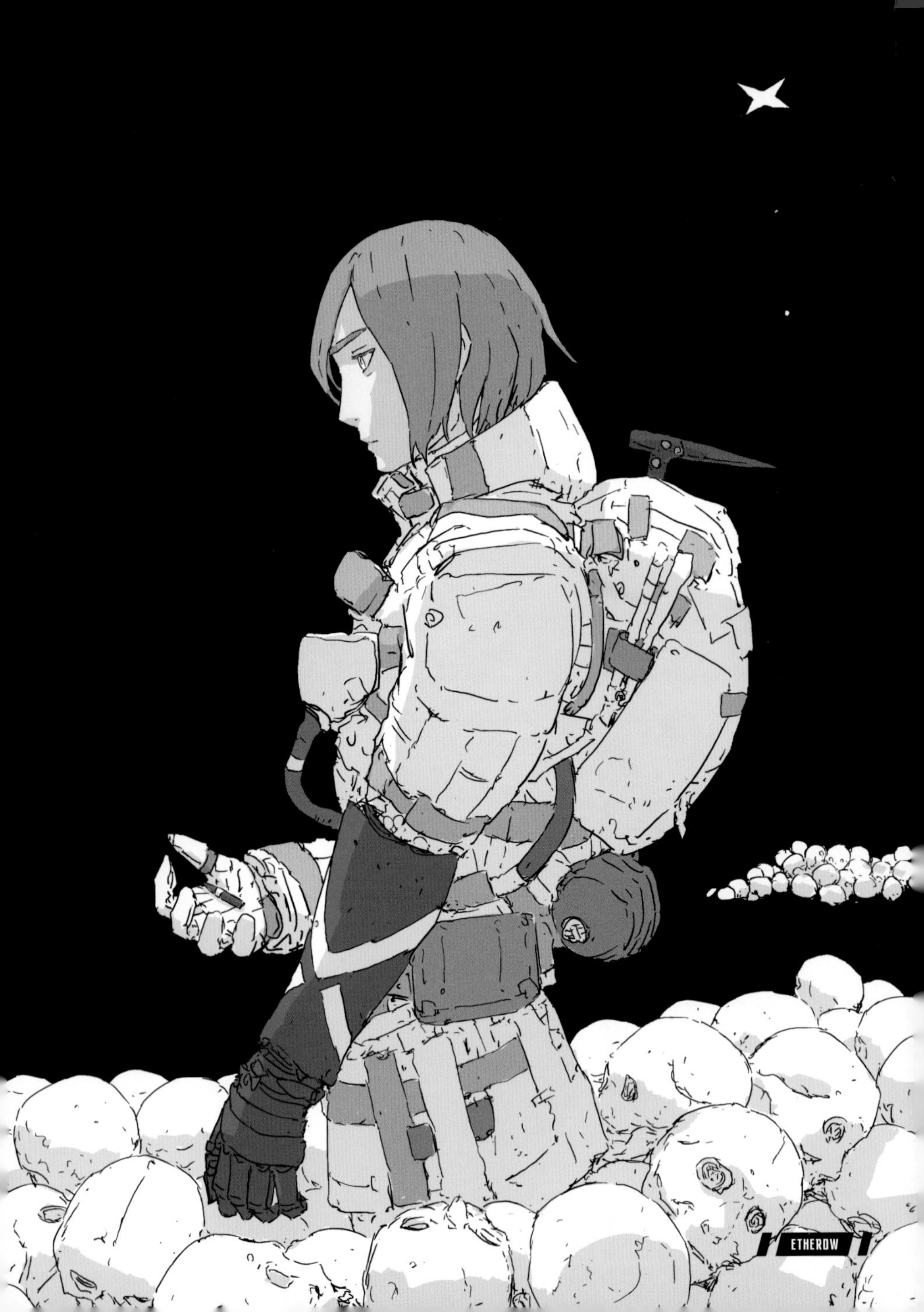
ETHEROW

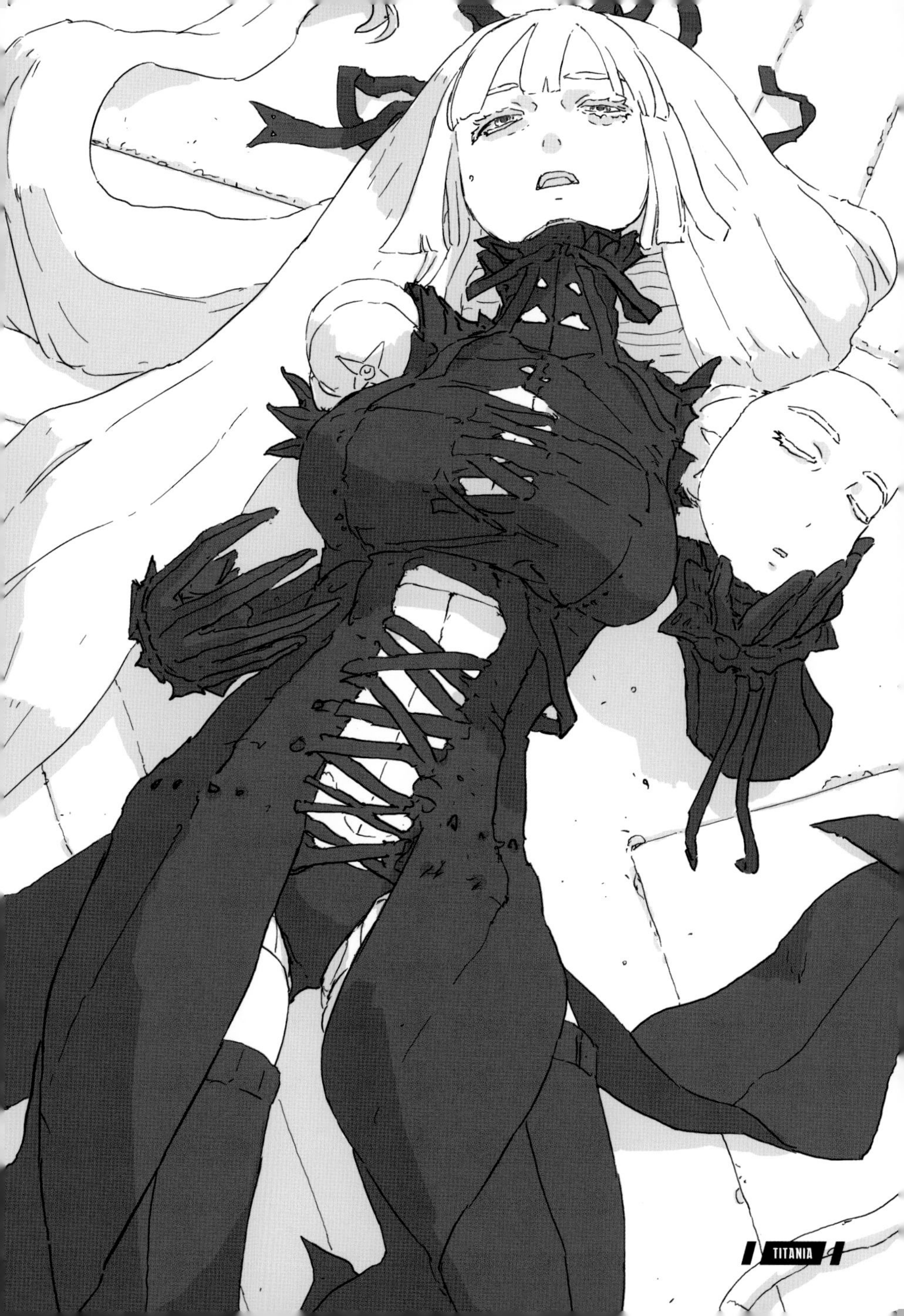
TITANIA

A P O S I M Z

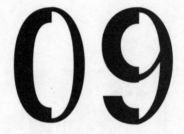

**TSUTOMU
NIHEI**

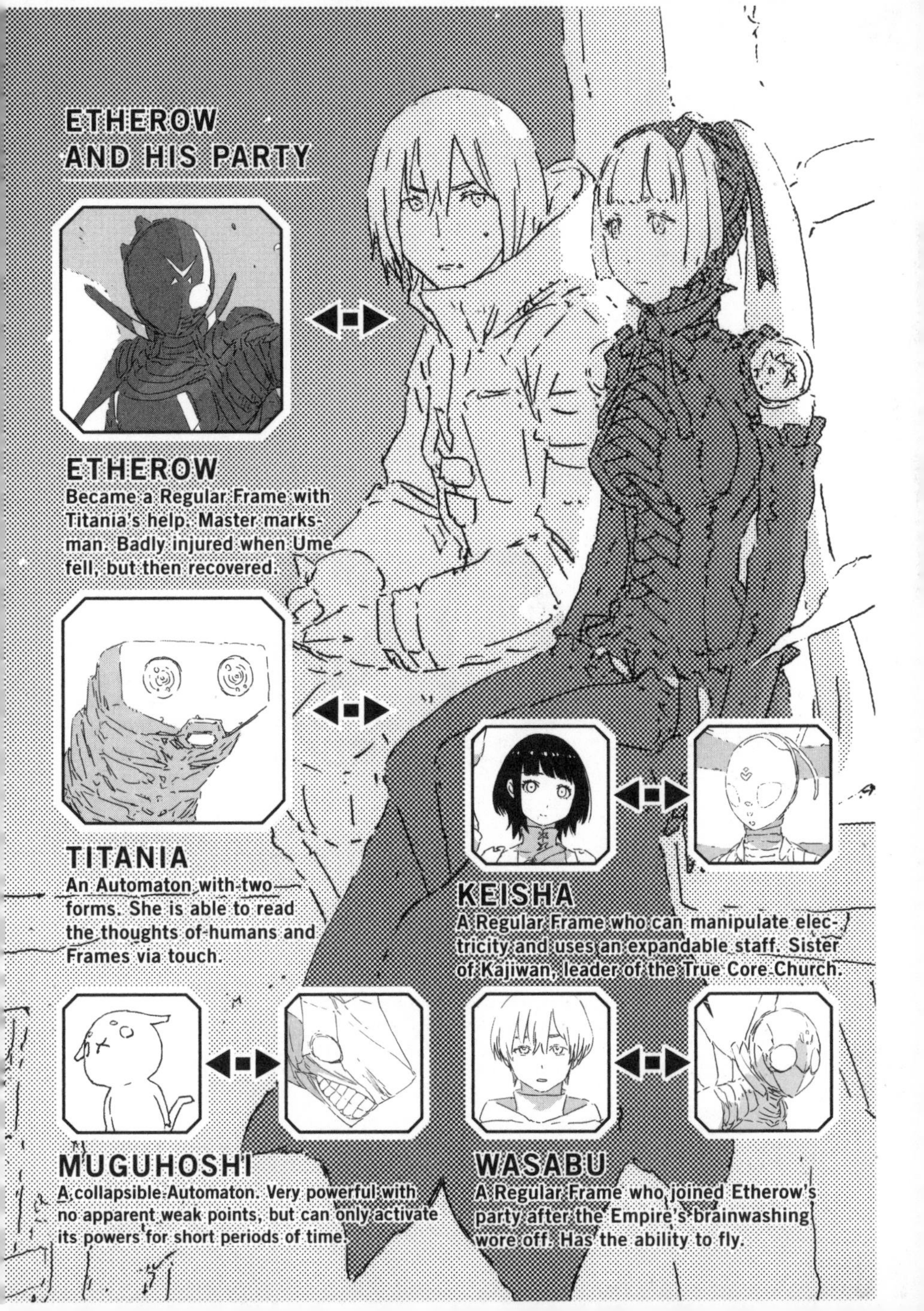
ETHEROW AND HIS PARTY
ETHEROW
Became a Regular Frame with Titania's help. Master marksman. Badly injured when Ume fell, but then recovered.
TITANIA
An Automaton with two forms. She is able to read the thoughts of humans and Frames via touch.
KEISHA
A Regular Frame who can manipulate electricity and uses an expandable staff. Sister of Kajiwan, leader of the True Core Church.
MUGUHOSHI
A collapsible Automaton. Very powerful with no apparent weak points, but can only activate its powers for short periods of time.
WASABU
A Regular Frame who joined Etherow's party after the Empire's brainwashing wore off. Has the ability to fly.

PLOT AND CHARACTER INTRO

REBEDOAN EMPIRE

A militant state with powerful, heavily-armed forces that continues to invade various regions. Has many Regular Frames in its ranks.

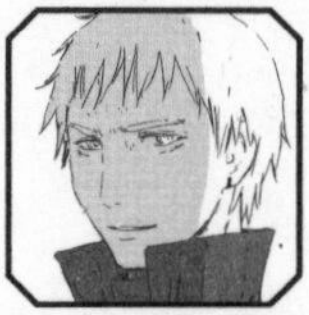

NICHIKO SUOU

The Emperor of Rebedoa. Has the ability to predict the future.

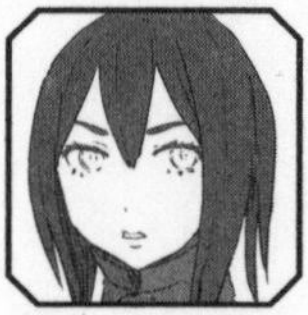

JATE

A high-level Reincarnated of the Rebedoan Empire. Has the ability to manipulate Automatons.

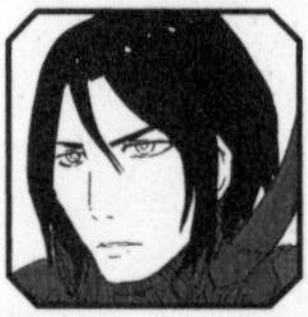

TOSU

A high-level Reincarnated of the Rebedoan Empire. Has the ability to manipulate metal.

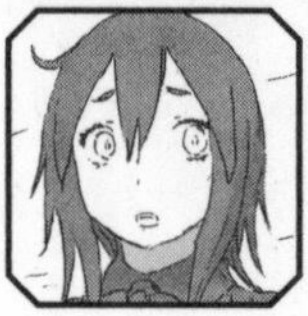

AJATE

A clone of Jate created via artificial Code. She looks like a giant version of Jate.

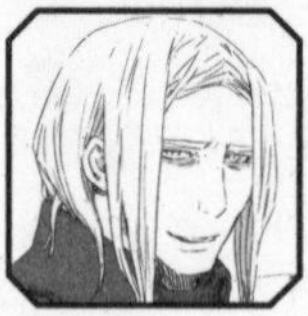

RINAI

Reincarnated.
An old friend of Jate's.
Has the ability to transfer matter.

TRUE CORE CHURCH

Organization created by Kajiwan to gather those afflicted with Frame disease. Bestows certain sufferers with knowledge and power, turning them into "Regenerateds." Views both the Empire and humans as enemies.

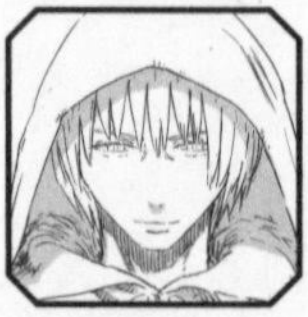

KAJIWAN

The last King of Irf Nikk. Using the powers of the mysterious Frame created from Titania's stolen arm, he became a Regular Frame himself. Has the ability to produce fireballs.

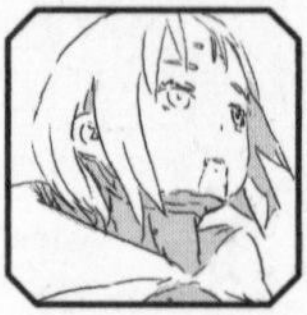

JINATA

Regenerated member of the True Core Church. Her only power is the ability to fight back against Regular Frames.

Previously

Imperial soldiers took Wasabu hostage in order to force Etherow to negotiate. However, Dokobu of the Execution Squad takes over their ship. When Etherow becomes distraught over his friend being captured, Titania—in a voice unlike any she has used before—tells Etherow she can grant him three wishes. But just then, Wasabu reappears, badly injured by the torture he endured at the hands of the Empire...

APOSIMZ

CHAPTER 49

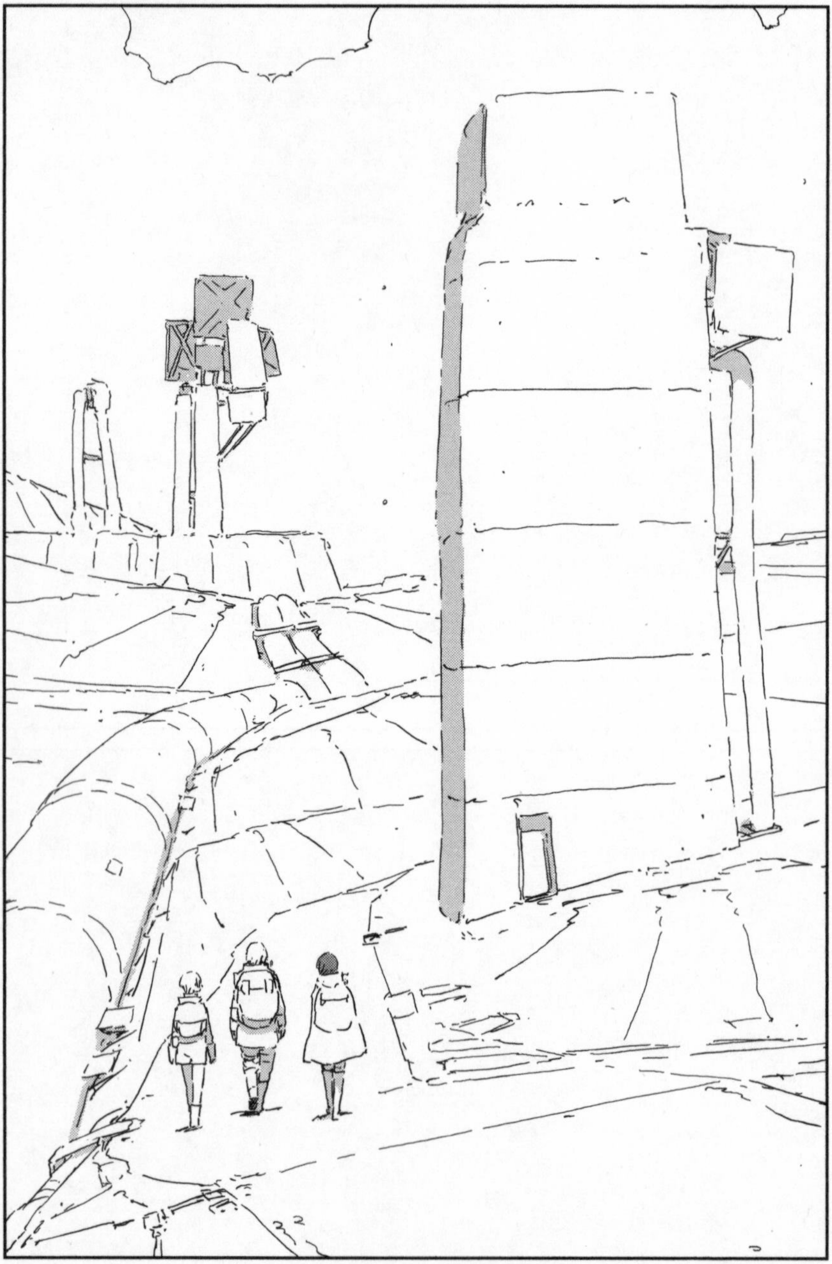

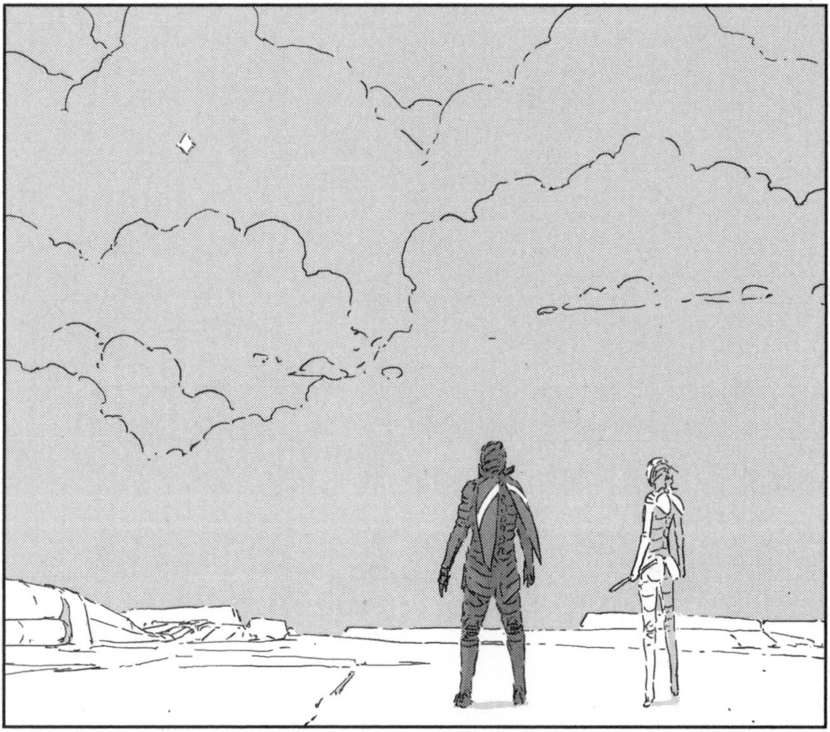

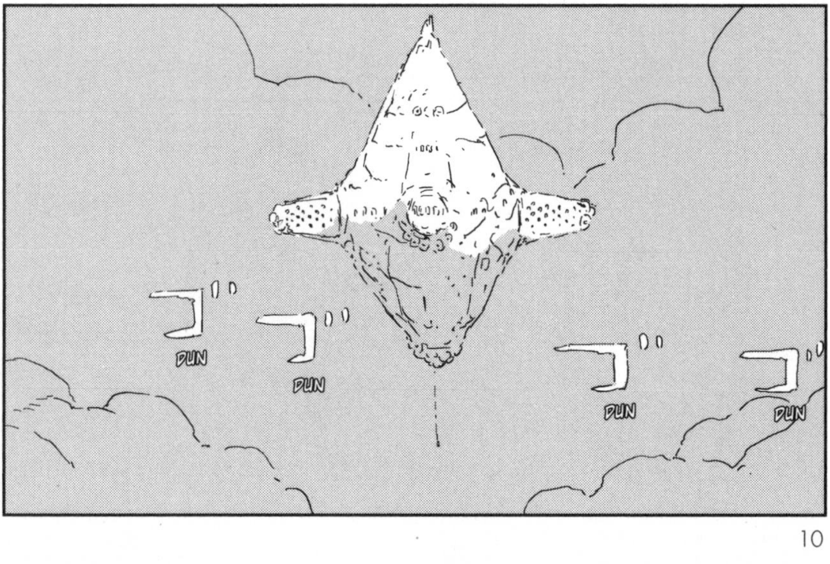
ゴ
DUN
ゴ
DUN
ゴ
DUN
ゴ
DUN

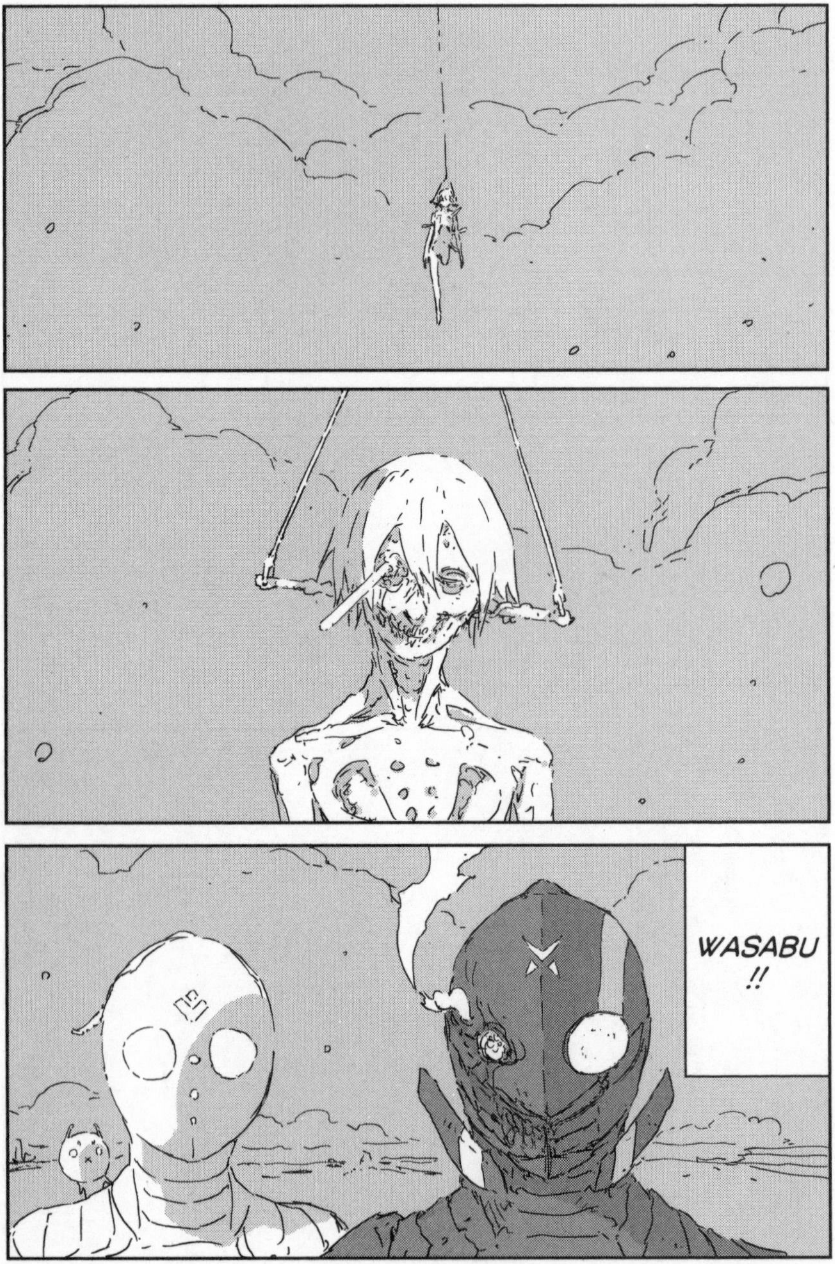
WASABU
!!

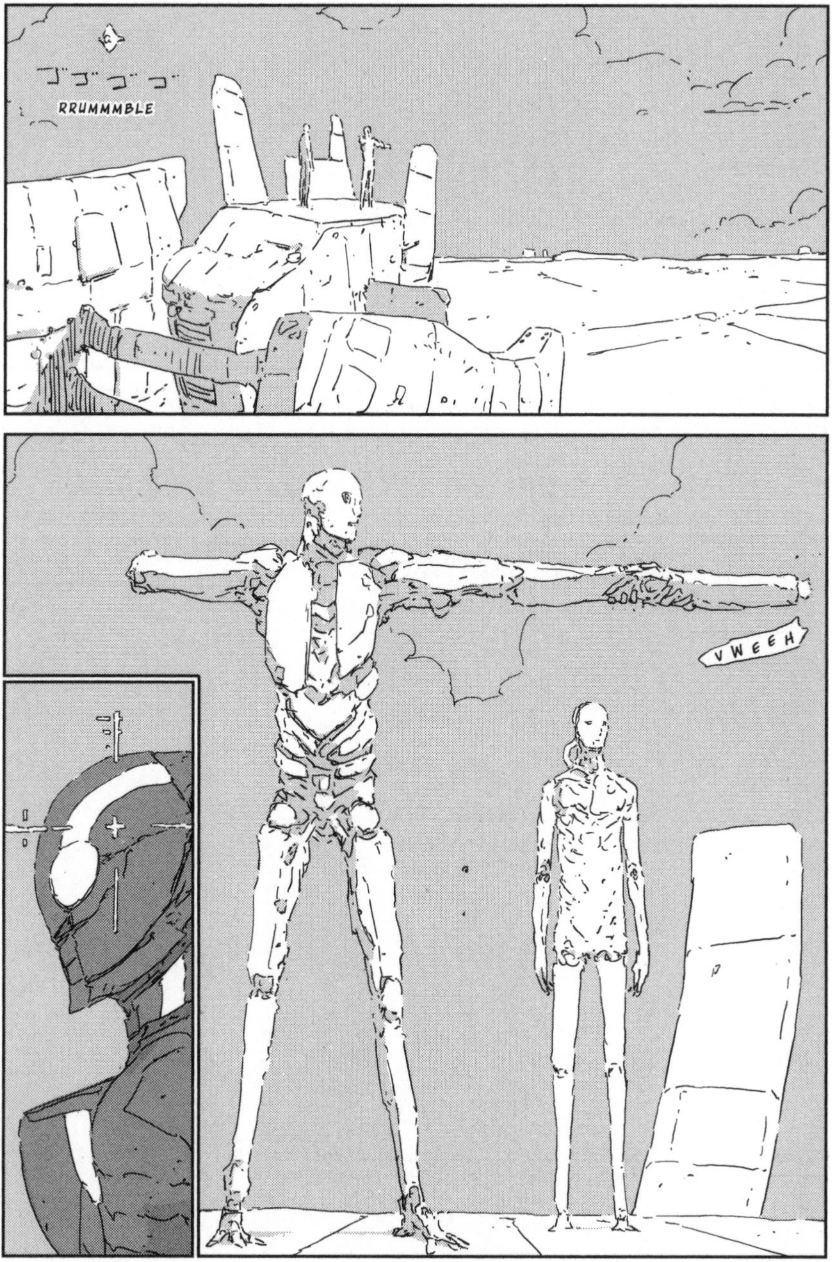
ゴゴゴゴ
RRUMMMBLE
VWEEH

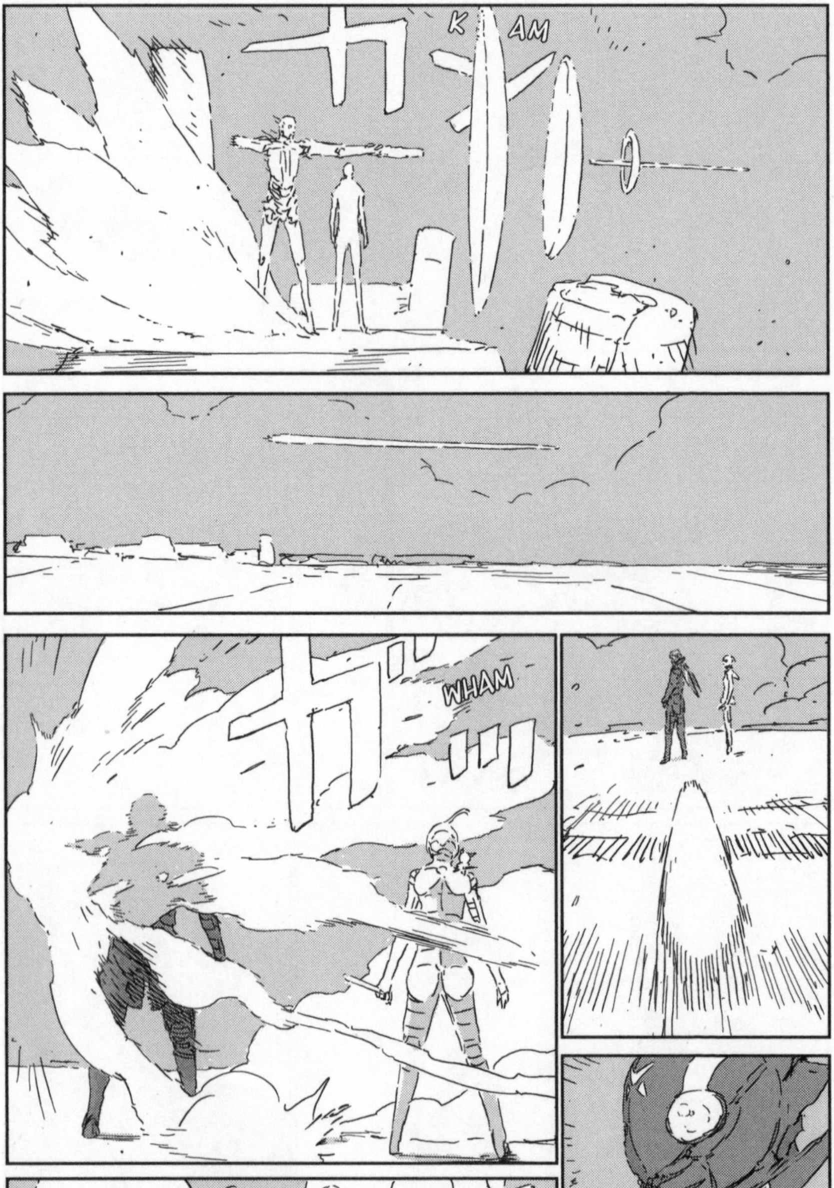
K AM
WHAM
!

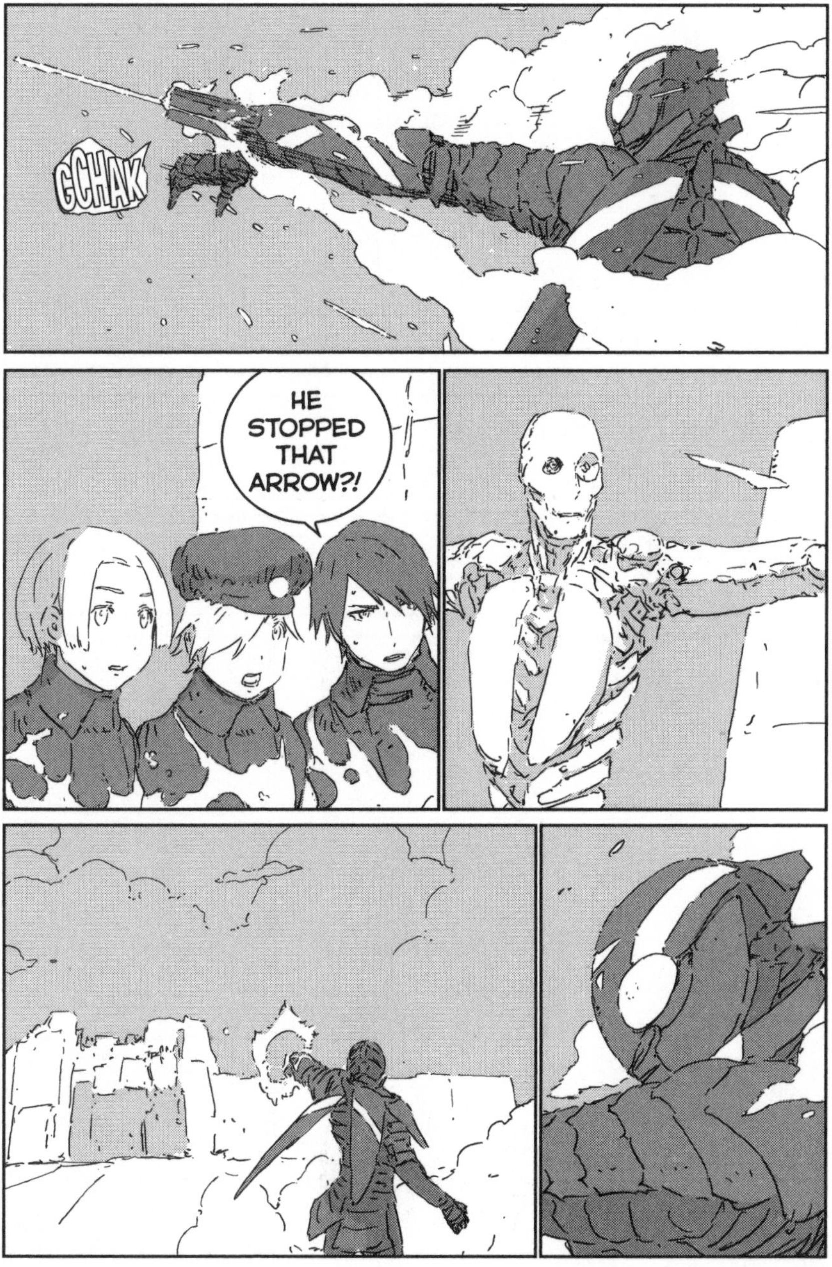
GCHAK
HE STOPPED THAT ARROW?!

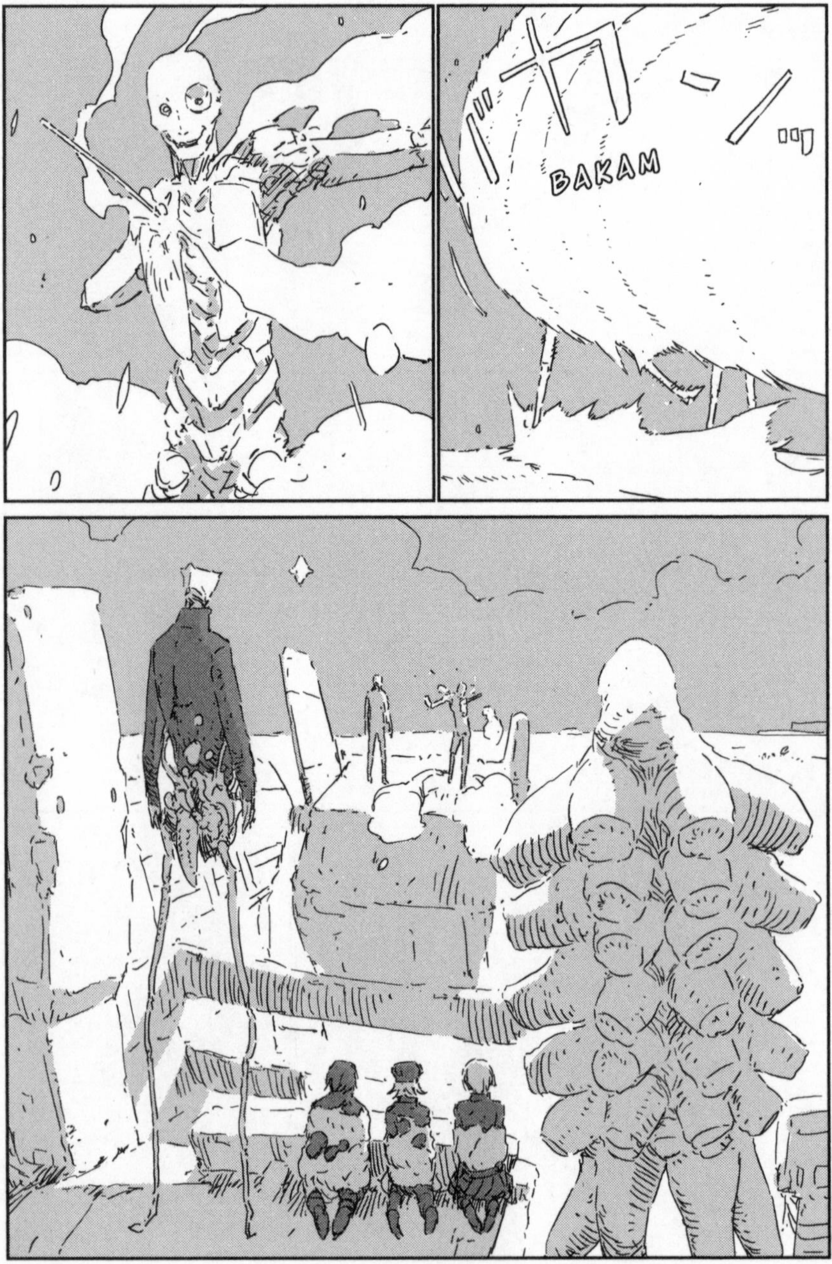
BAKAM

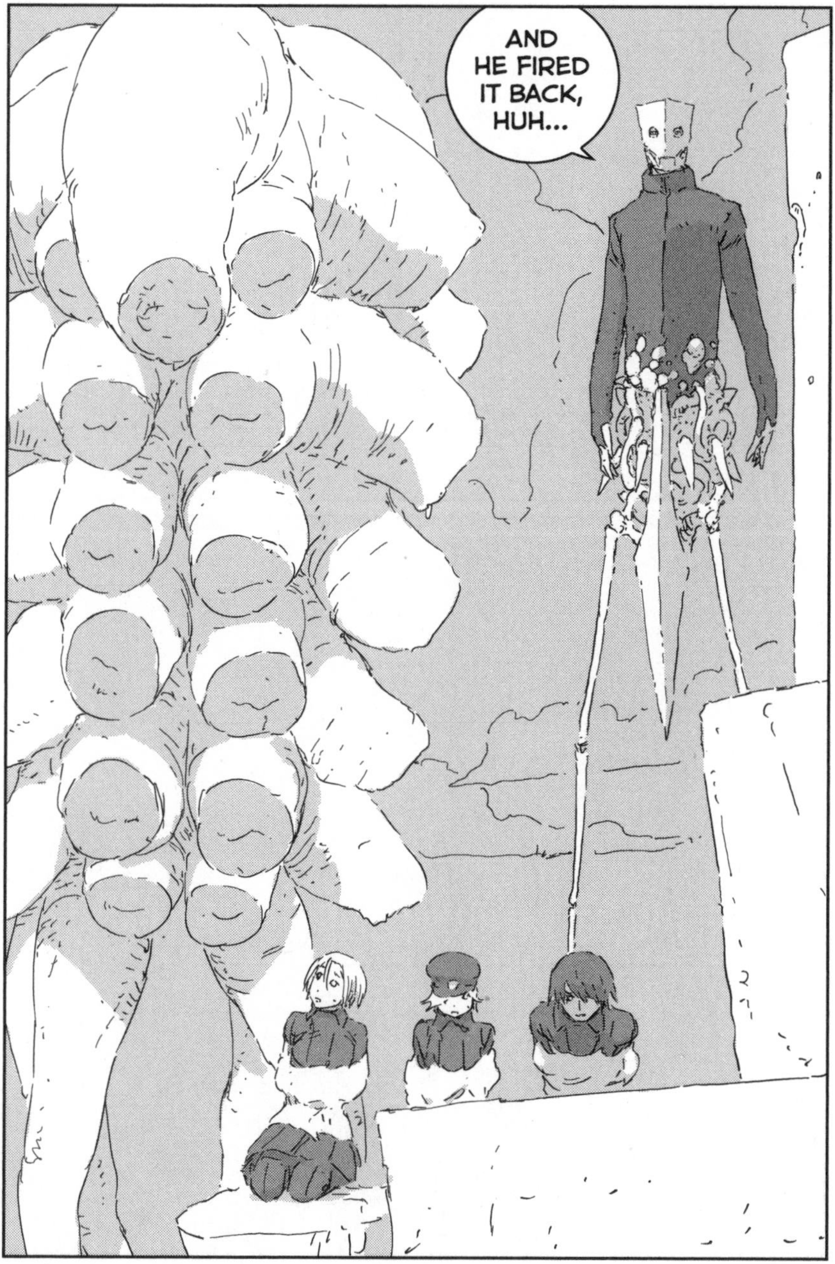
AND HE FIRED IT BACK, HUH...

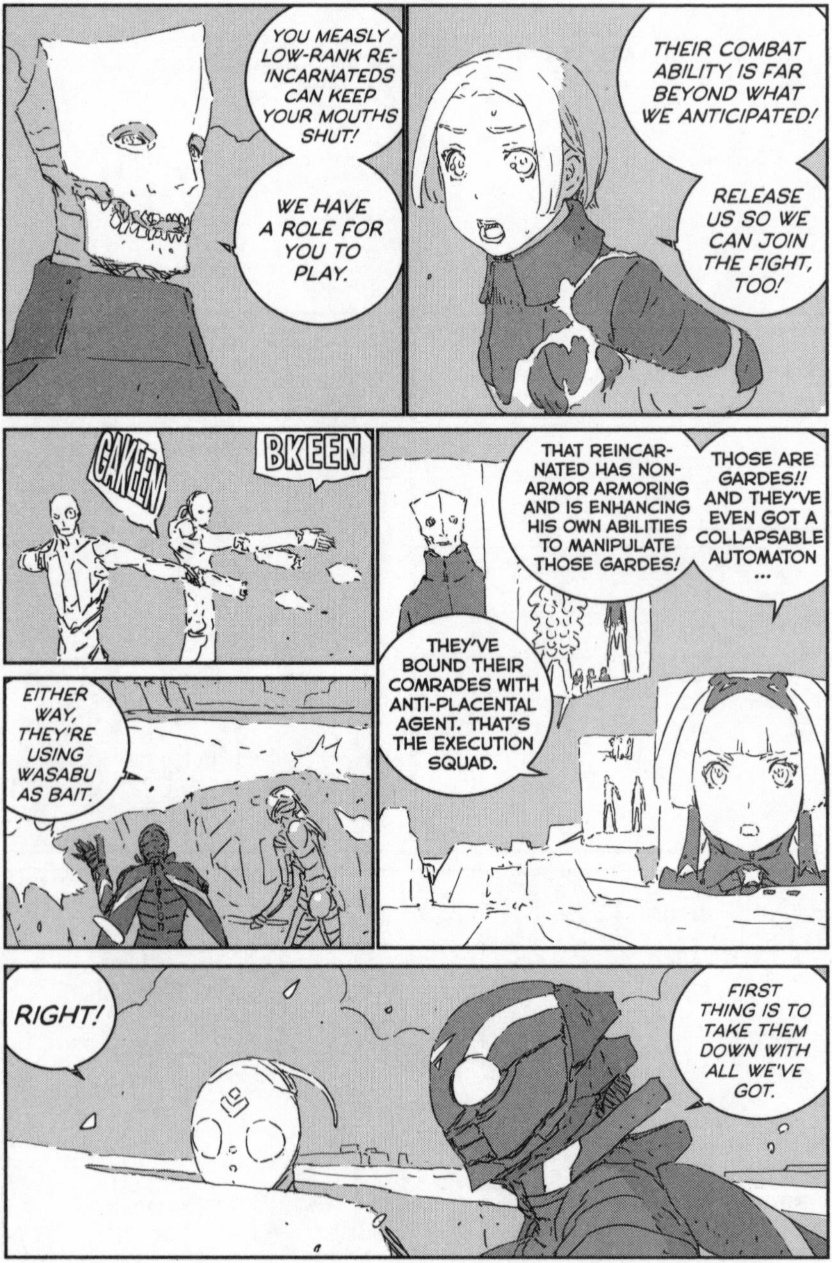
THEIR COMBAT ABILITY IS FAR BEYOND WHAT WE ANTICIPATED!
RELEASE US SO WE CAN JOIN THE FIGHT, TOO!
YOU MEASLY LOW-RANK RE-INCARNATEDS CAN KEEP YOUR MOUTHS SHUT!
WE HAVE A ROLE FOR YOU TO PLAY.
THOSE ARE GARDES!! AND THEY'VE EVEN GOT A COLLAPSABLE AUTOMATON ...
THAT REINCARNATED HAS NON-ARMOR ARMORING AND IS ENHANCING HIS OWN ABILITIES TO MANIPULATE THOSE GARDES!
THEY'VE BOUND THEIR COMRADES WITH ANTI-PLACENTAL AGENT. THAT'S THE EXECUTION SQUAD.
BKEEN
GAKEEN
EITHER WAY, THEY'RE USING WASABU AS BAIT.
FIRST THING IS TO TAKE THEM DOWN WITH ALL WE'VE GOT.
RIGHT!

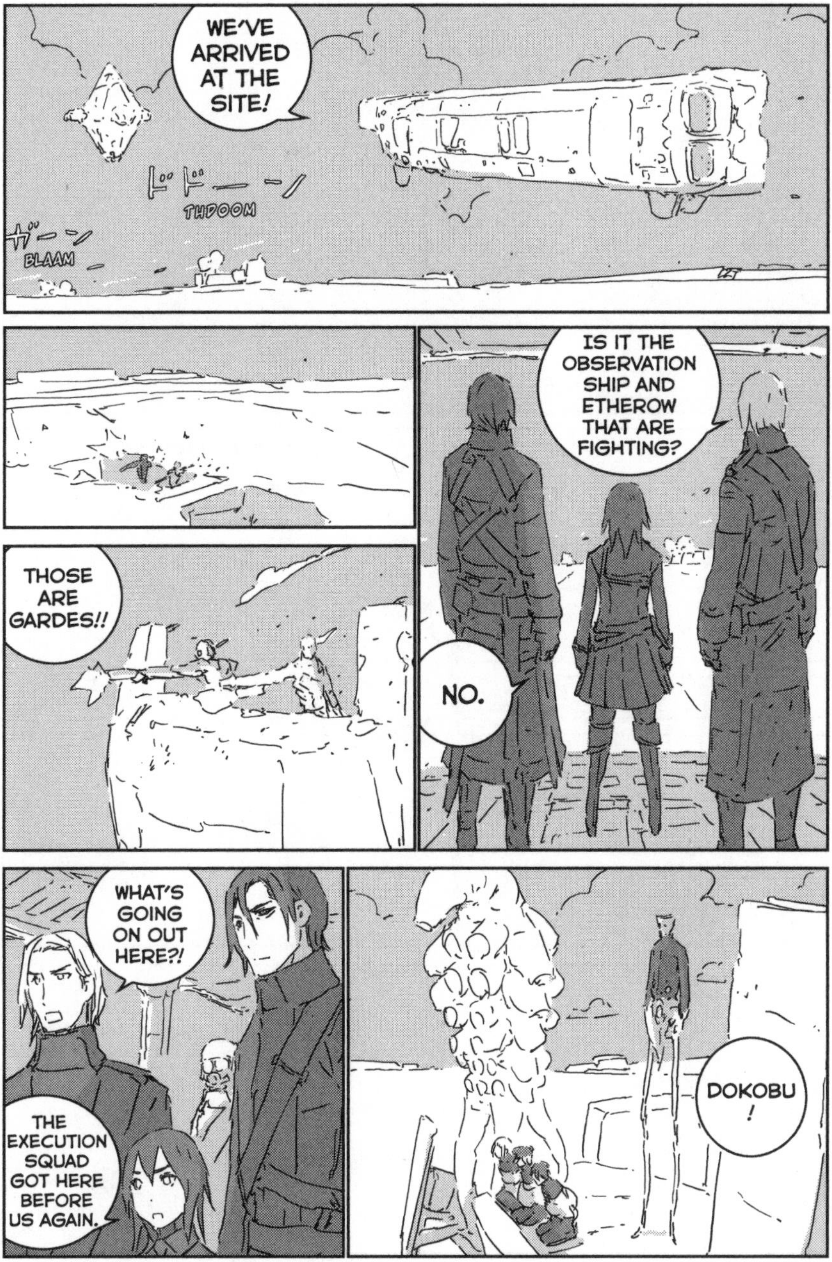

WE'VE ARRIVED AT THE SITE!
ドドーーン
THDOOM
ガーン
BLAAM
IS IT THE OBSERVATION SHIP AND ETHEROW THAT ARE FIGHTING?
NO.
THOSE ARE GARDES!!
DOKOBU!
WHAT'S GOING ON OUT HERE?!
THE EXECUTION SQUAD GOT HERE BEFORE US AGAIN.

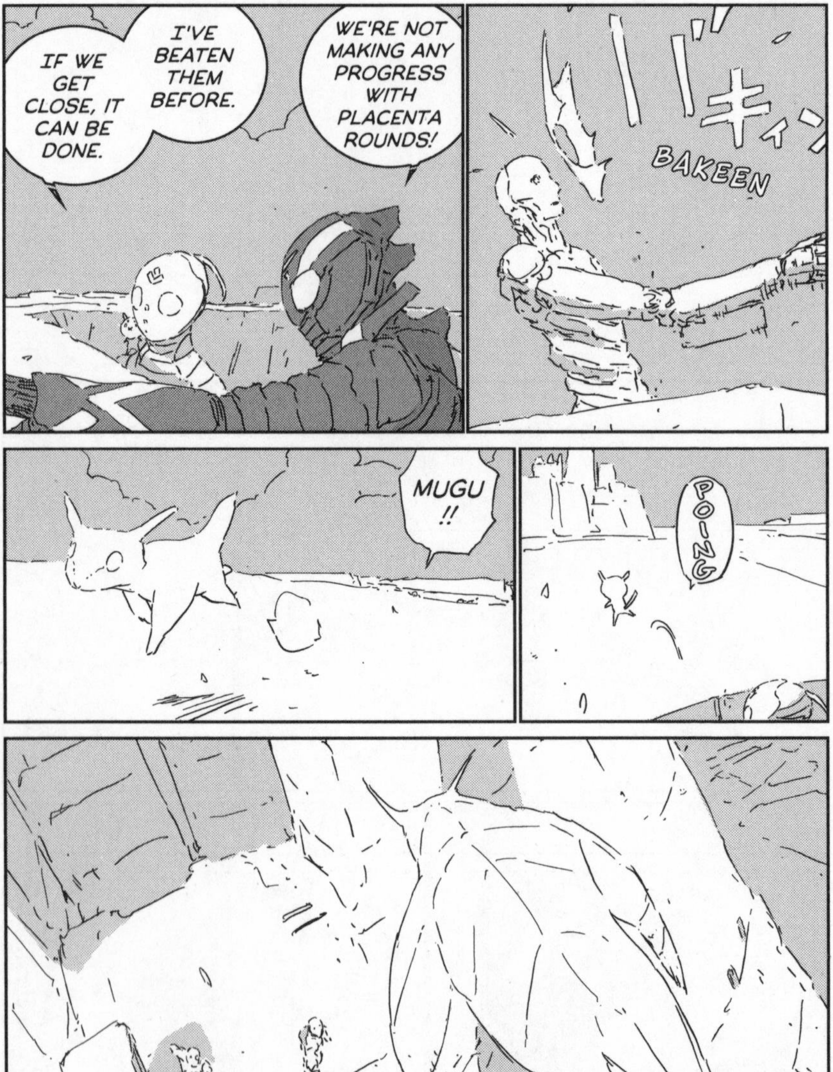
BAKEEN
WE'RE NOT MAKING ANY PROGRESS WITH PLACENTA ROUNDS!
I'VE BEATEN THEM BEFORE.
IF WE GET CLOSE, IT CAN BE DONE.
POING
MUGU !!

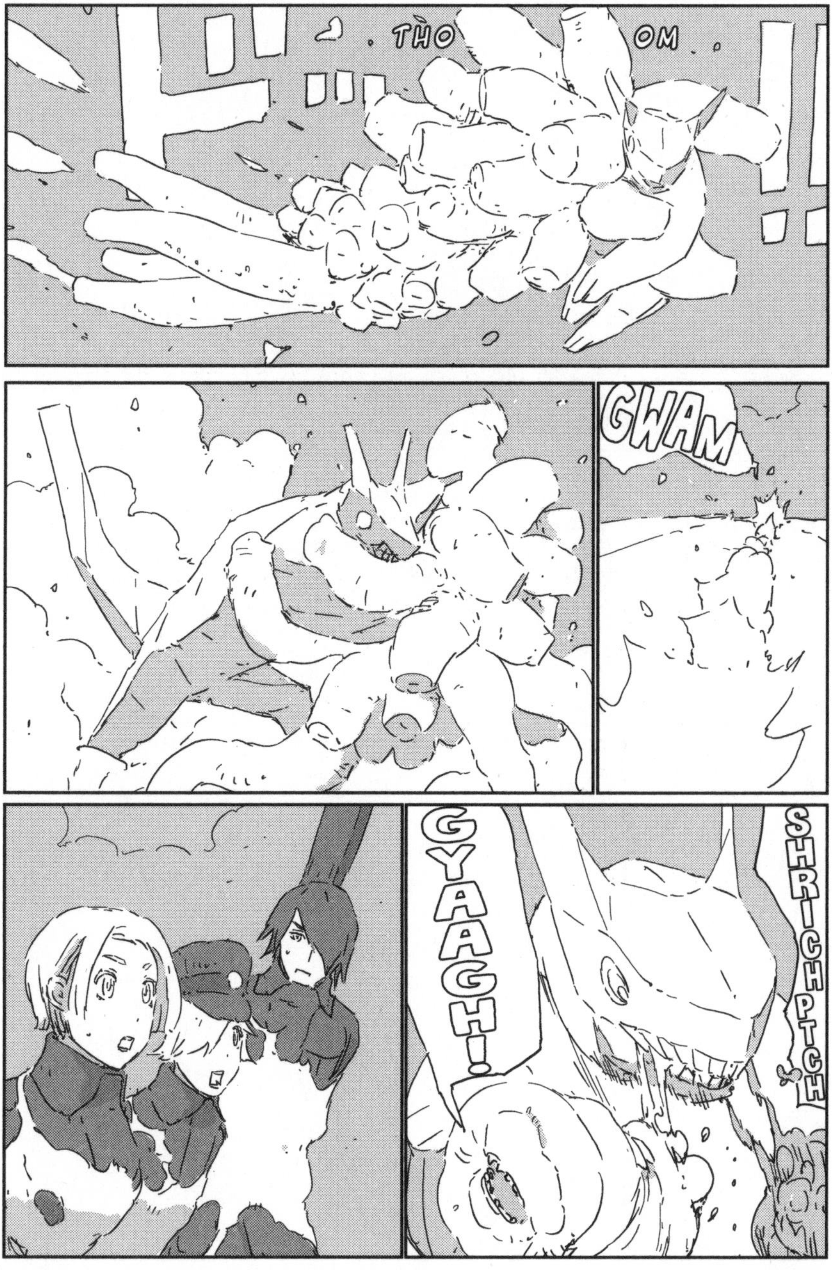
THO OM
GWAM
SHRICHPTCH
GYAAGH!

HAVE SOME FOOD, FRIEND.
CHOMP CHOMP
YATSUMA !!

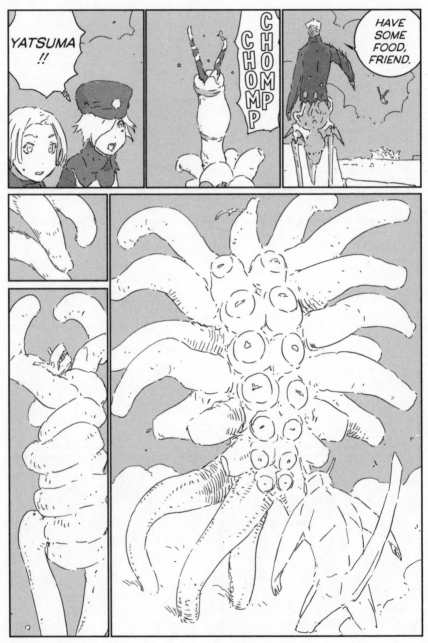

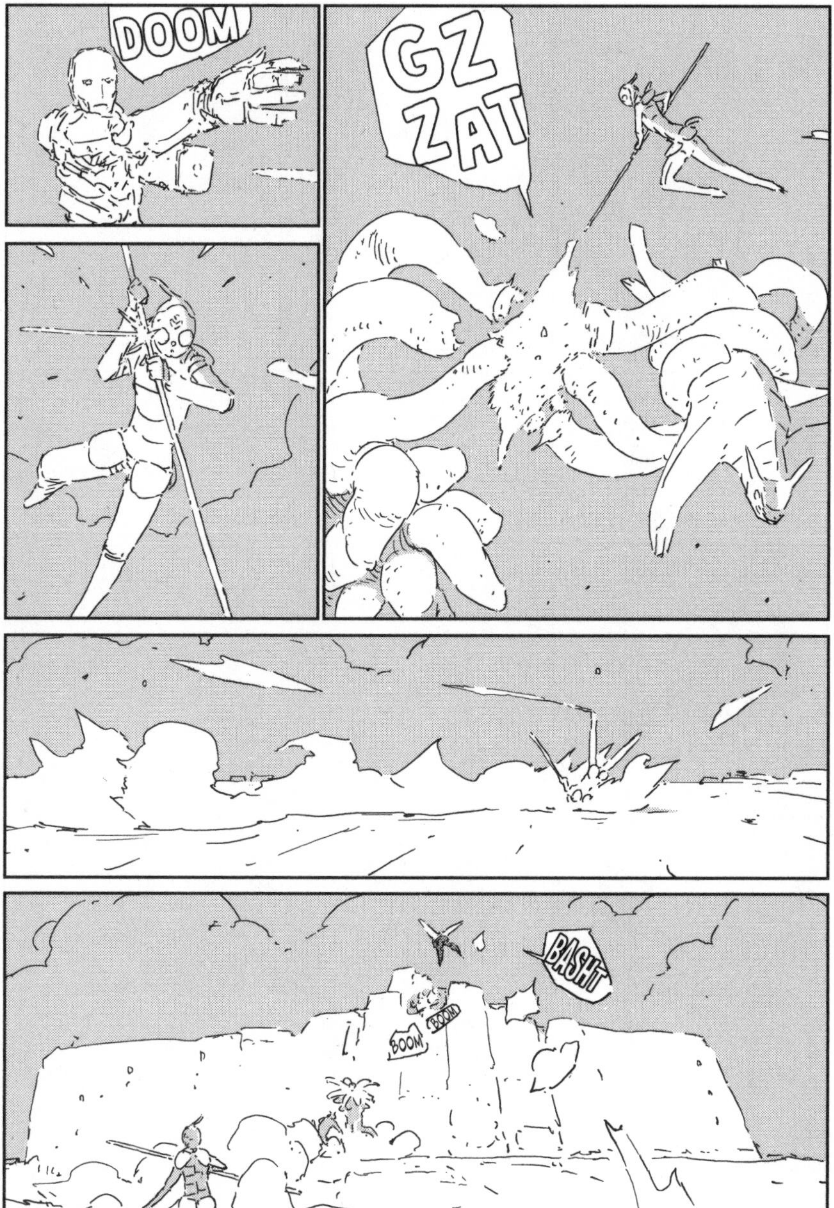
GZ ZAT
DOOM
BASHT
BOOM
BOOM

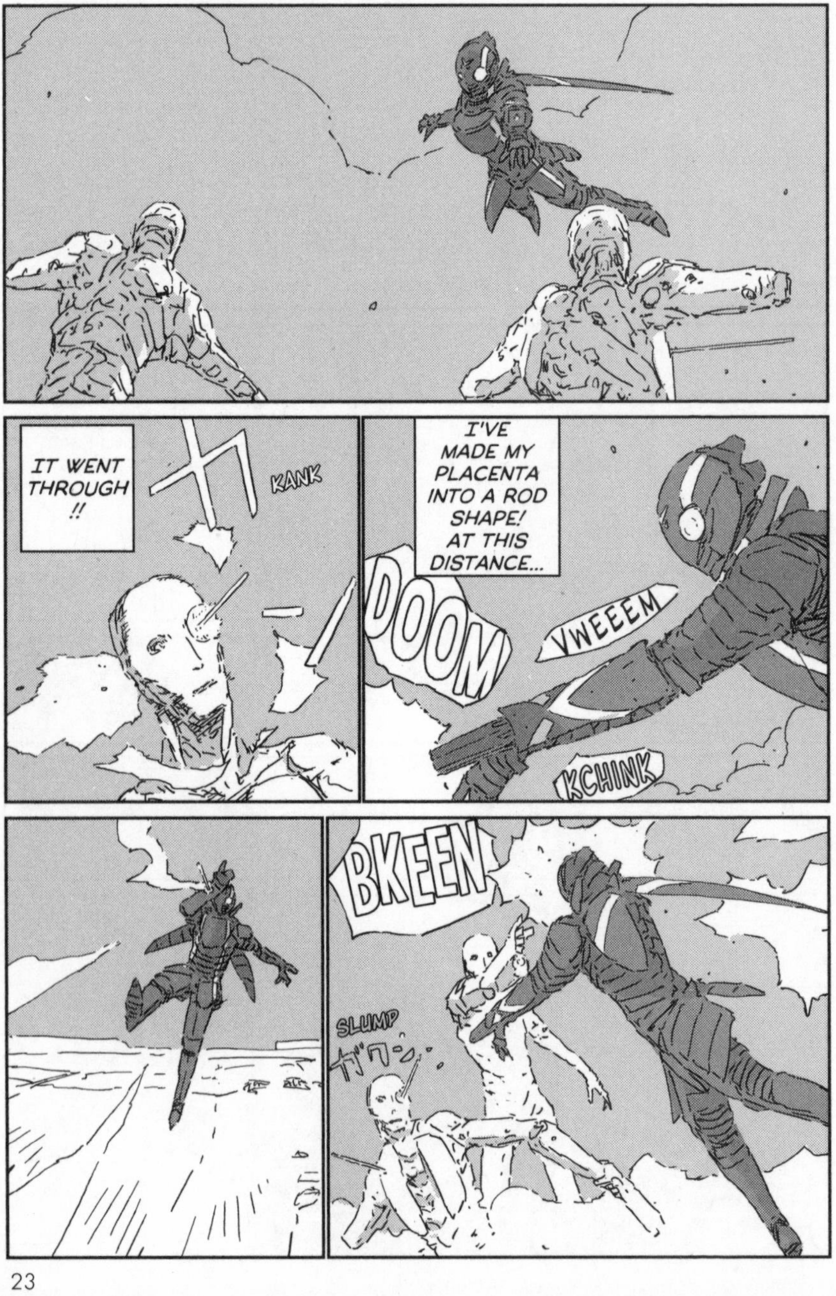
I'VE MADE MY PLACENTA INTO A ROD SHAPE! AT THIS DISTANCE...
DOOM
VWEEEM
KCHINK
IT WENT THROUGH !!
KANK
BKEEN
SLUMP

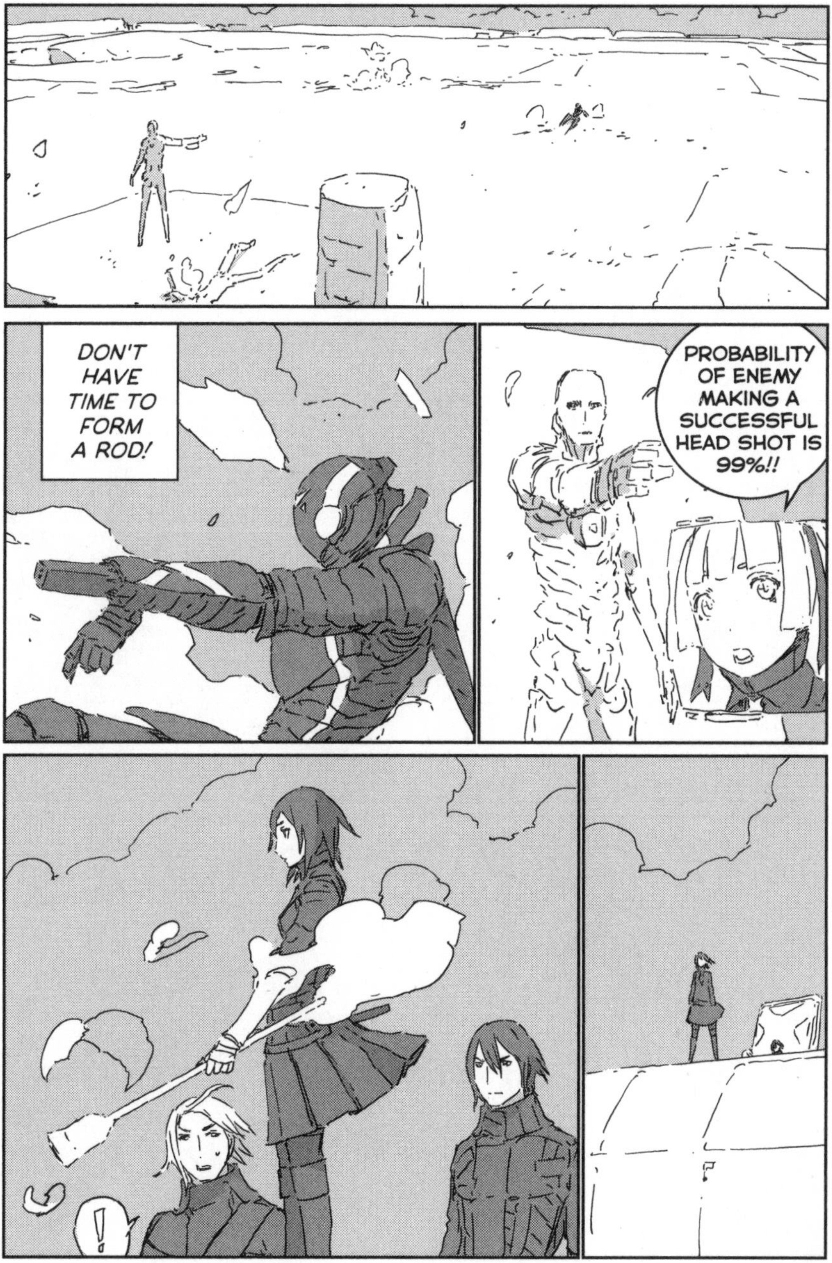
PROBABILITY OF ENEMY MAKING A SUCCESSFUL HEAD SHOT IS 99%!!
DON'T HAVE TIME TO FORM A ROD!
!

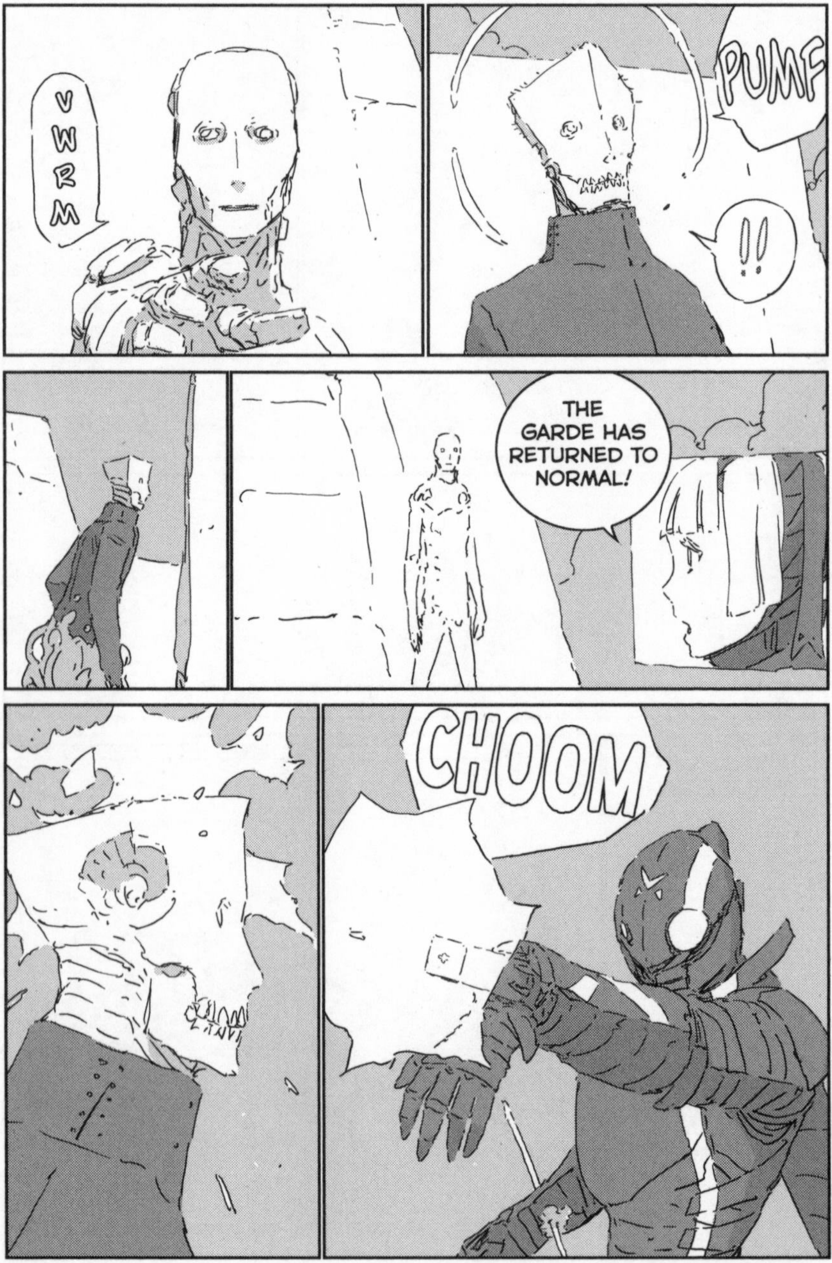
PUMF
!!
VWRM
THE GARDE HAS RETURNED TO NORMAL!
CHOOM

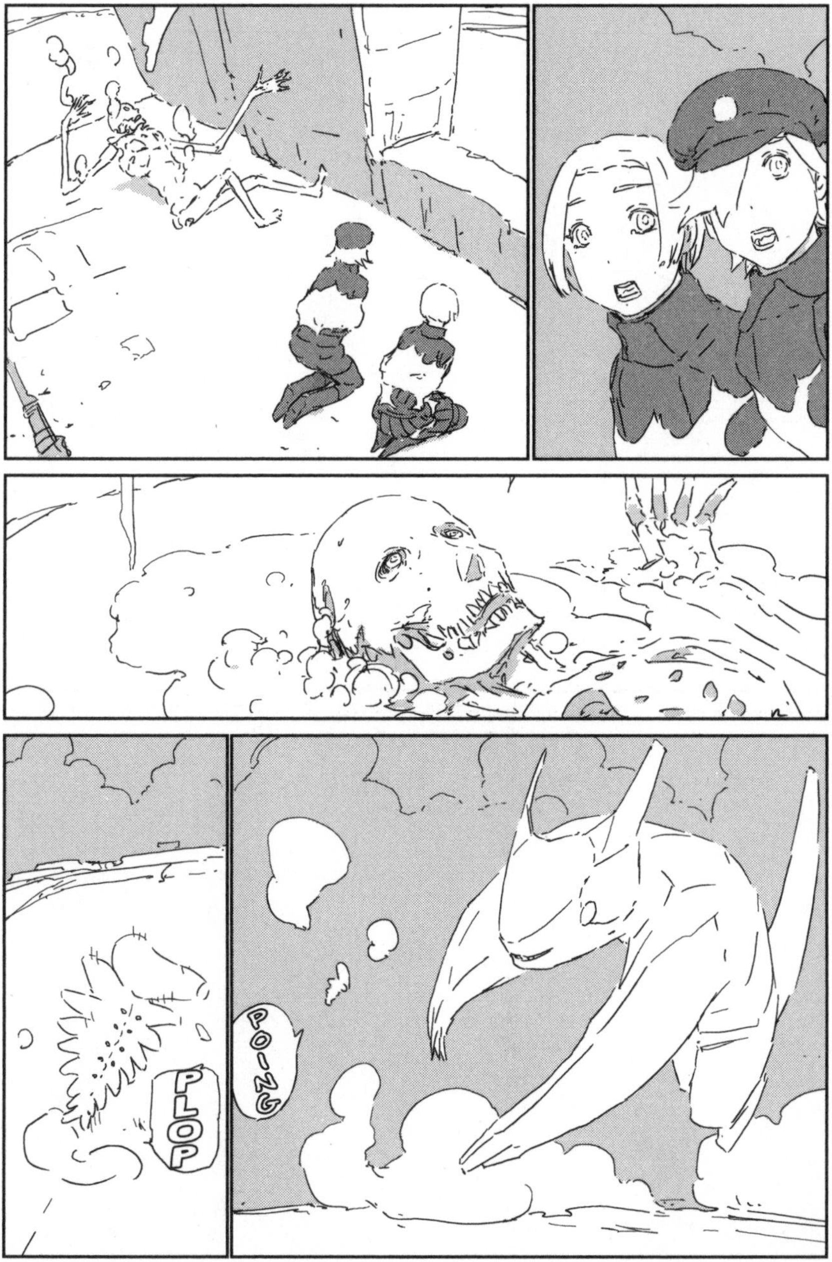
POING
PLOP

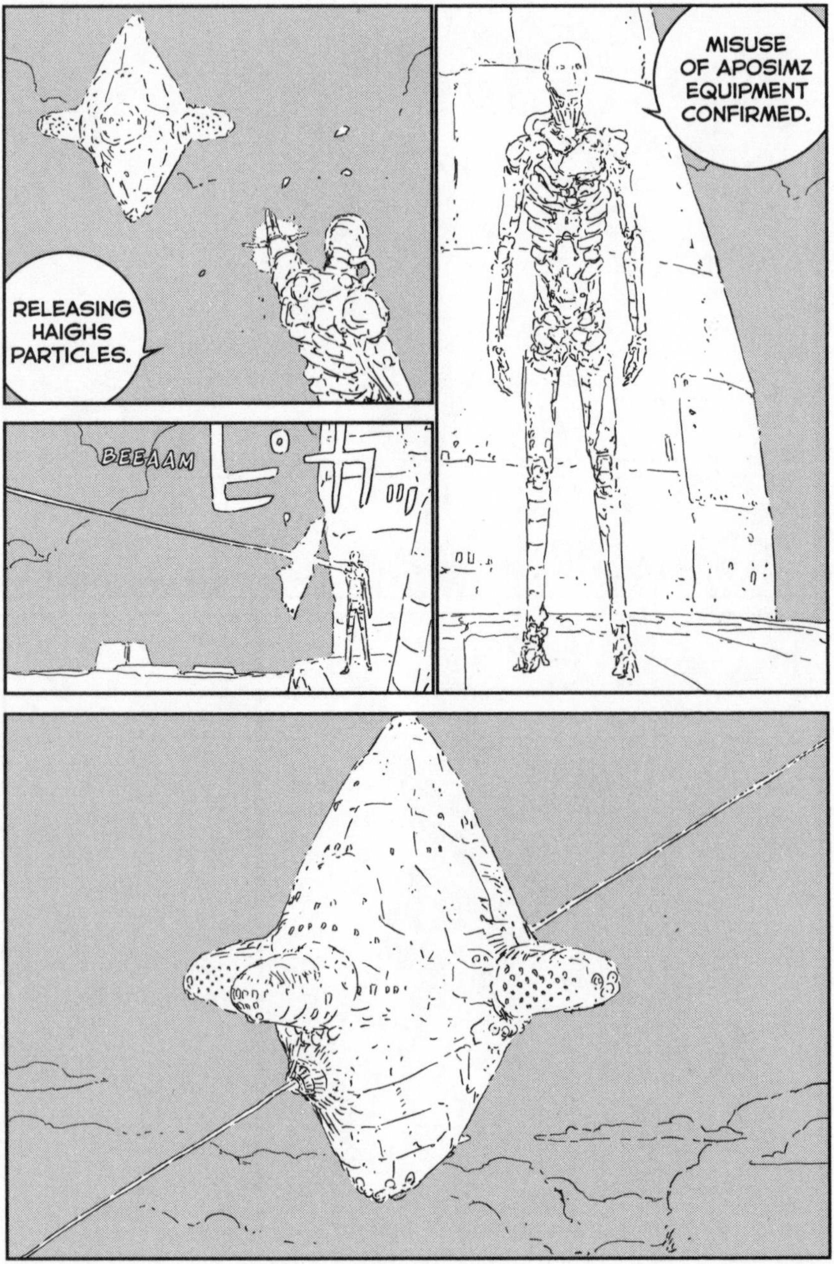
MISUSE OF APOSIMZ EQUIPMENT CONFIRMED.
RELEASING HAIGHS PARTICLES.
BEEAAM
ピカ

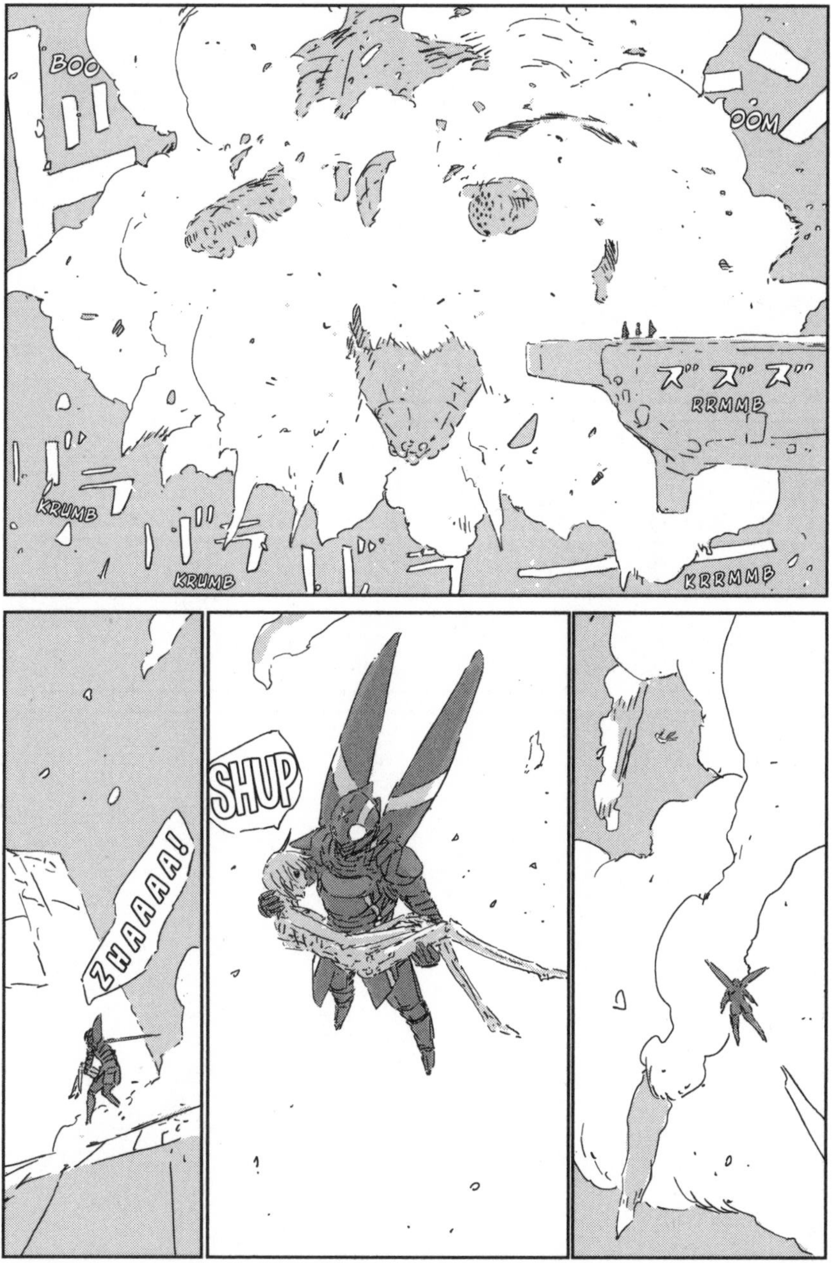
BOO
OOM
ズズズ
RRMMB
KRRMMB
KRUMB
KRUMB
SHUP
ZHAAAAA!

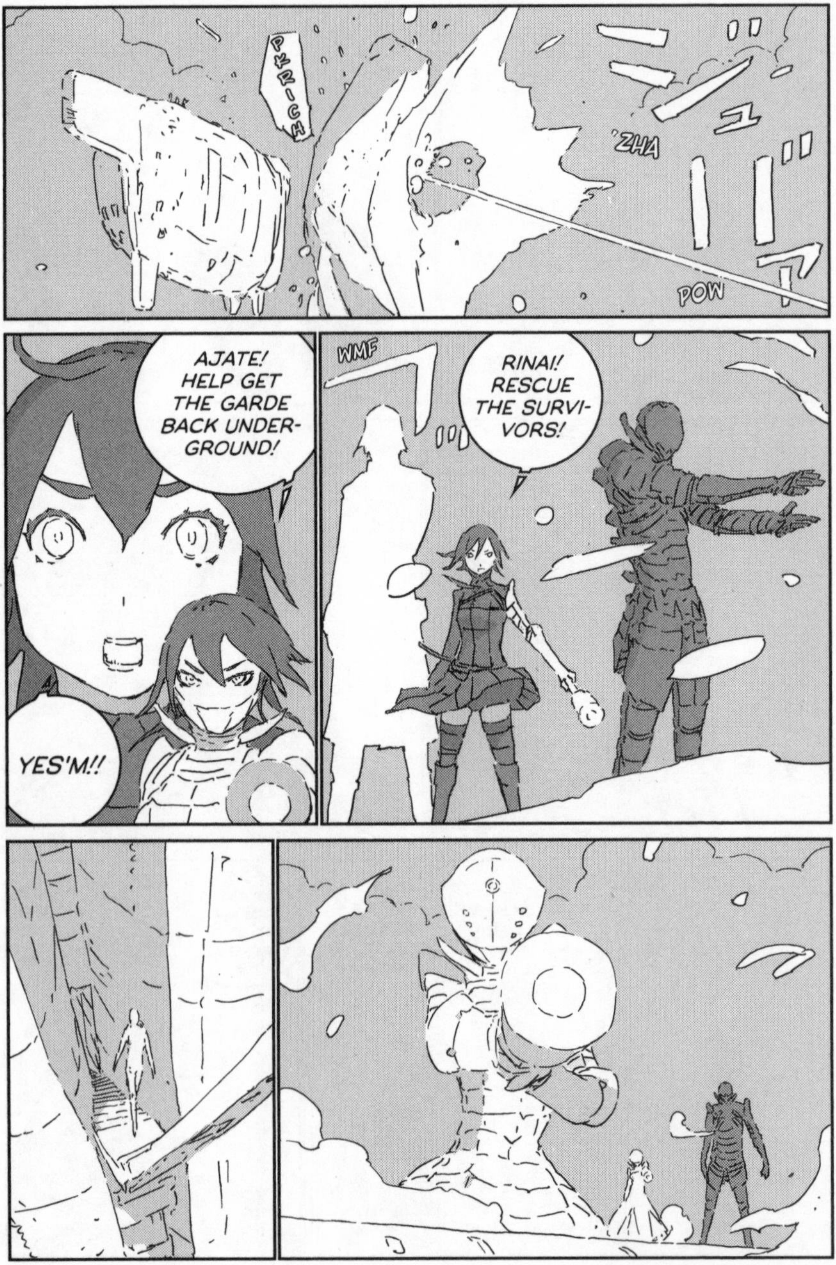

'ZHA
PKRICH
POW
WMF
RINAI! RESCUE THE SURVIVORS!
AJATE! HELP GET THE GARDE BACK UNDERGROUND!
YES'M!!

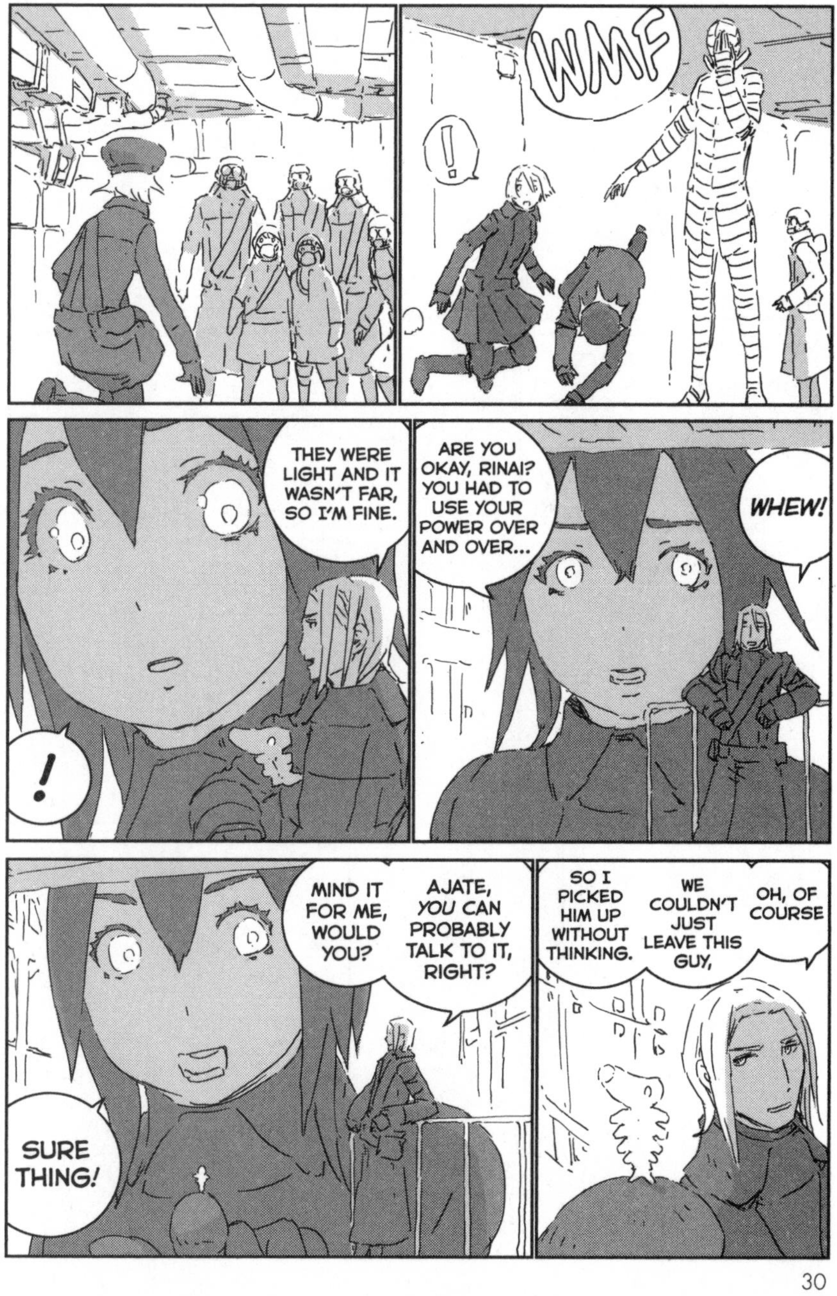
WMF
!
WHEW!
ARE YOU OKAY, RINAI? YOU HAD TO USE YOUR POWER OVER AND OVER...
THEY WERE LIGHT AND IT WASN'T FAR, SO I'M FINE.
!
OH, OF COURSE
WE COULDN'T JUST LEAVE THIS GUY,
SO I PICKED HIM UP WITHOUT THINKING.
AJATE, *YOU* CAN PROBABLY TALK TO IT, RIGHT?
MIND IT FOR ME, WOULD YOU?
SURE THING!

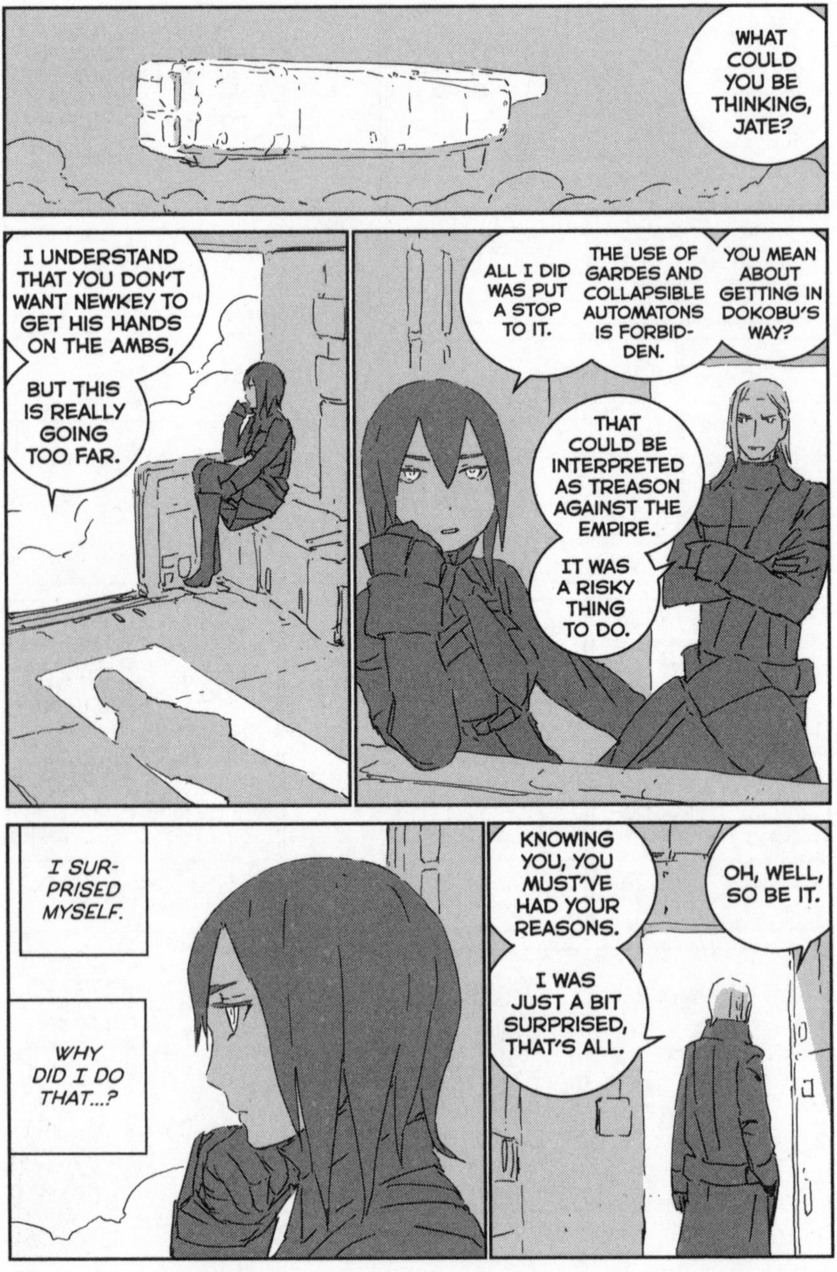
WHAT COULD YOU BE THINKING, JATE?
YOU MEAN ABOUT GETTING IN DOKOBU'S WAY?
THE USE OF GARDES AND COLLAPSIBLE AUTOMATONS IS FORBIDDEN.
ALL I DID WAS PUT A STOP TO IT.
THAT COULD BE INTERPRETED AS TREASON AGAINST THE EMPIRE.
IT WAS A RISKY THING TO DO.
I UNDERSTAND THAT YOU DON'T WANT NEWKEY TO GET HIS HANDS ON THE AMBS,
BUT THIS IS REALLY GOING TOO FAR.
OH, WELL, SO BE IT.
KNOWING YOU, YOU MUST'VE HAD YOUR REASONS.
I WAS JUST A BIT SURPRISED, THAT'S ALL.
I SURPRISED MYSELF.
WHY DID I DO THAT...?

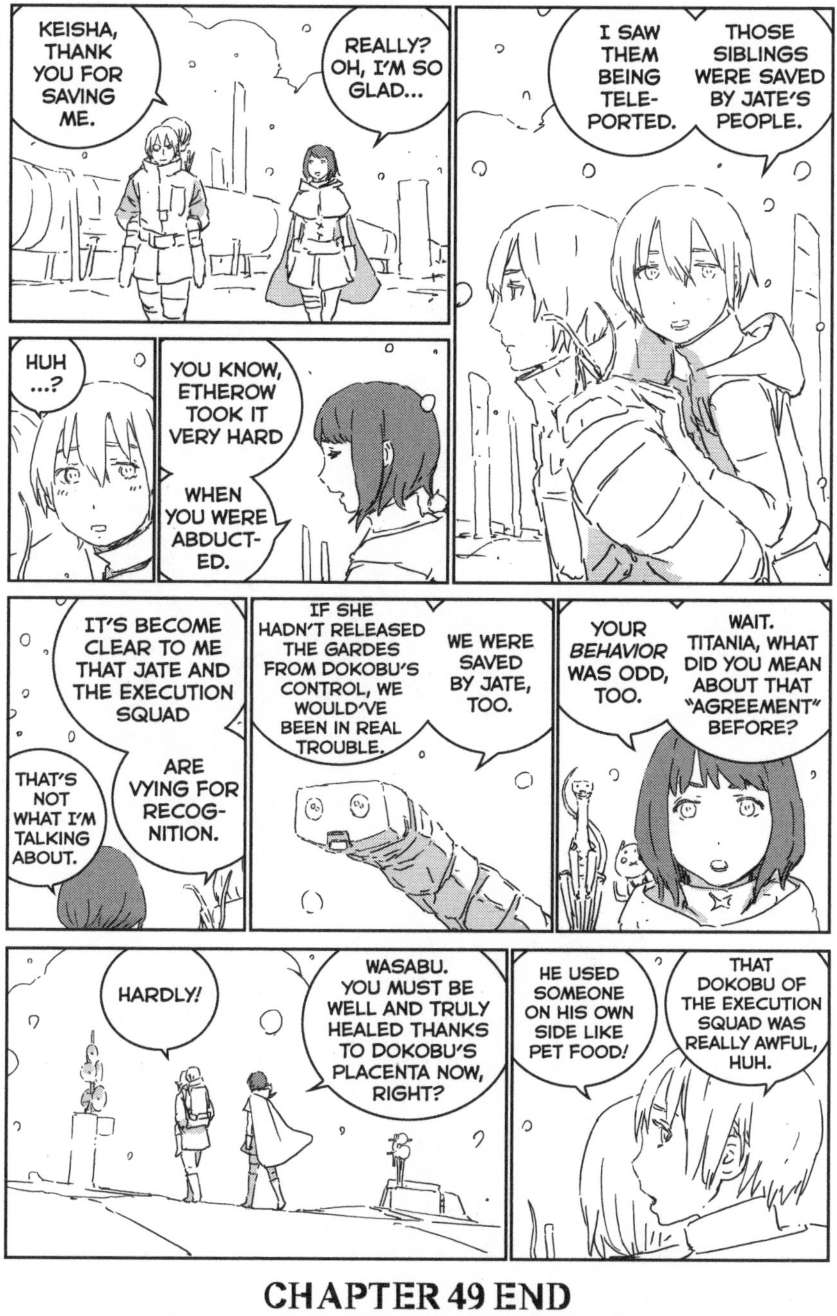
THOSE SIBLINGS WERE SAVED BY JATE'S PEOPLE.
I SAW THEM BEING TELE-PORTED.
REALLY? OH, I'M SO GLAD...
KEISHA, THANK YOU FOR SAVING ME.
YOU KNOW, ETHEROW TOOK IT VERY HARD
WHEN YOU WERE ABDUCT-ED.
HUH ...?
WAIT. TITANIA, WHAT DID YOU MEAN ABOUT THAT "AGREEMENT" BEFORE?
YOUR *BEHAVIOR* WAS ODD, TOO.
WE WERE SAVED BY JATE, TOO.
IF SHE HADN'T RELEASED THE GARDES FROM DOKOBU'S CONTROL, WE WOULD'VE BEEN IN REAL TROUBLE.
IT'S BECOME CLEAR TO ME THAT JATE AND THE EXECUTION SQUAD
ARE VYING FOR RECOG-NITION.
THAT'S NOT WHAT I'M TALKING ABOUT.
THAT DOKOBU OF THE EXECUTION SQUAD WAS REALLY AWFUL, HUH.
HE USED SOMEONE ON HIS OWN SIDE LIKE PET FOOD!
WASABU. YOU MUST BE WELL AND TRULY HEALED THANKS TO DOKOBU'S PLACENTA NOW, RIGHT?
HARDLY!

CHAPTER 49 END

APOSIMZ

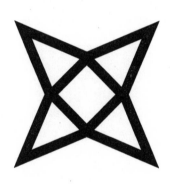

CHAPTER 50

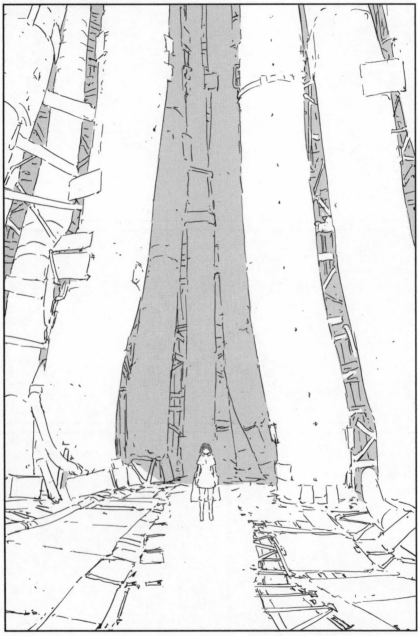

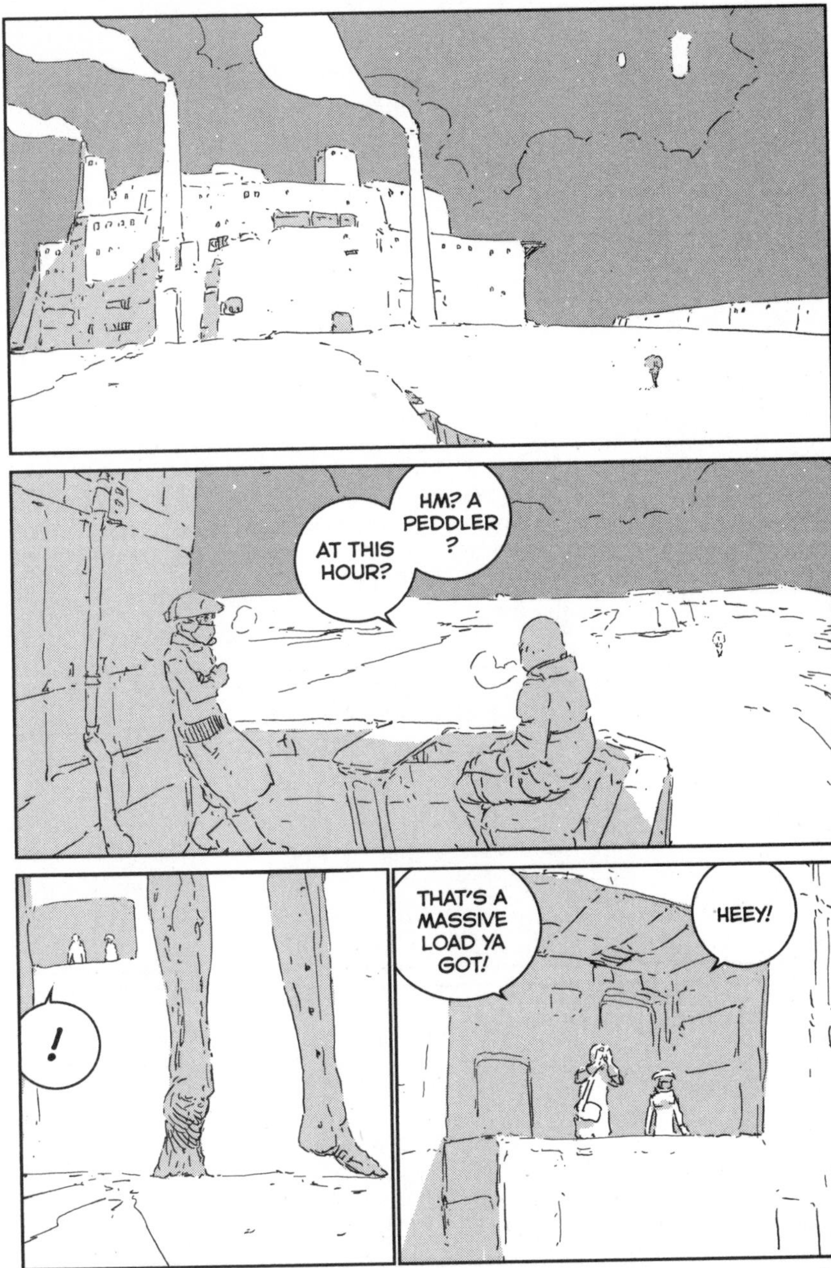
HM? A PEDDLER ?
AT THIS HOUR?
HEEY!
THAT'S A MASSIVE LOAD YA GOT!
!

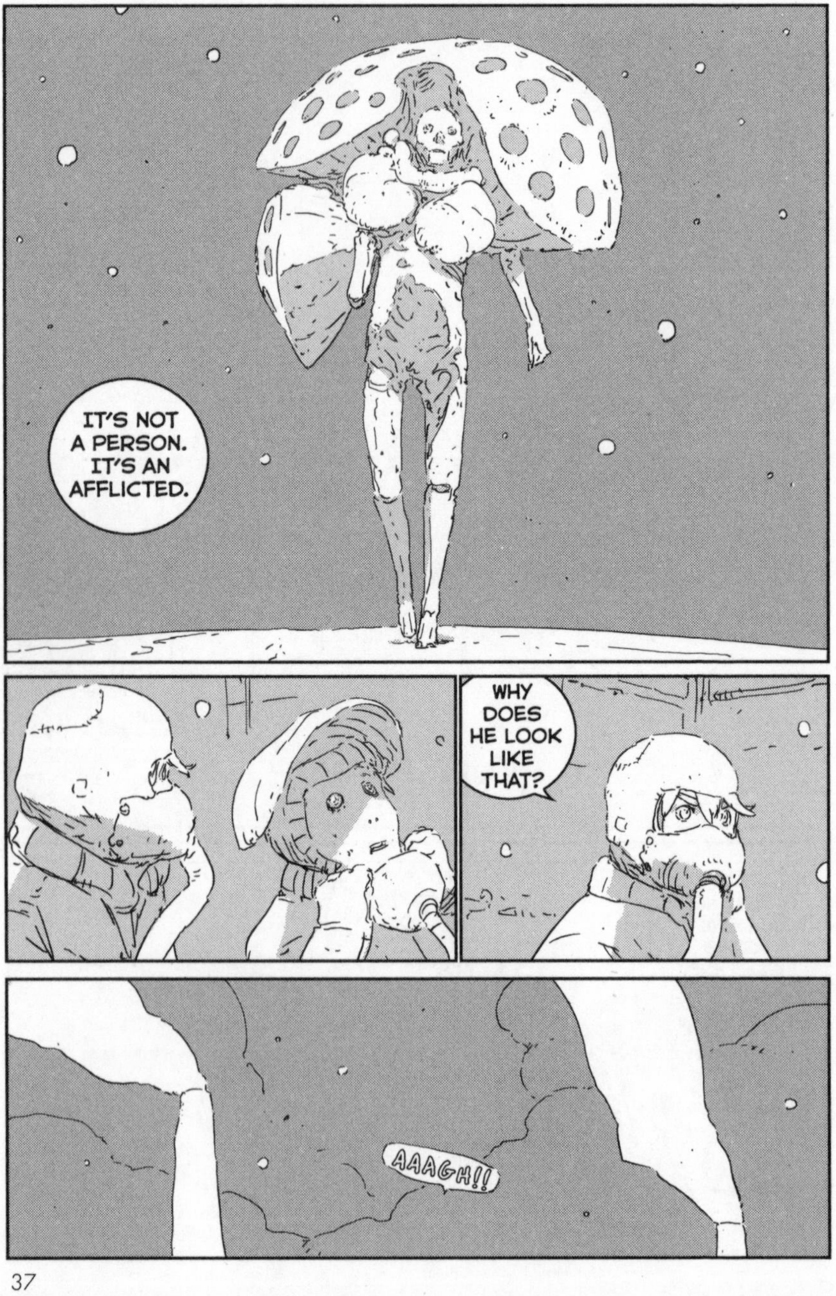
IT'S NOT A PERSON. IT'S AN AFFLICTED.
WHY DOES HE LOOK LIKE THAT?
AAAGH!!

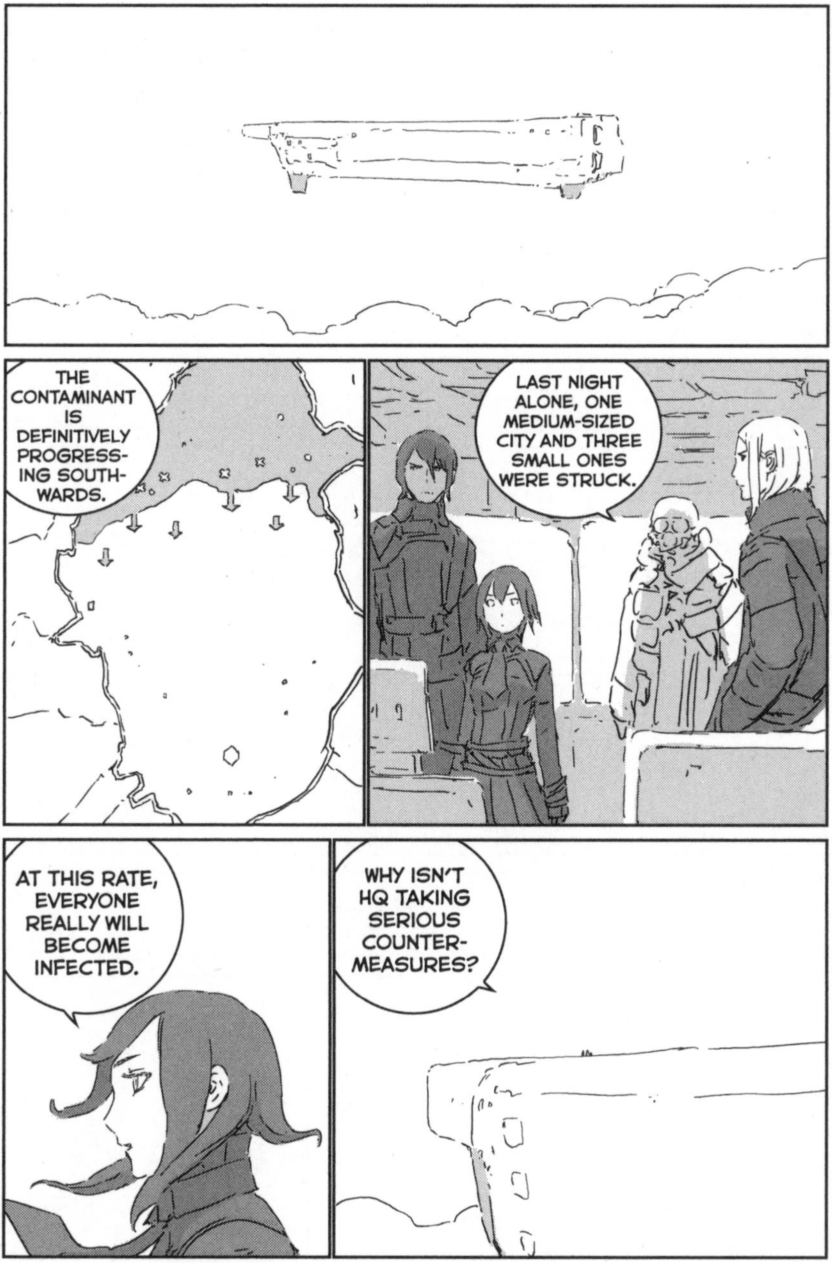
LAST NIGHT ALONE, ONE MEDIUM-SIZED CITY AND THREE SMALL ONES WERE STRUCK.
THE CONTAMINANT IS DEFINITIVELY PROGRESSING SOUTHWARDS.
WHY ISN'T HQ TAKING SERIOUS COUNTERMEASURES?
AT THIS RATE, EVERYONE REALLY WILL BECOME INFECTED.

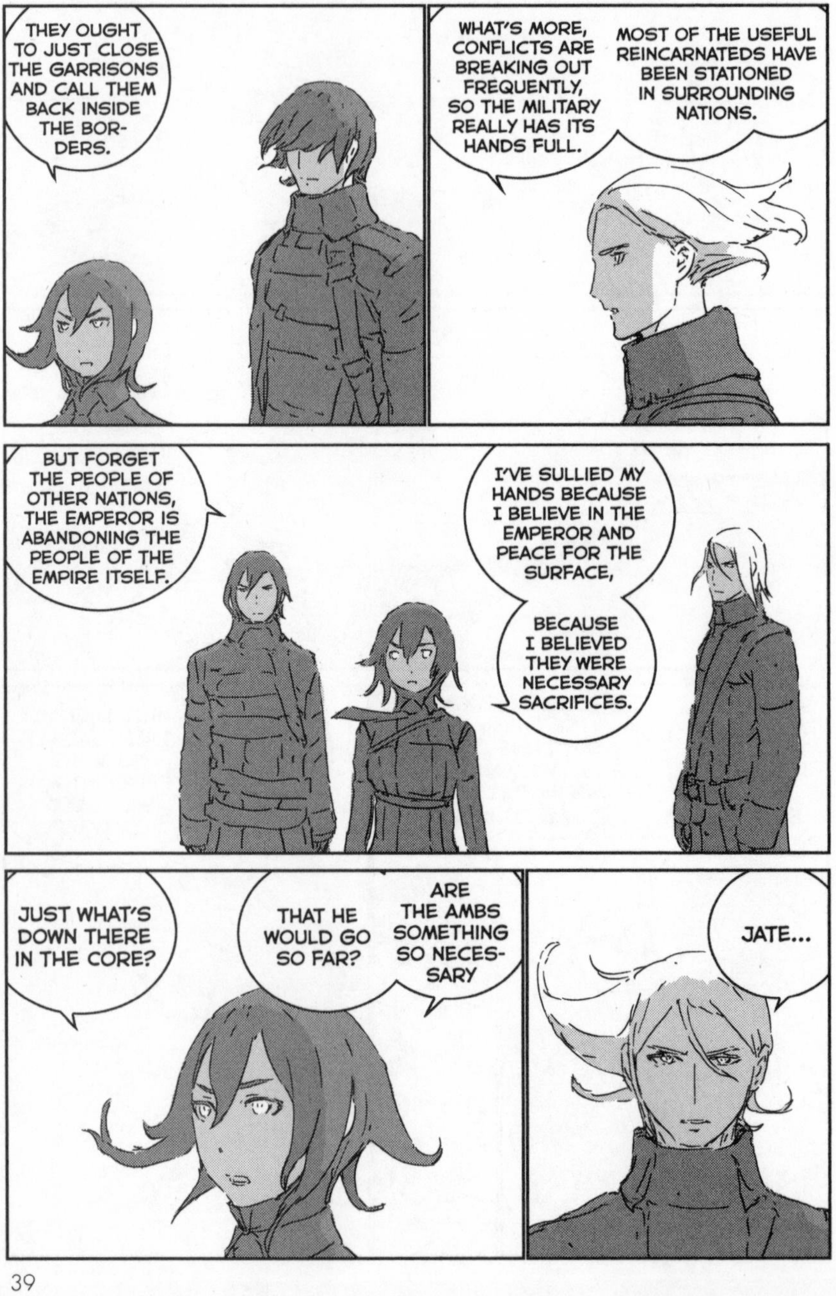
MOST OF THE USEFUL REINCARNATEDS HAVE BEEN STATIONED IN SURROUNDING NATIONS.
WHAT'S MORE, CONFLICTS ARE BREAKING OUT FREQUENTLY, SO THE MILITARY REALLY HAS ITS HANDS FULL.
THEY OUGHT TO JUST CLOSE THE GARRISONS AND CALL THEM BACK INSIDE THE BOR-DERS.
I'VE SULLIED MY HANDS BECAUSE I BELIEVE IN THE EMPEROR AND PEACE FOR THE SURFACE,
BECAUSE I BELIEVED THEY WERE NECESSARY SACRIFICES.
BUT FORGET THE PEOPLE OF OTHER NATIONS, THE EMPEROR IS ABANDONING THE PEOPLE OF THE EMPIRE ITSELF.
JATE...
ARE THE AMBS SOMETHING SO NECES-SARY
THAT HE WOULD GO SO FAR?
JUST WHAT'S DOWN THERE IN THE CORE?

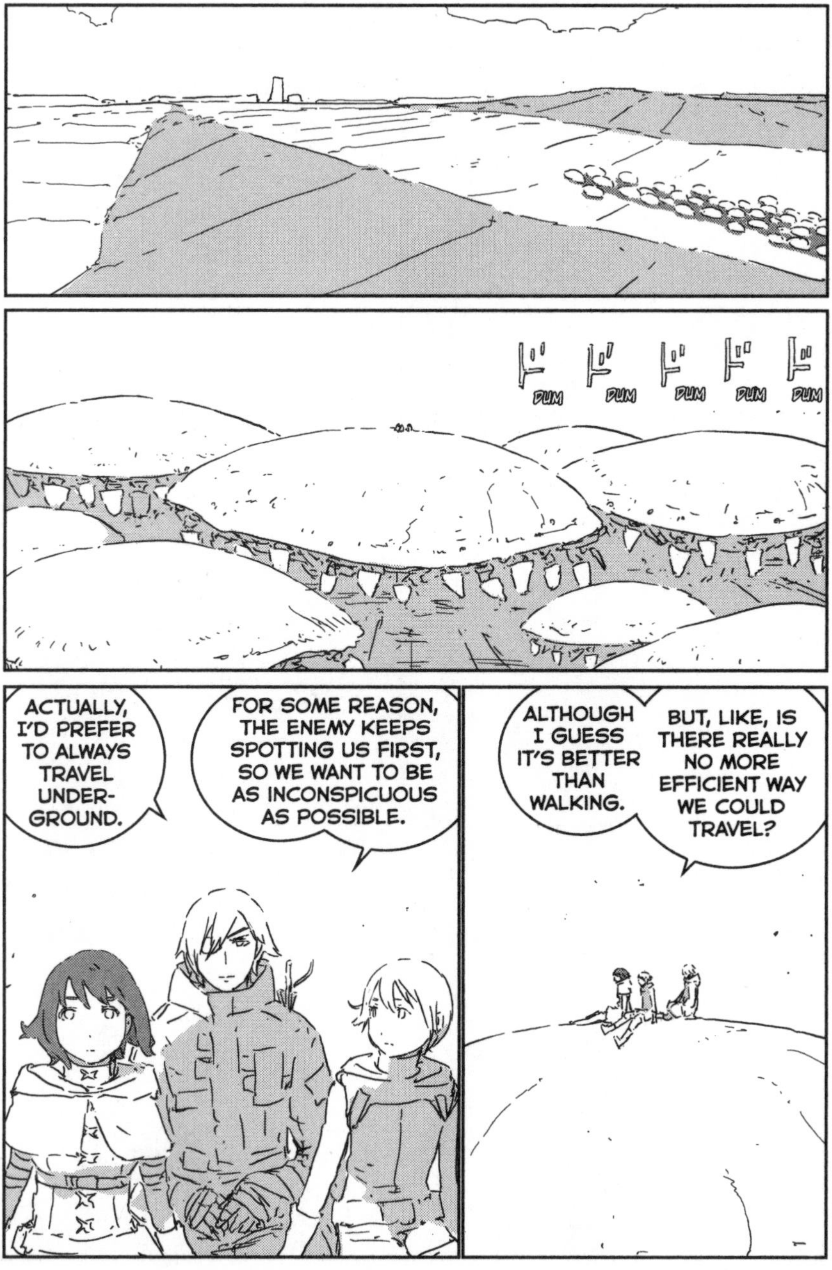
ドドドドド
DUM DUM DUM DUM DUM
BUT, LIKE, IS THERE REALLY NO MORE EFFICIENT WAY WE COULD TRAVEL?
ALTHOUGH I GUESS IT'S BETTER THAN WALKING.
FOR SOME REASON, THE ENEMY KEEPS SPOTTING US FIRST, SO WE WANT TO BE AS INCONSPICUOUS AS POSSIBLE.
ACTUALLY, I'D PREFER TO ALWAYS TRAVEL UNDER-GROUND.

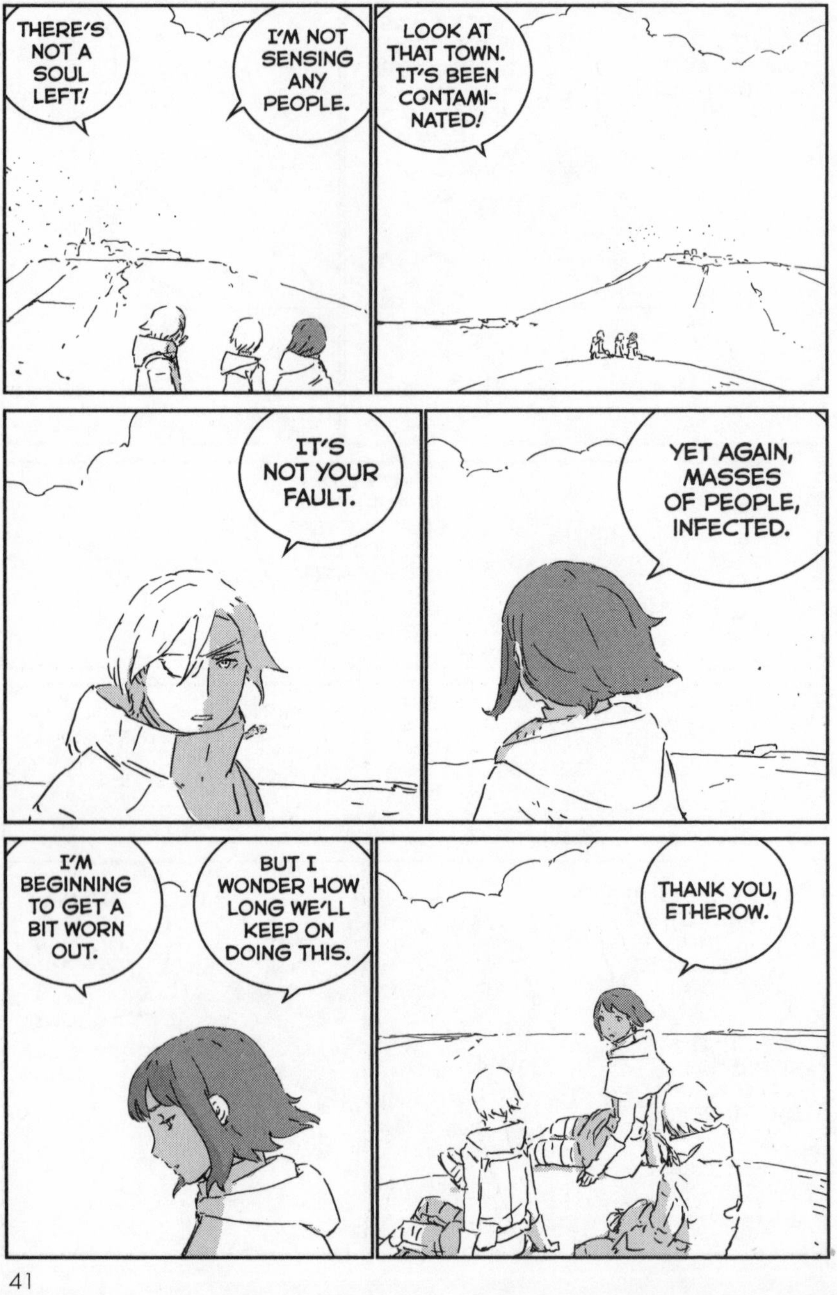
LOOK AT THAT TOWN. IT'S BEEN CONTAMI-NATED!
I'M NOT SENSING ANY PEOPLE.
THERE'S NOT A SOUL LEFT!
YET AGAIN, MASSES OF PEOPLE, INFECTED.
IT'S NOT YOUR FAULT.
THANK YOU, ETHEROW.
BUT I WONDER HOW LONG WE'LL KEEP ON DOING THIS.
I'M BEGINNING TO GET A BIT WORN OUT.

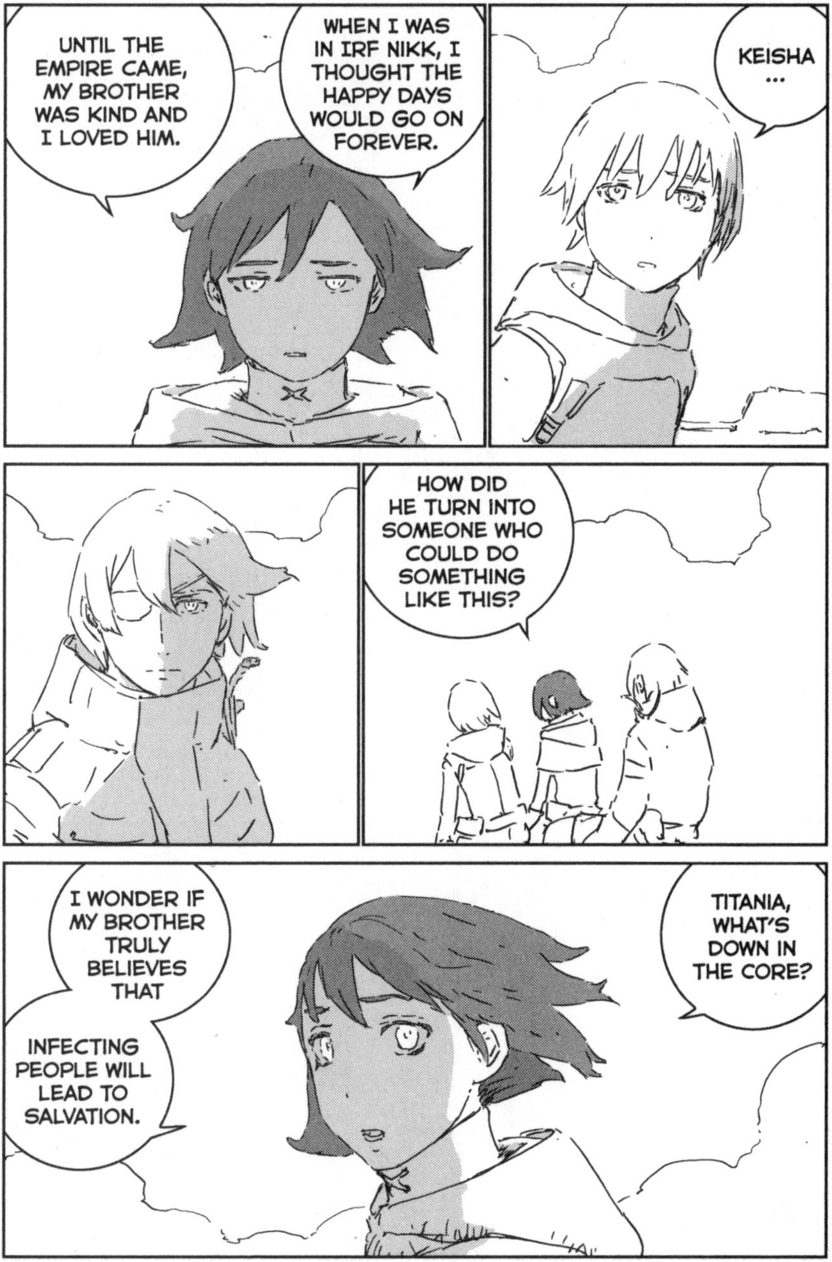
KEISHA ...
WHEN I WAS IN IRF NIKK, I THOUGHT THE HAPPY DAYS WOULD GO ON FOREVER.
UNTIL THE EMPIRE CAME, MY BROTHER WAS KIND AND I LOVED HIM.
HOW DID HE TURN INTO SOMEONE WHO COULD DO SOMETHING LIKE THIS?
TITANIA, WHAT'S DOWN IN THE CORE?
I WONDER IF MY BROTHER TRULY BELIEVES THAT
INFECTING PEOPLE WILL LEAD TO SALVATION.

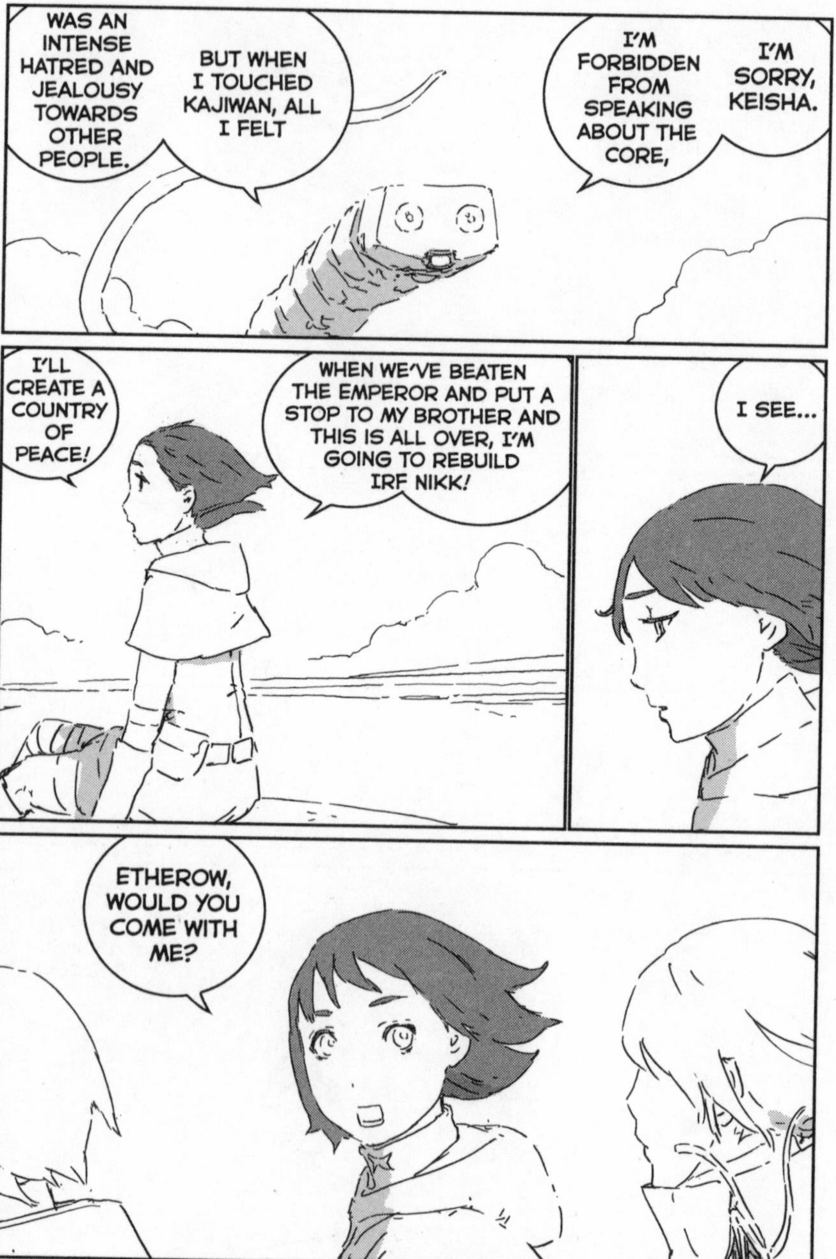
I'M SORRY, KEISHA.
I'M FORBIDDEN FROM SPEAKING ABOUT THE CORE,
BUT WHEN I TOUCHED KAJIWAN, ALL I FELT
WAS AN INTENSE HATRED AND JEALOUSY TOWARDS OTHER PEOPLE.
I SEE...
WHEN WE'VE BEATEN THE EMPEROR AND PUT A STOP TO MY BROTHER AND THIS IS ALL OVER, I'M GOING TO REBUILD IRF NIKK!
I'LL CREATE A COUNTRY OF PEACE!
ETHEROW, WOULD YOU COME WITH ME?

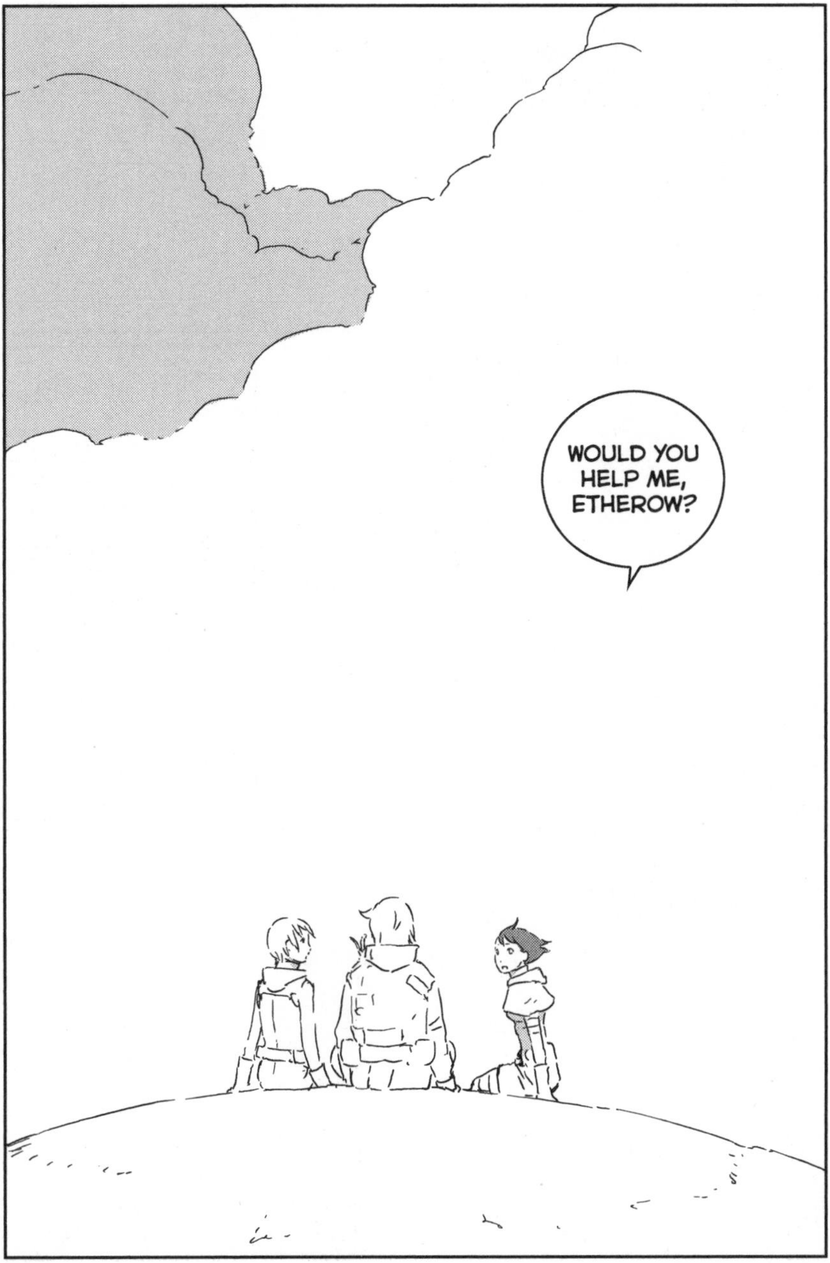
WOULD YOU HELP ME, ETHEROW?

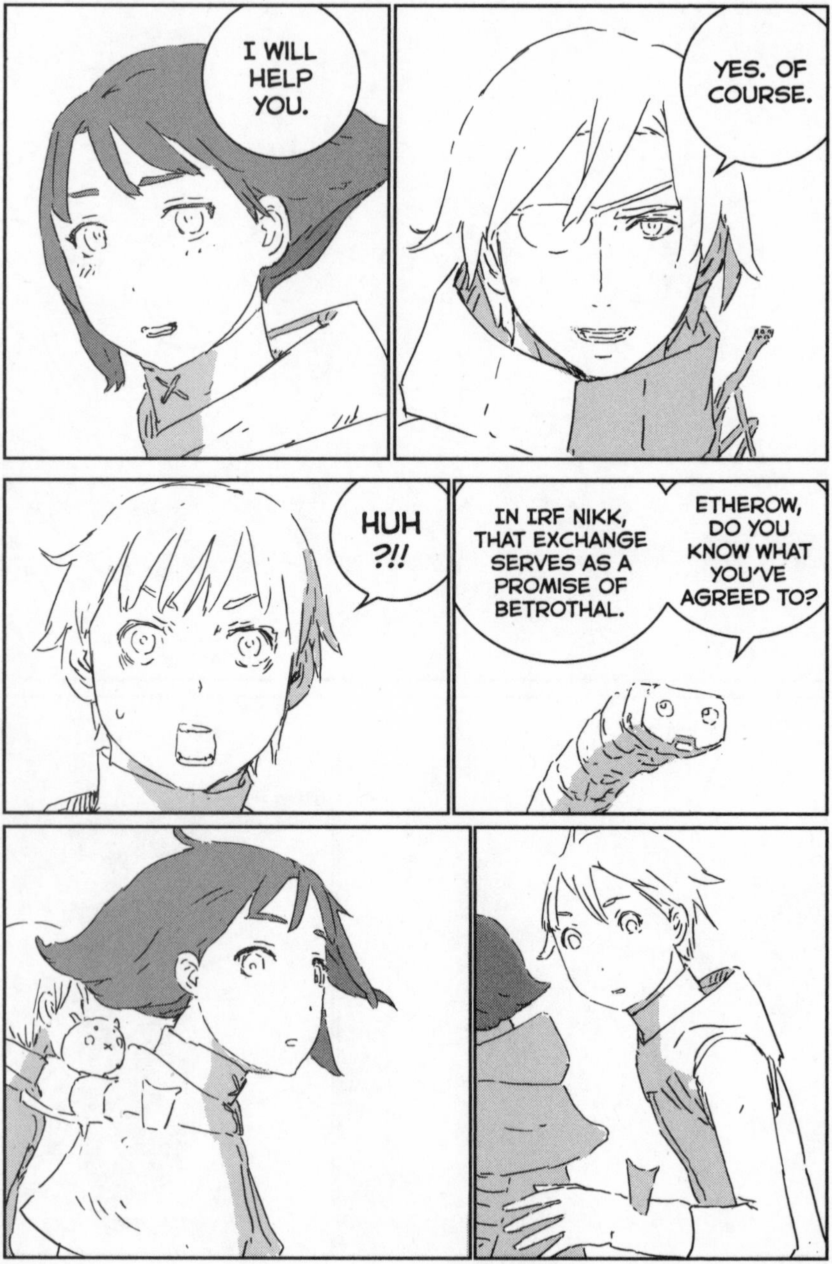
YES. OF COURSE.
I WILL HELP YOU.
ETHEROW, DO YOU KNOW WHAT YOU'VE AGREED TO?
IN IRF NIKK, THAT EXCHANGE SERVES AS A PROMISE OF BETROTHAL.
HUH ?!!

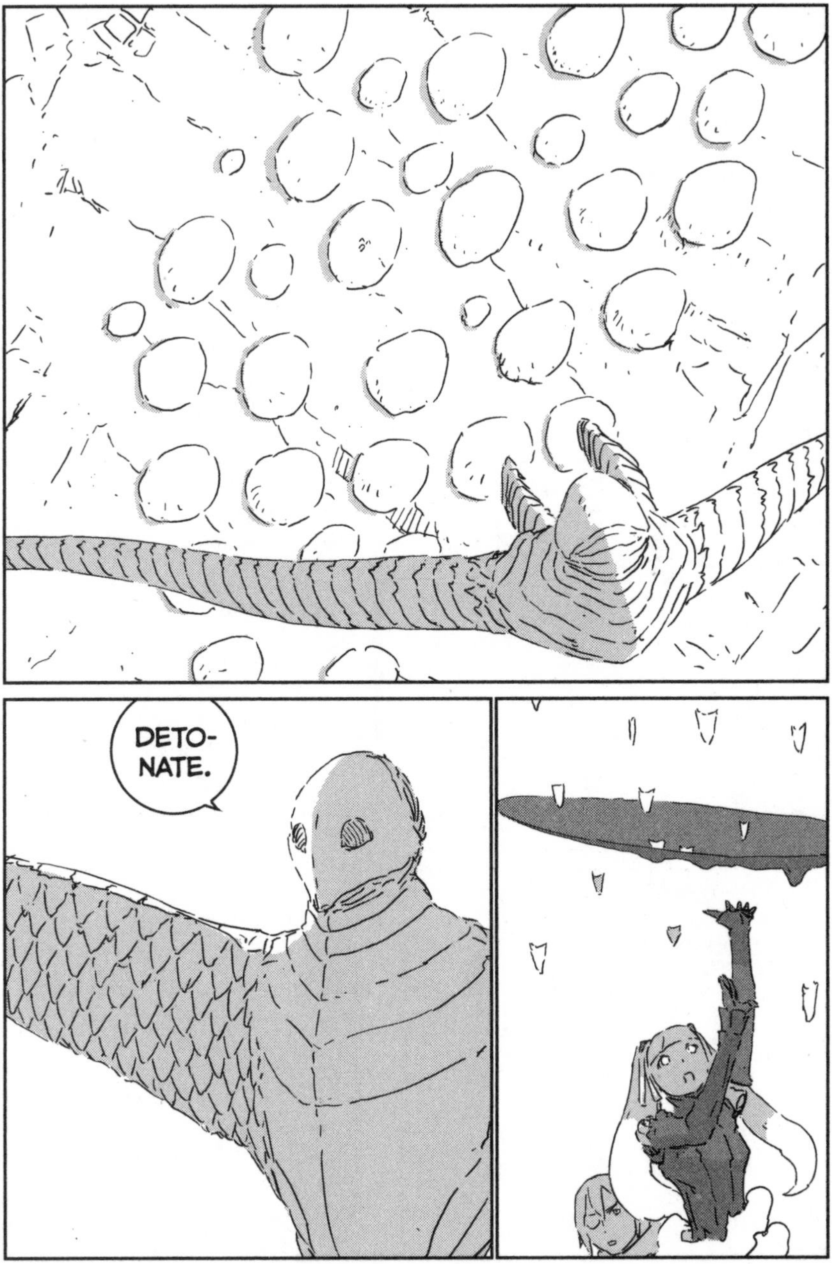
DETO-
NATE.

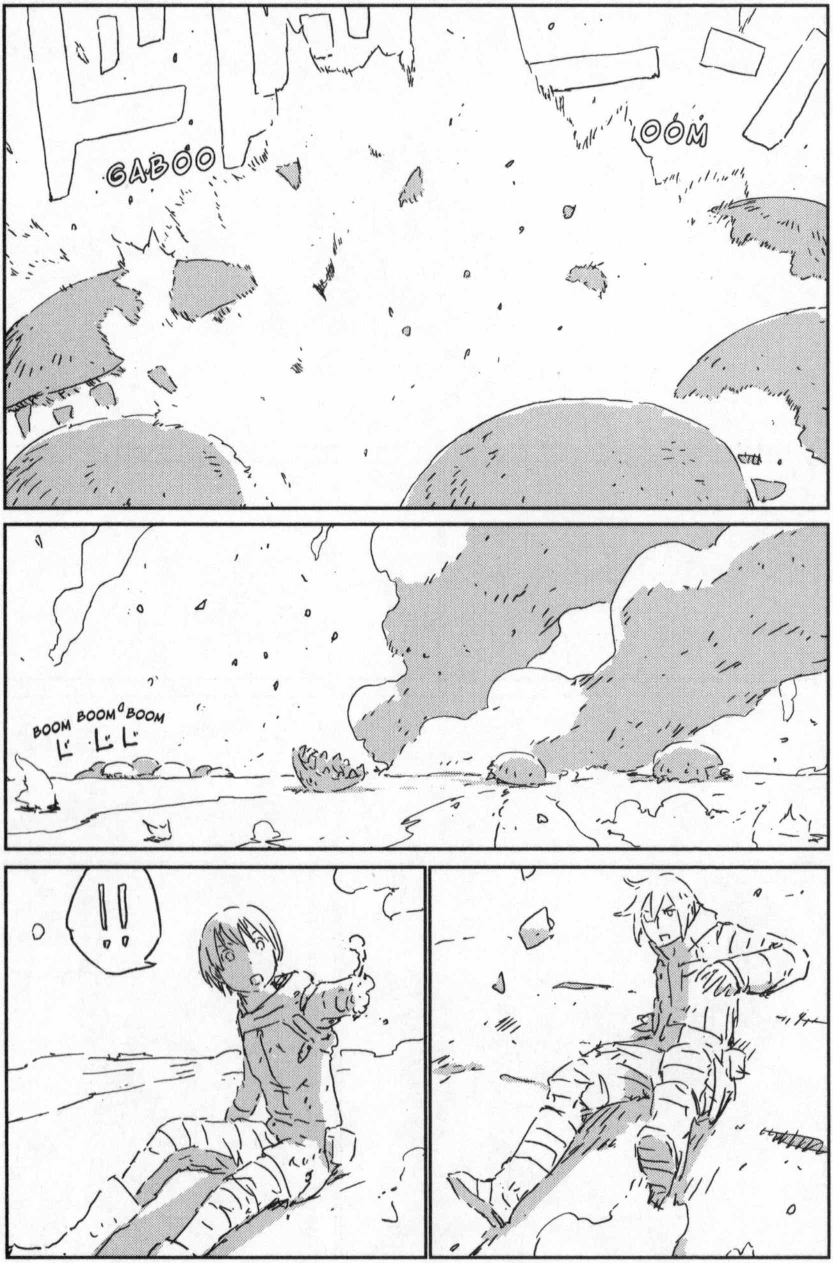
GABOO
OOM
BOOM BOOM BOOM
!!

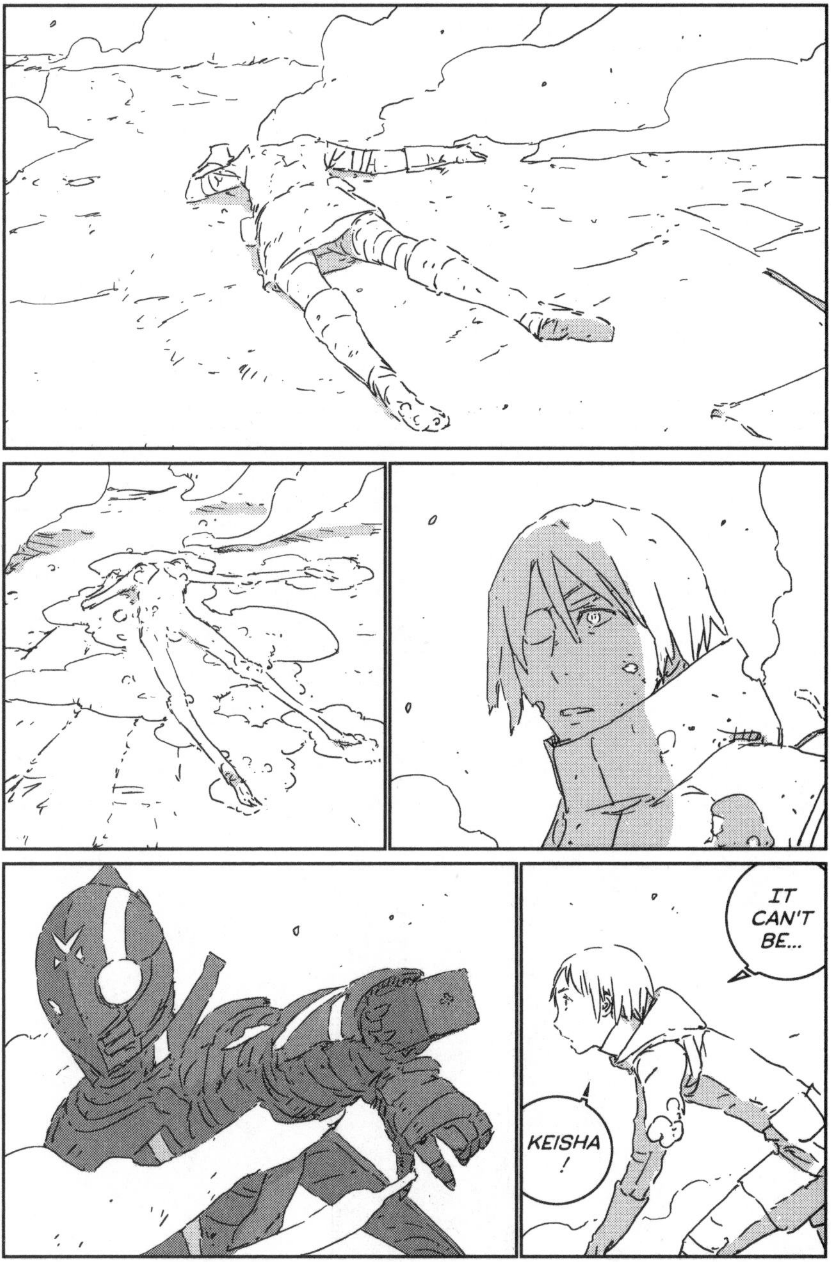
IT CAN'T BE...
KEISHA!

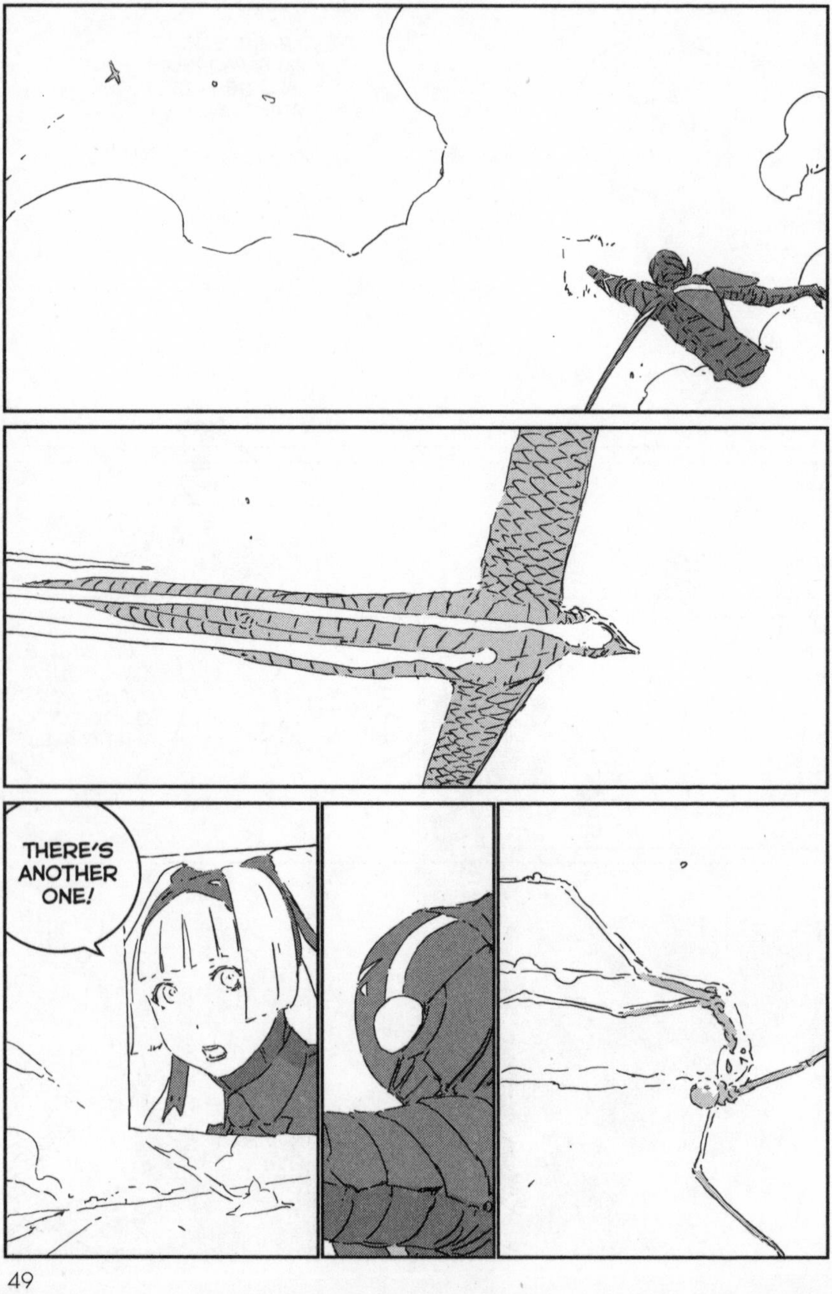
THERE'S ANOTHER ONE!

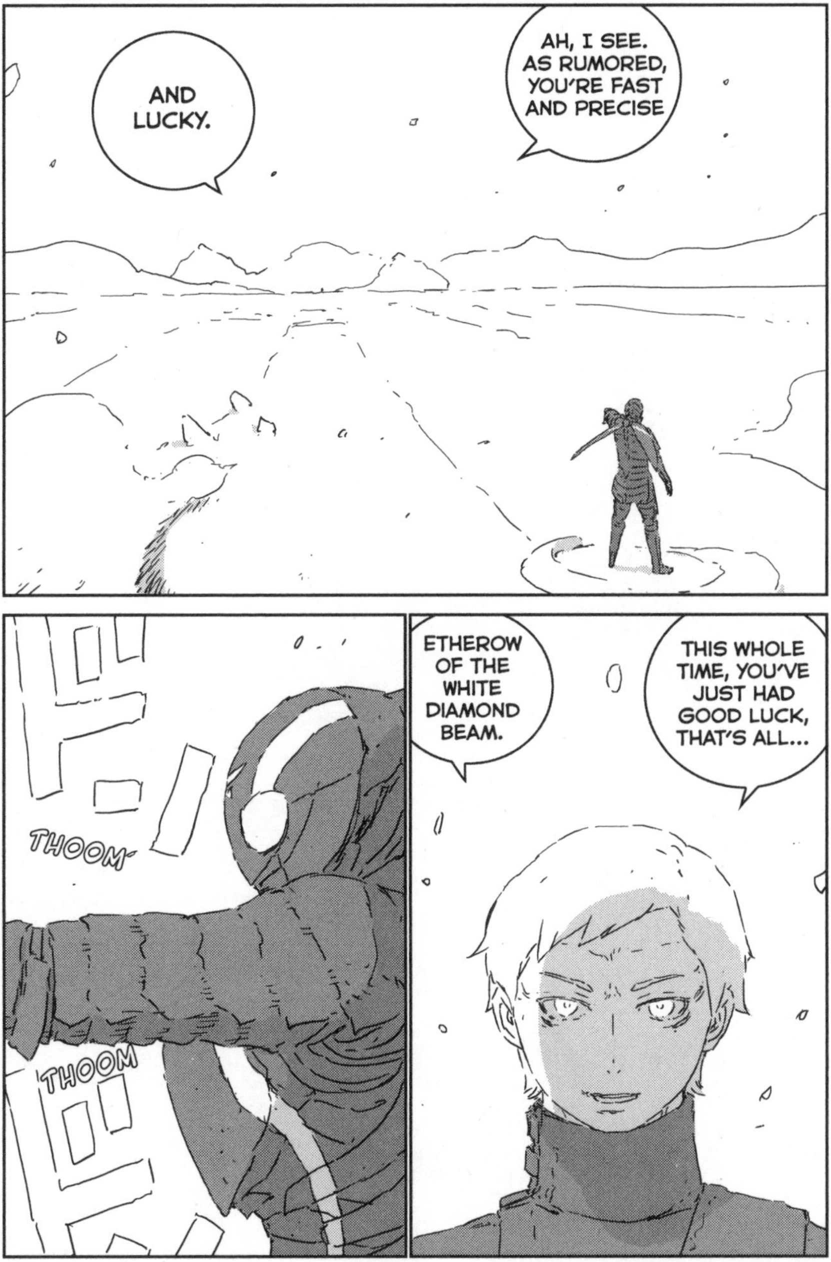
AH, I SEE. AS RUMORED, YOU'RE FAST AND PRECISE
AND LUCKY.
THIS WHOLE TIME, YOU'VE JUST HAD GOOD LUCK, THAT'S ALL...
ETHEROW OF THE WHITE DIAMOND BEAM.
THOOM
THOOM

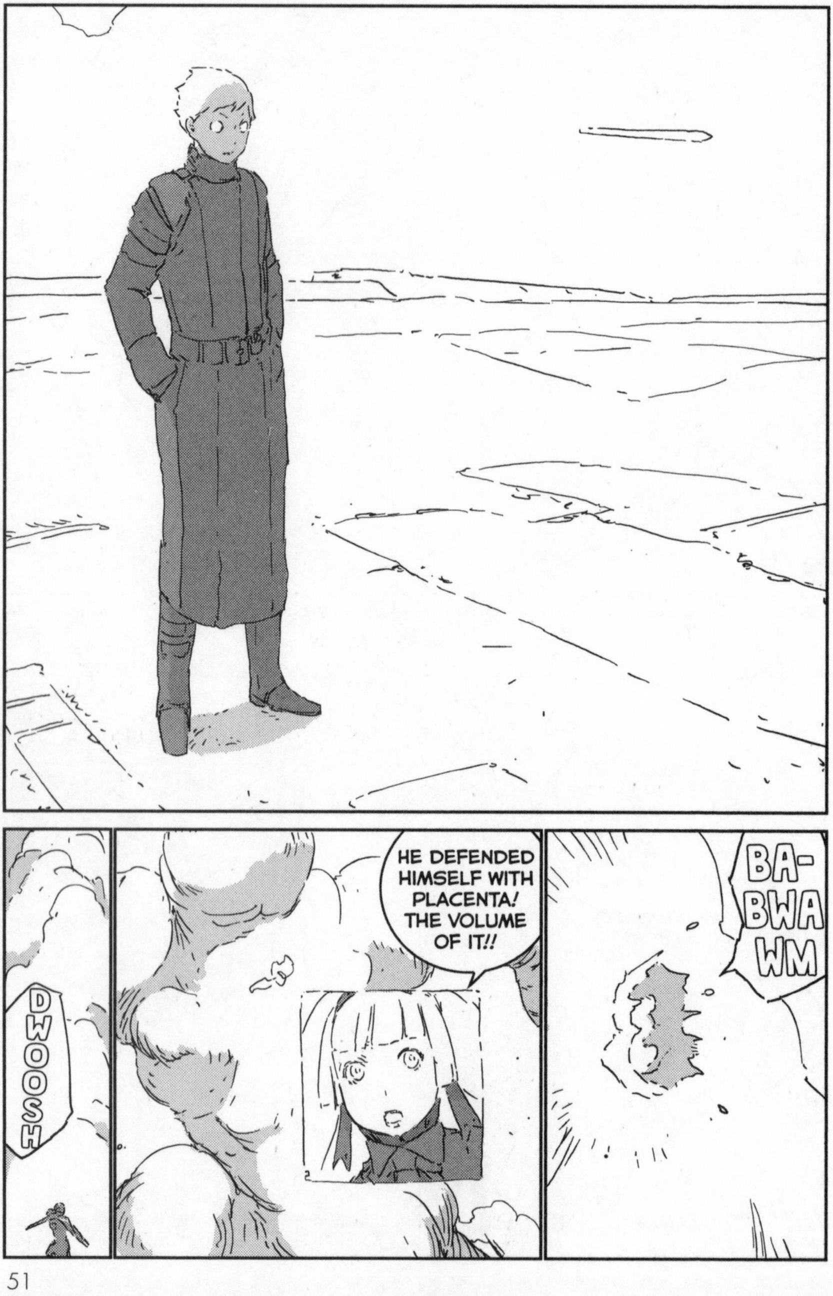
BA-BWAWM
HE DEFENDED HIMSELF WITH PLACENTA! THE VOLUME OF IT!!
DWOOSH

MUST BE TEN YEARS SINCE I PROPERLY ARMORED UP.
BUT NOW, BECAUSE YOU'VE KILLED FAR TOO MANY OF MY SUBORDI-NATES...

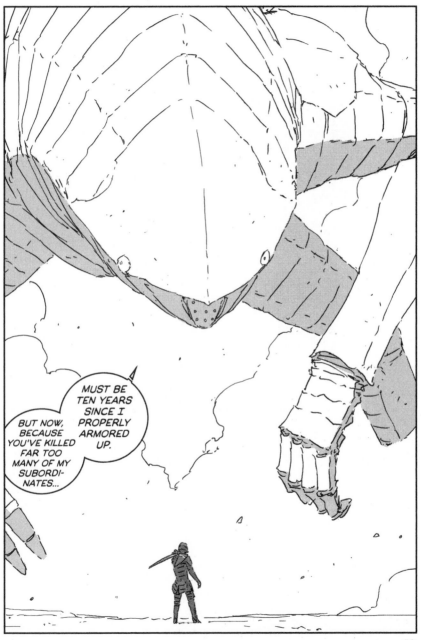

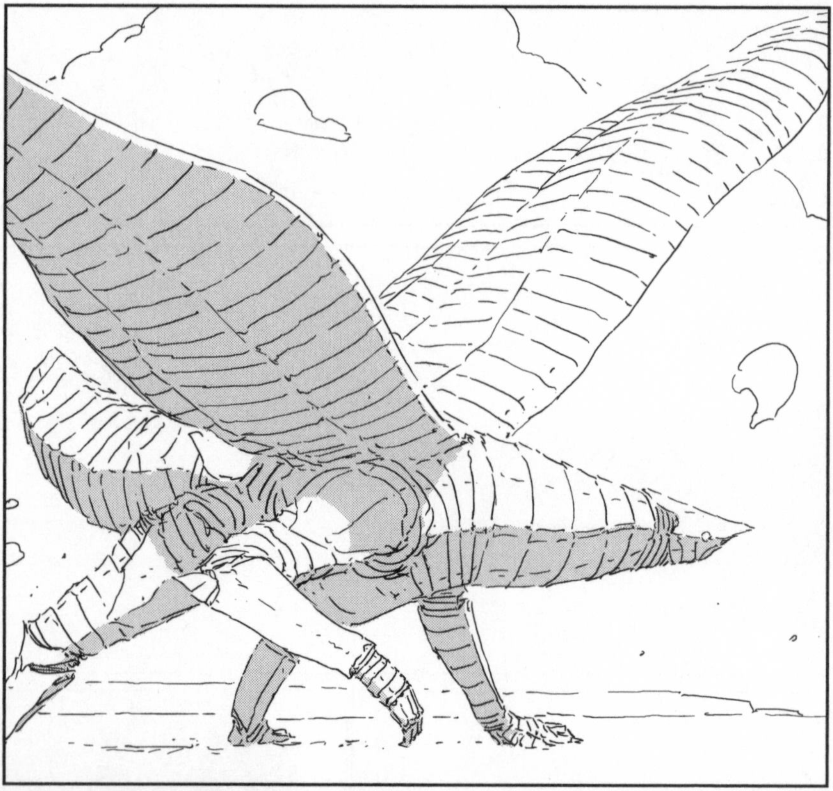

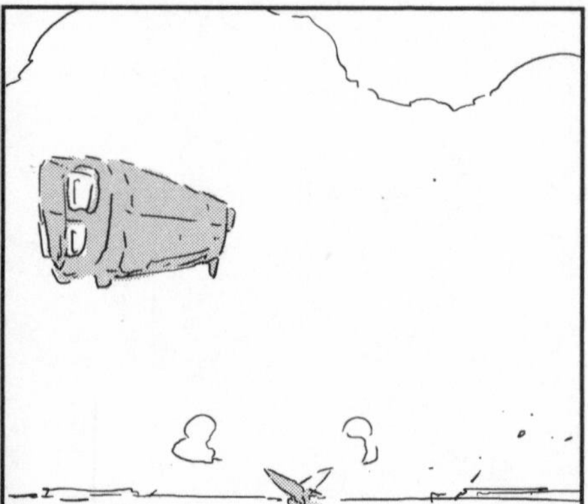

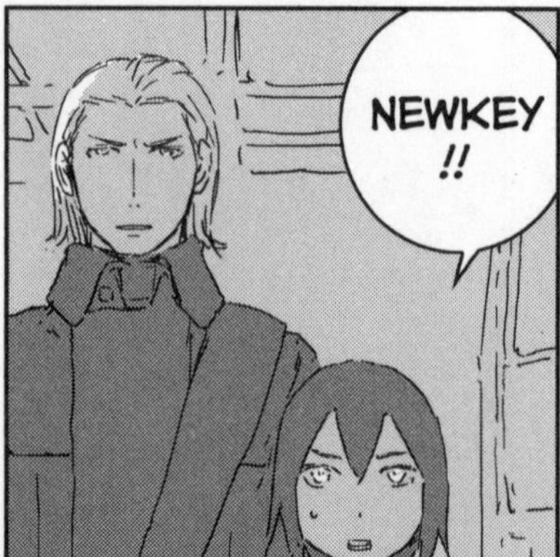
NEWKEY !!

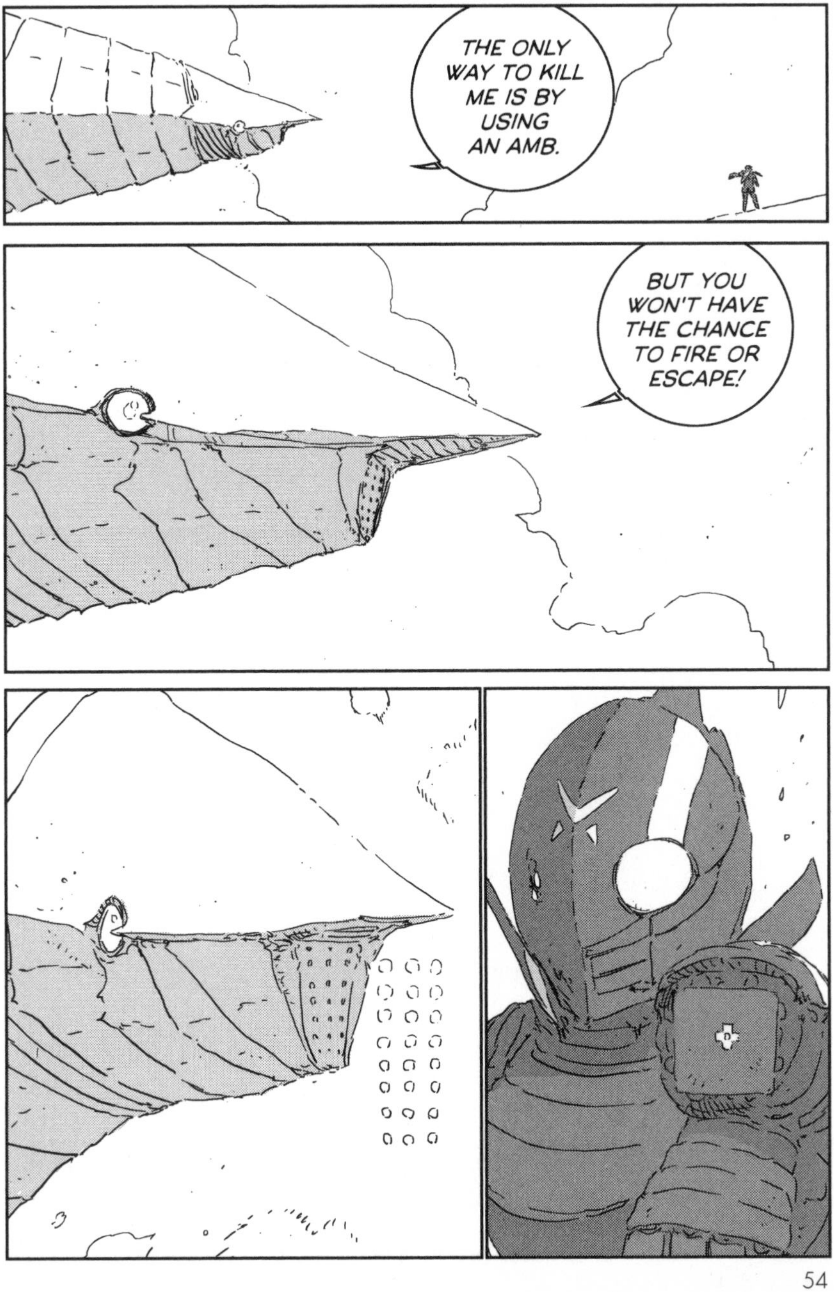
THE ONLY WAY TO KILL ME IS BY USING AN AMB.
BUT YOU WON'T HAVE THE CHANCE TO FIRE OR ESCAPE!

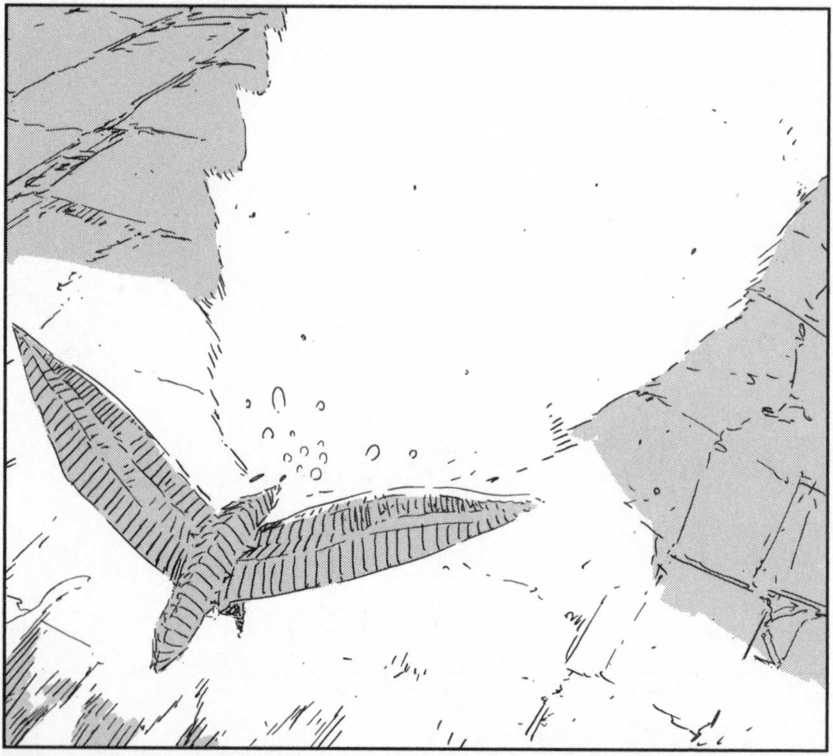

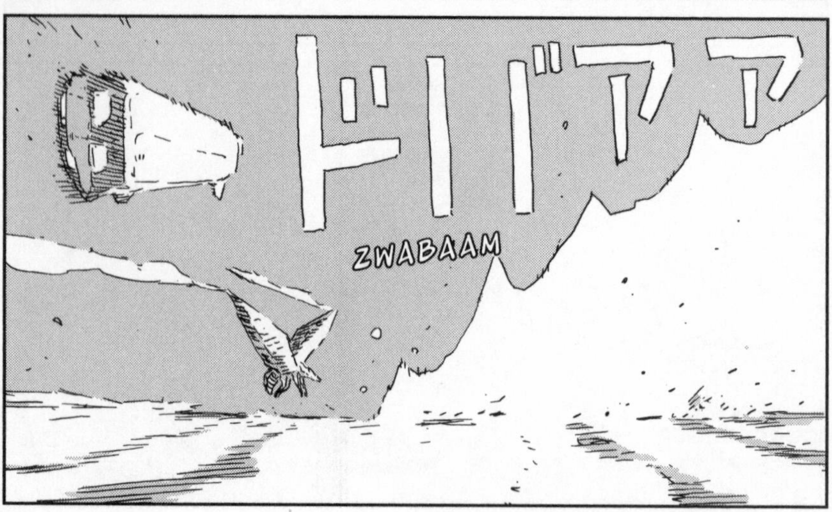
ドバアア
ZWABAAM

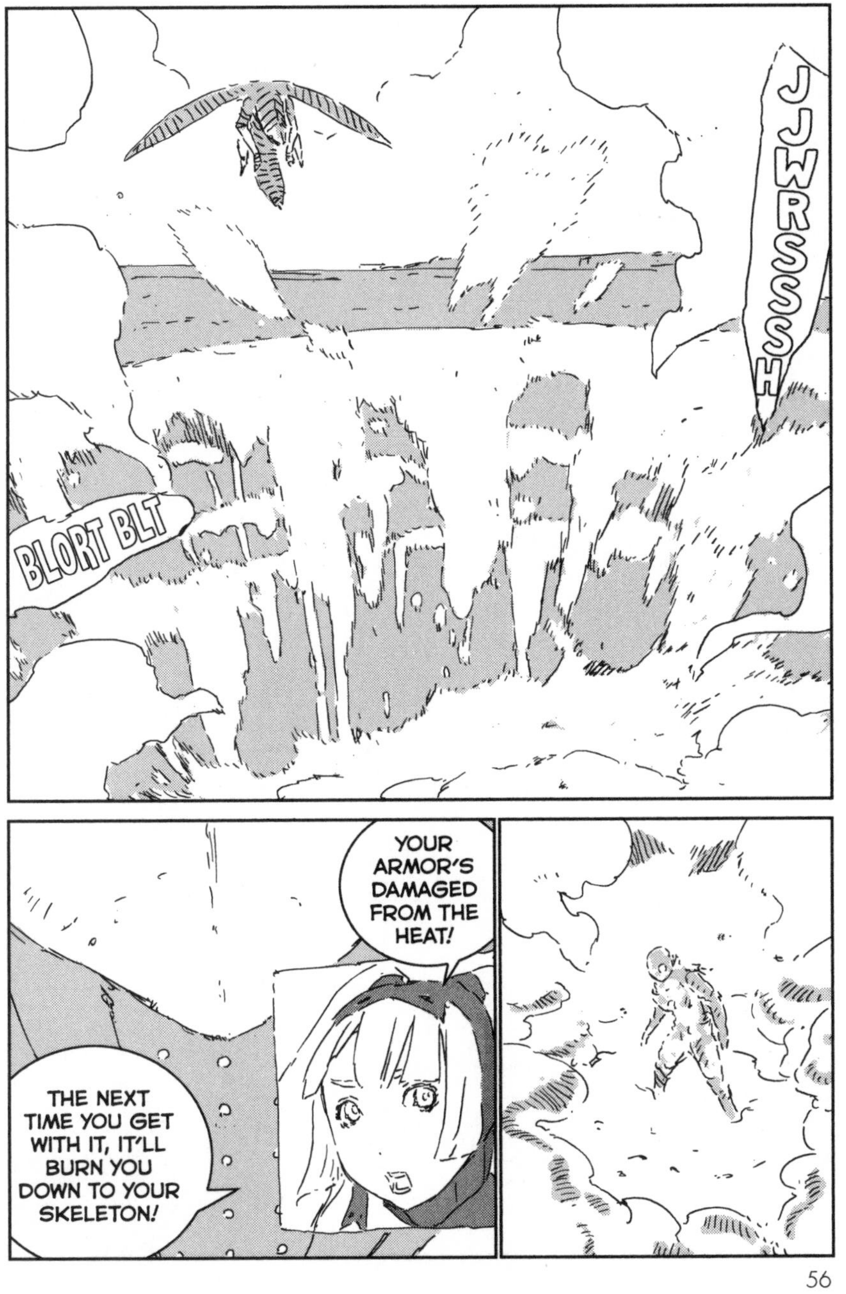
JJWRSSSSH
BLORT BLT
YOUR ARMOR'S DAMAGED FROM THE HEAT!
THE NEXT TIME YOU GET WITH IT, IT'LL BURN YOU DOWN TO YOUR SKELETON!

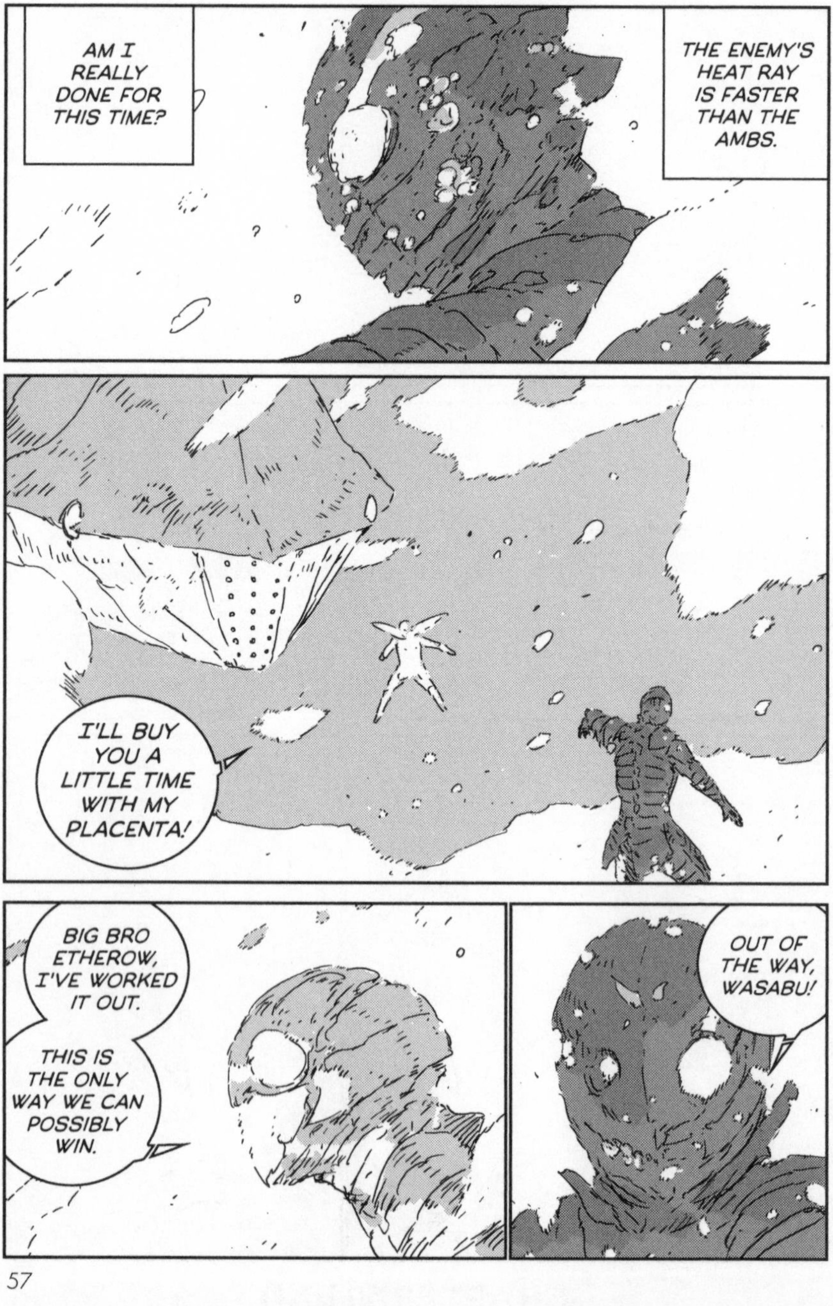
AM I REALLY DONE FOR THIS TIME?
THE ENEMY'S HEAT RAY IS FASTER THAN THE AMBS.
I'LL BUY YOU A LITTLE TIME WITH MY PLACENTA!
BIG BRO ETHEROW, I'VE WORKED IT OUT.
THIS IS THE ONLY WAY WE CAN POSSIBLY WIN.
OUT OF THE WAY, WASABU!

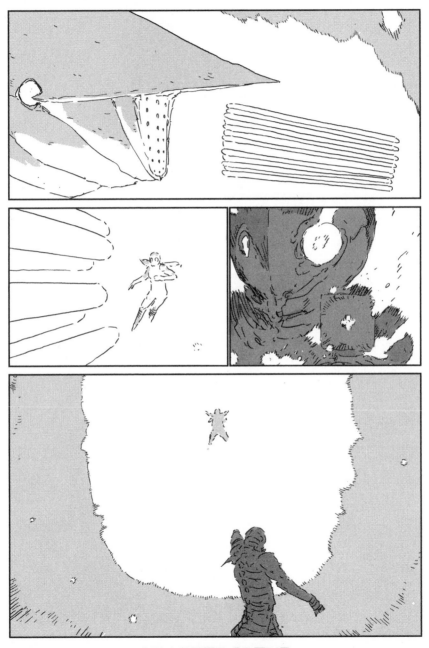

CHAPTER 50 END

APOSIMZ

X

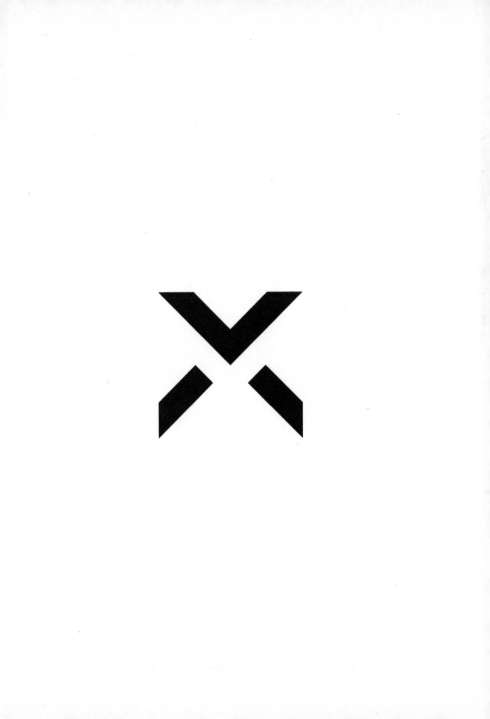

CHAPTER 51

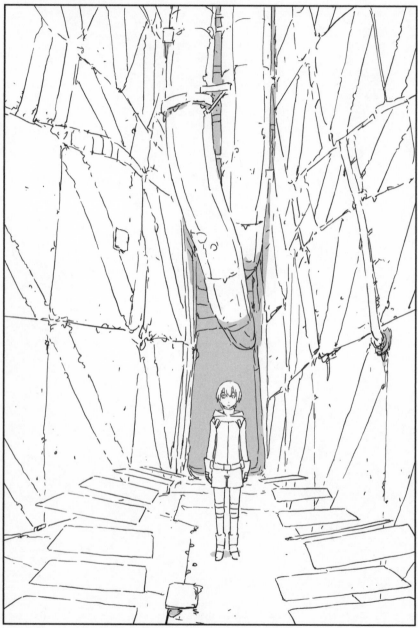

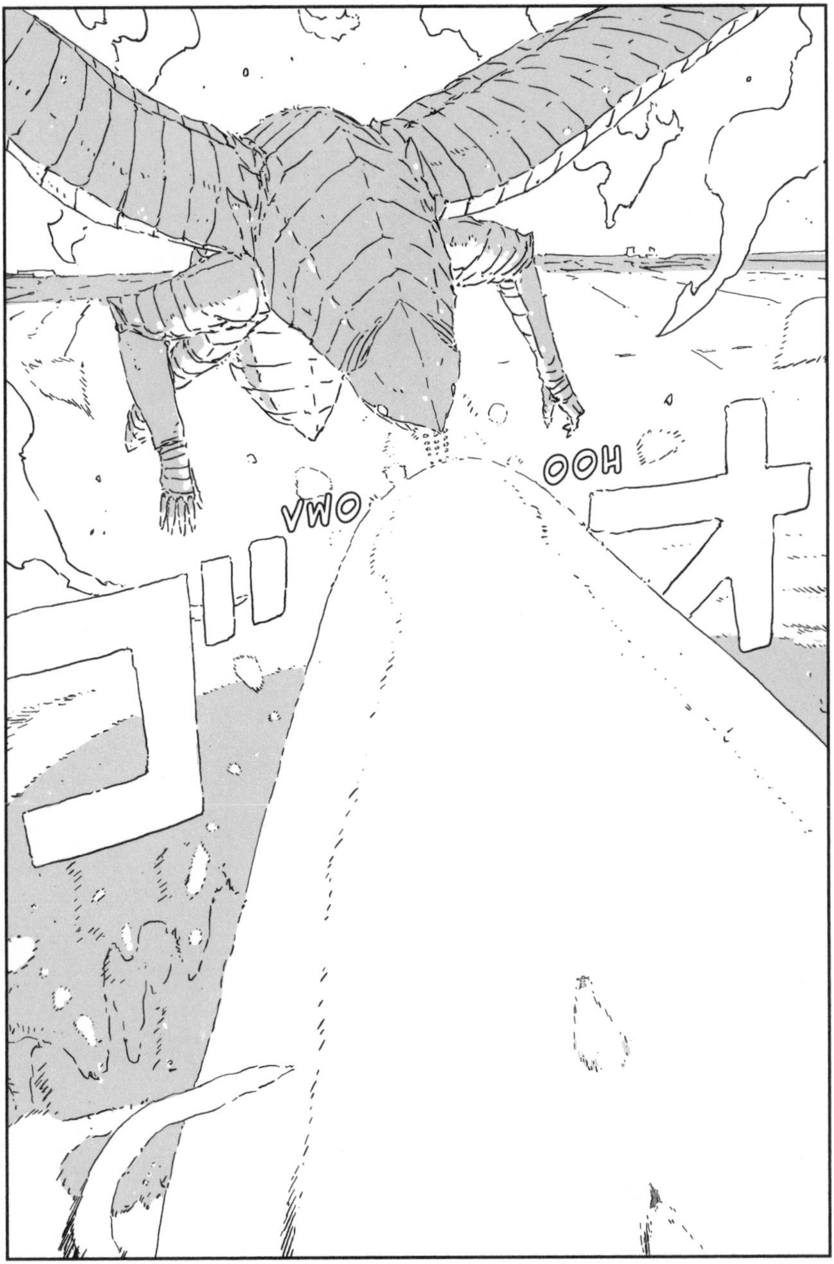
VWO
OOH
ゴ
オ

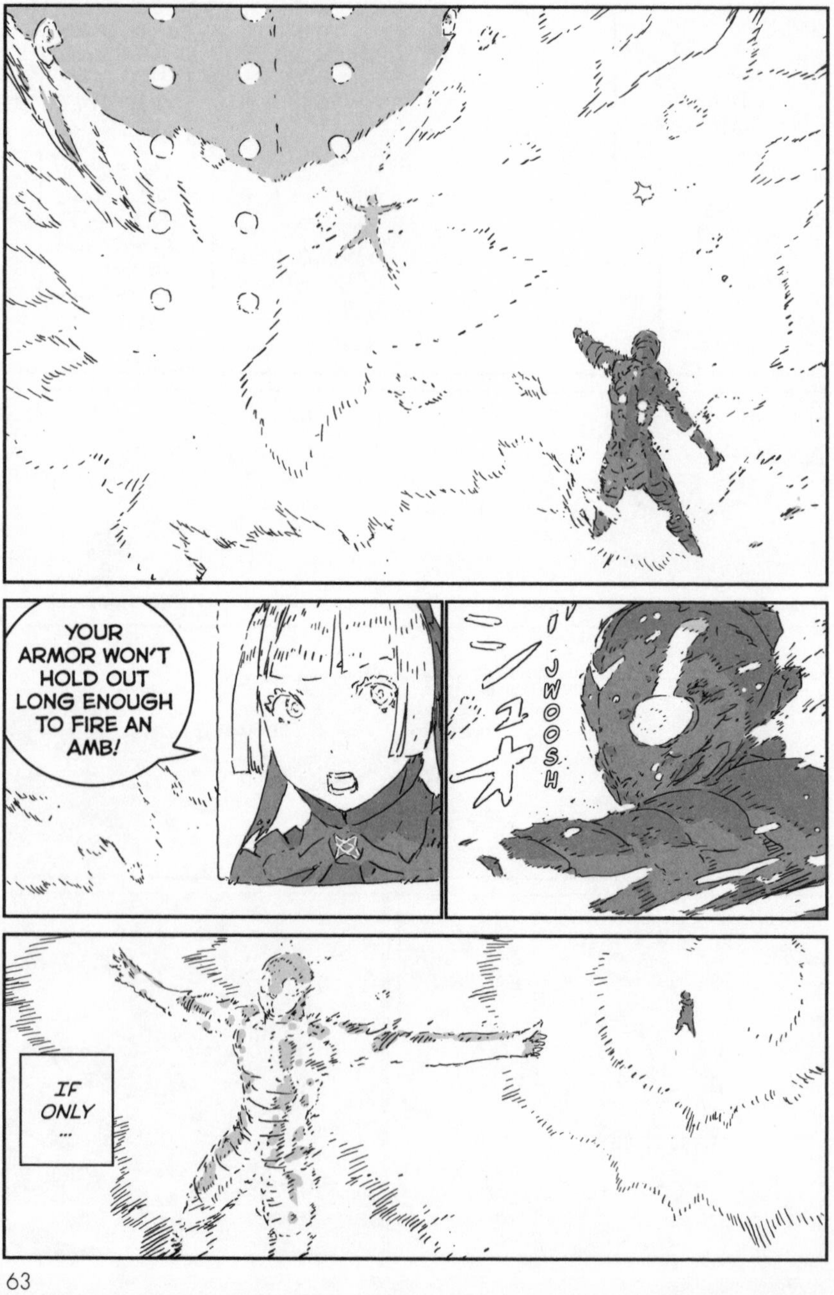
JWOOSH
YOUR ARMOR WON'T HOLD OUT LONG ENOUGH TO FIRE AN AMB!
IF ONLY ...

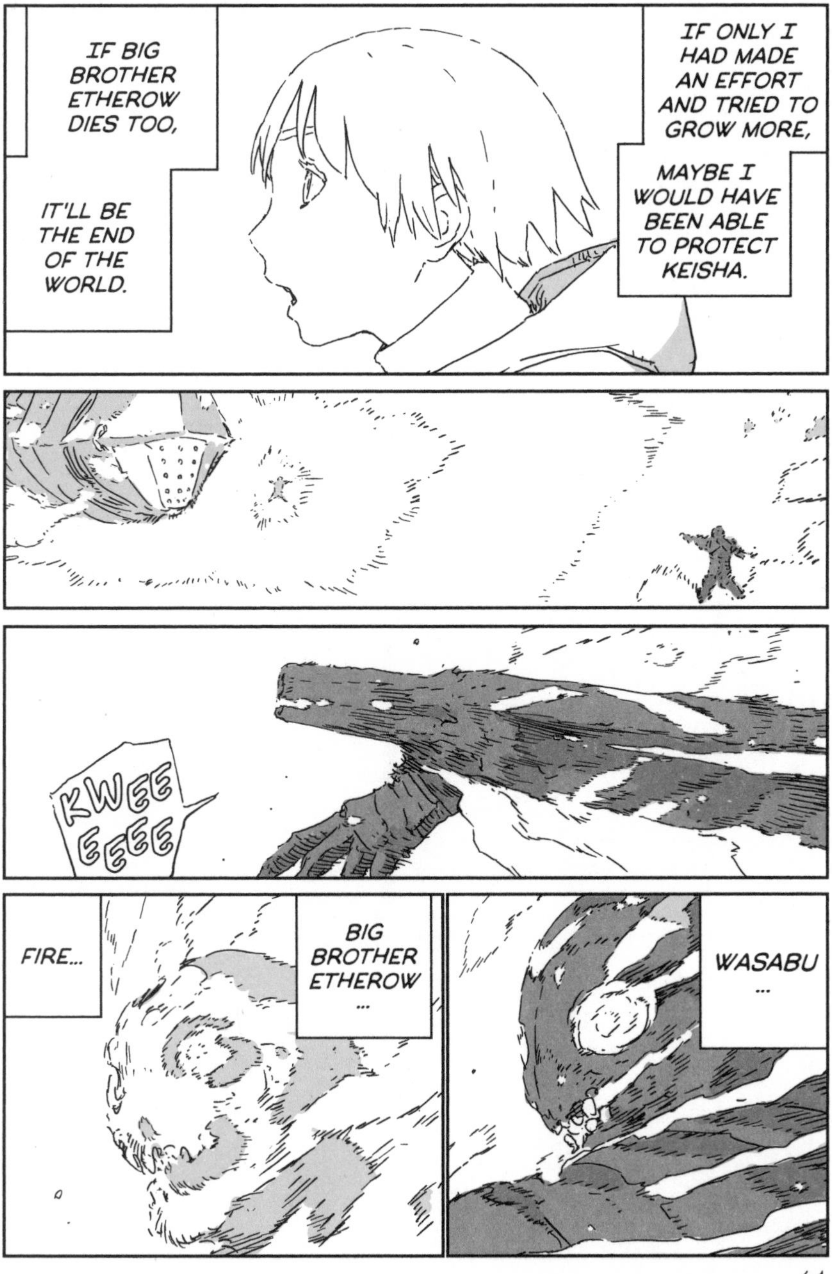
IF ONLY I HAD MADE AN EFFORT AND TRIED TO GROW MORE,
MAYBE I WOULD HAVE BEEN ABLE TO PROTECT KEISHA.
IF BIG BROTHER ETHEROW DIES TOO,
IT'LL BE THE END OF THE WORLD.
KWEE EEEE
WASABU ...
BIG BROTHER ETHEROW ...
FIRE...

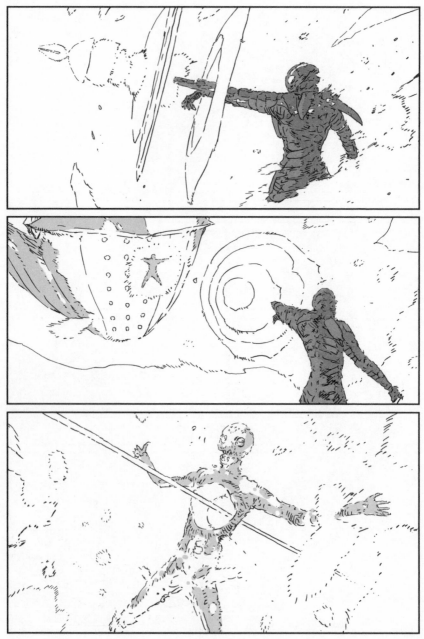

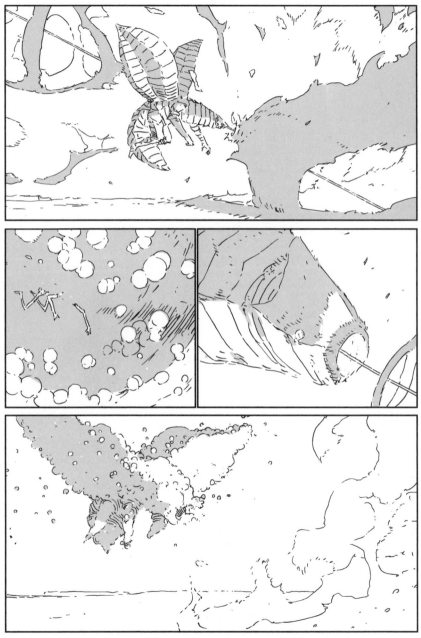

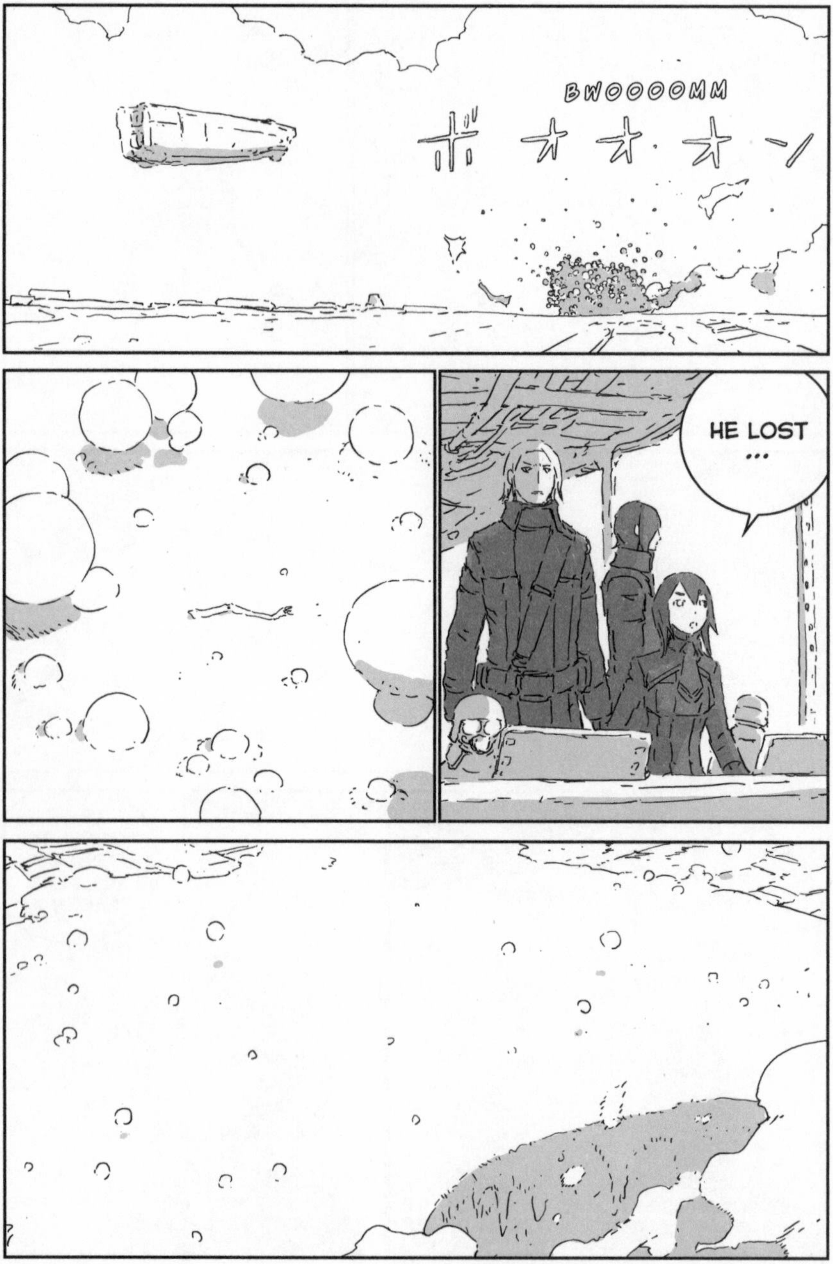
BWOOOOMM
ボオオ・オーン
HE LOST ...

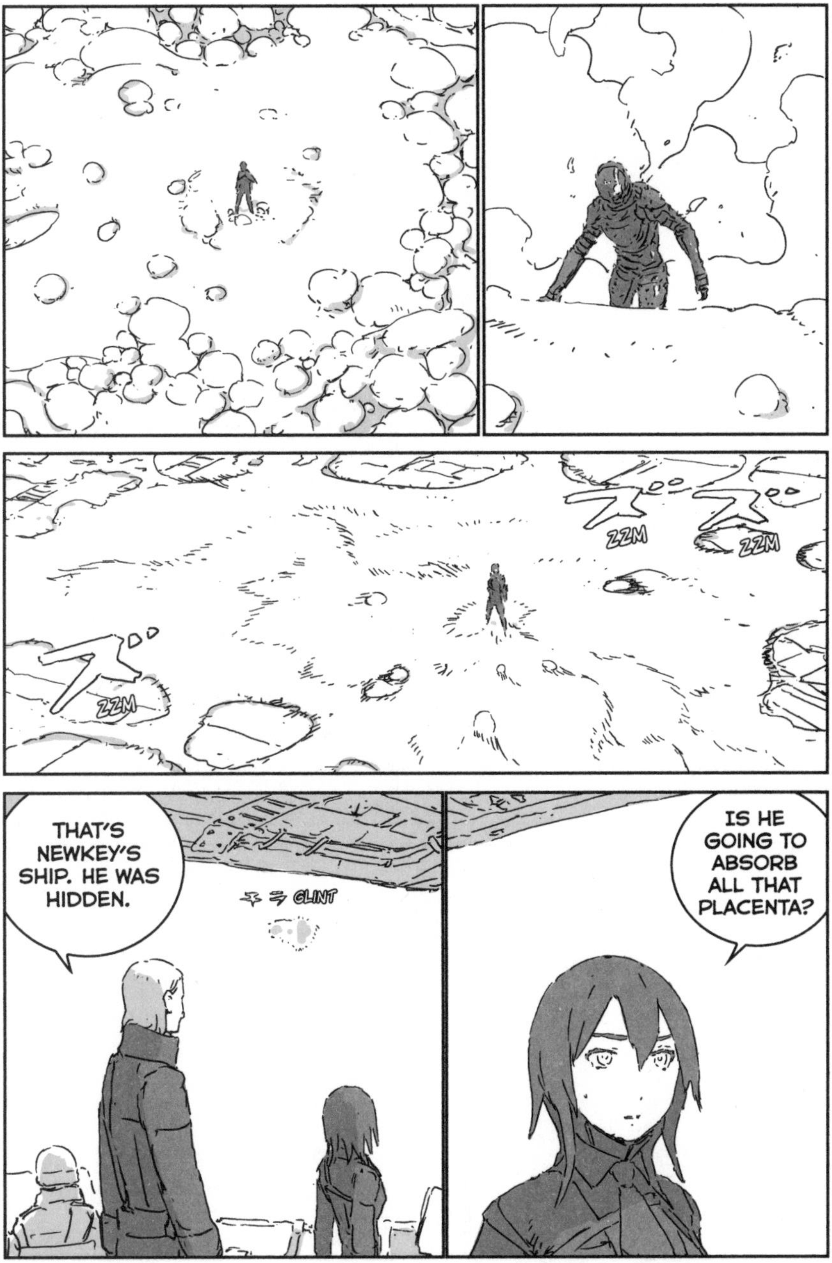
ZZM
ZZM
ZZM
IS HE GOING TO ABSORB ALL THAT PLACENTA?
THAT'S NEWKEY'S SHIP. HE WAS HIDDEN.
GLINT

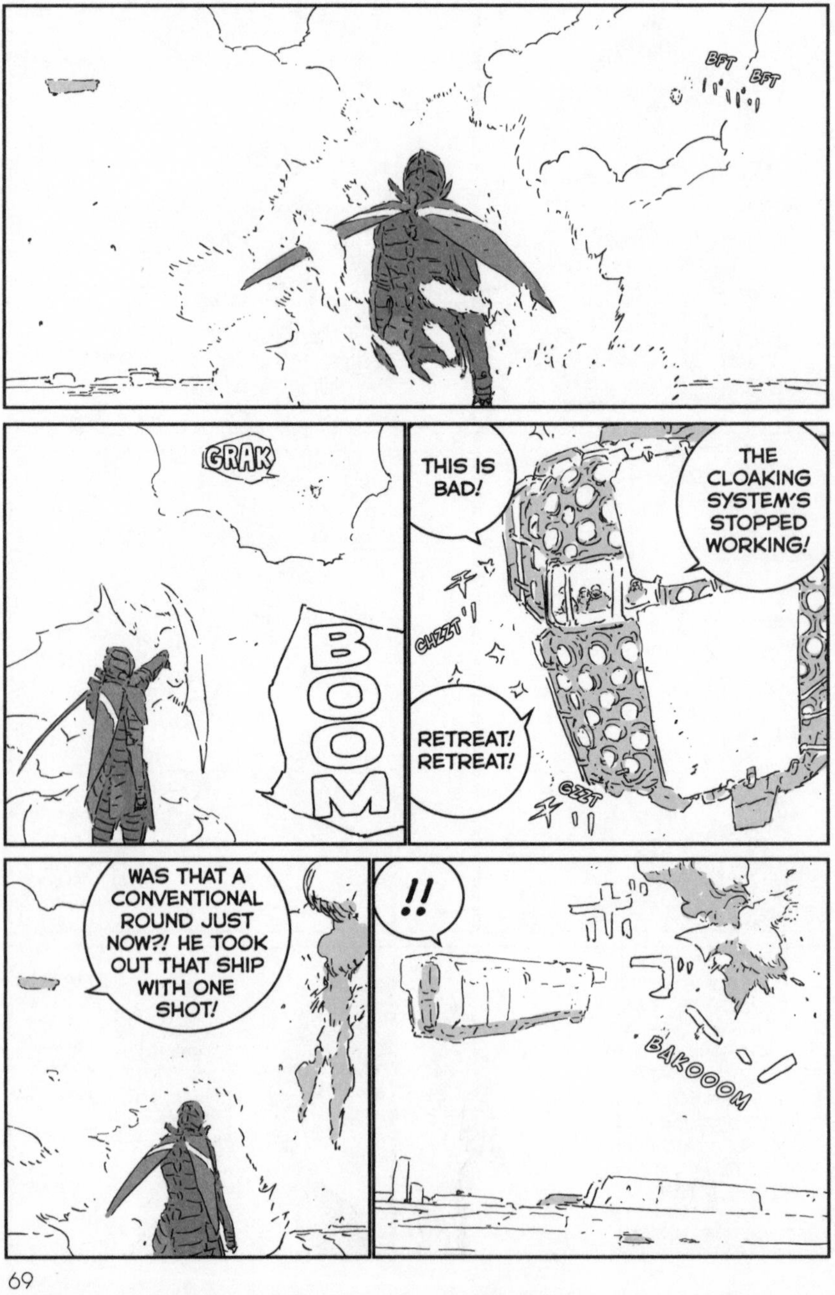
BFT BFT
THE CLOAKING SYSTEM'S STOPPED WORKING!
THIS IS BAD!
CHZZT
RETREAT! RETREAT!
GZZT
GRAK
BOOM
!!
BAKOOOM
WAS THAT A CONVENTIONAL ROUND JUST NOW?! HE TOOK OUT THAT SHIP WITH ONE SHOT!

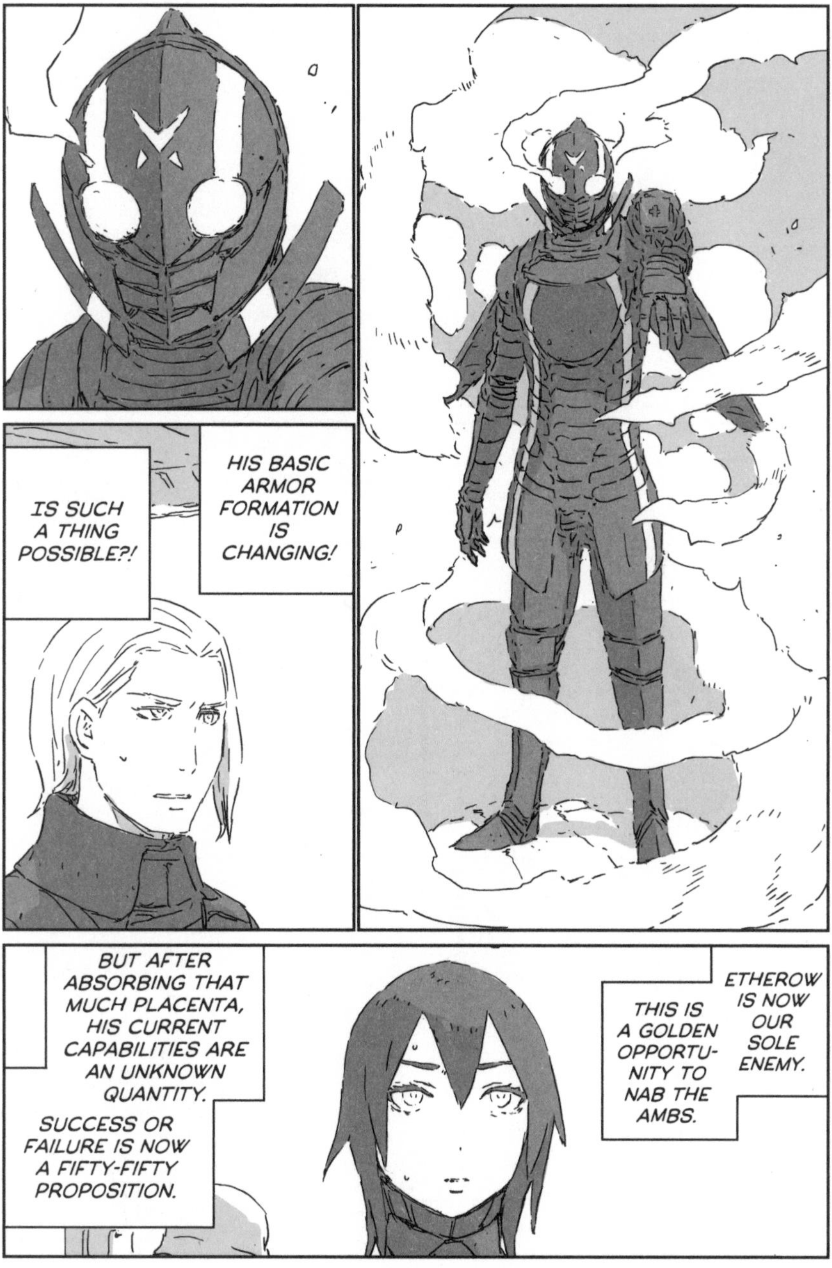
HIS BASIC ARMOR FORMATION IS CHANGING!
IS SUCH A THING POSSIBLE?!
ETHEROW IS NOW OUR SOLE ENEMY.
THIS IS A GOLDEN OPPORTU-NITY TO NAB THE AMBS.
BUT AFTER ABSORBING THAT MUCH PLACENTA, HIS CURRENT CAPABILITIES ARE AN UNKNOWN QUANTITY.
SUCCESS OR FAILURE IS NOW A FIFTY-FIFTY PROPOSITION.

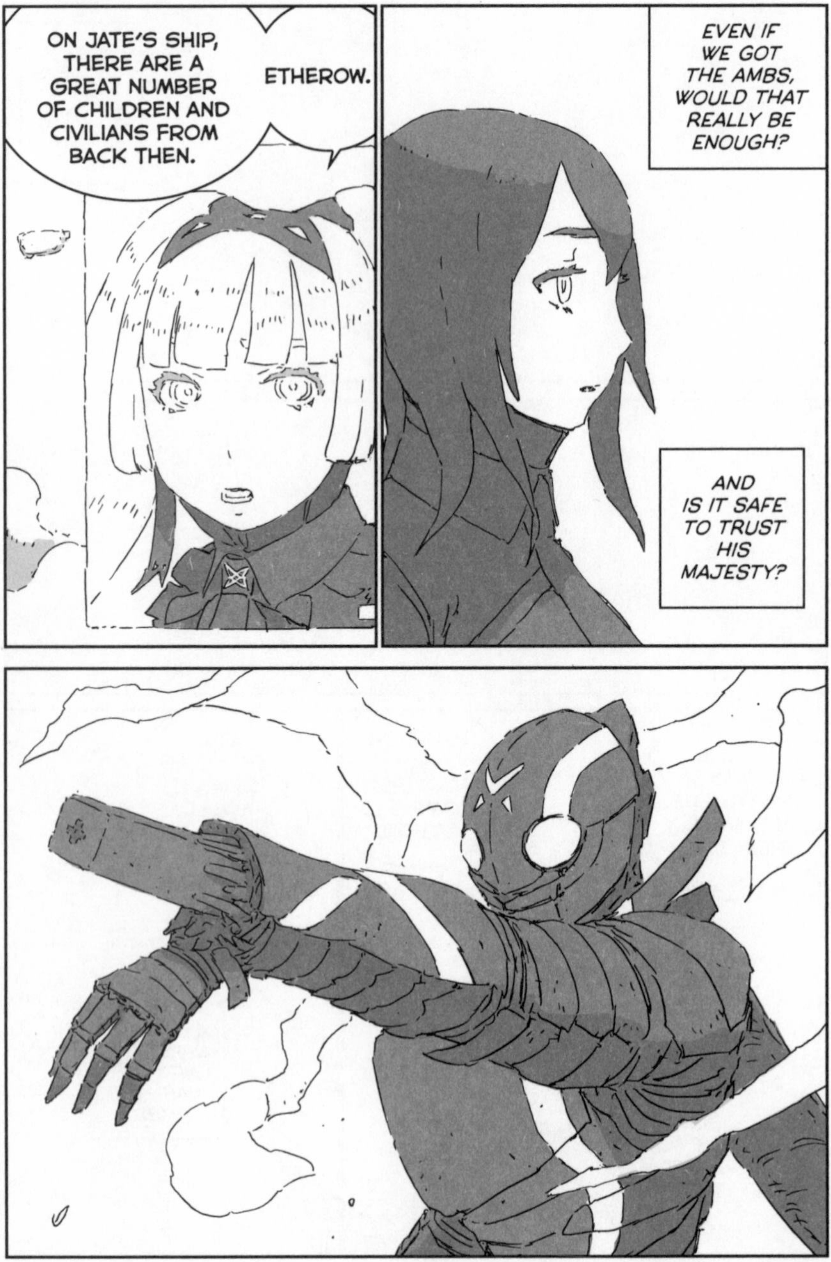
EVEN IF WE GOT THE AMBS, WOULD THAT REALLY BE ENOUGH?
AND IS IT SAFE TO TRUST HIS MAJESTY?
ETHEROW.
ON JATE'S SHIP, THERE ARE A GREAT NUMBER OF CHILDREN AND CIVILIANS FROM BACK THEN.

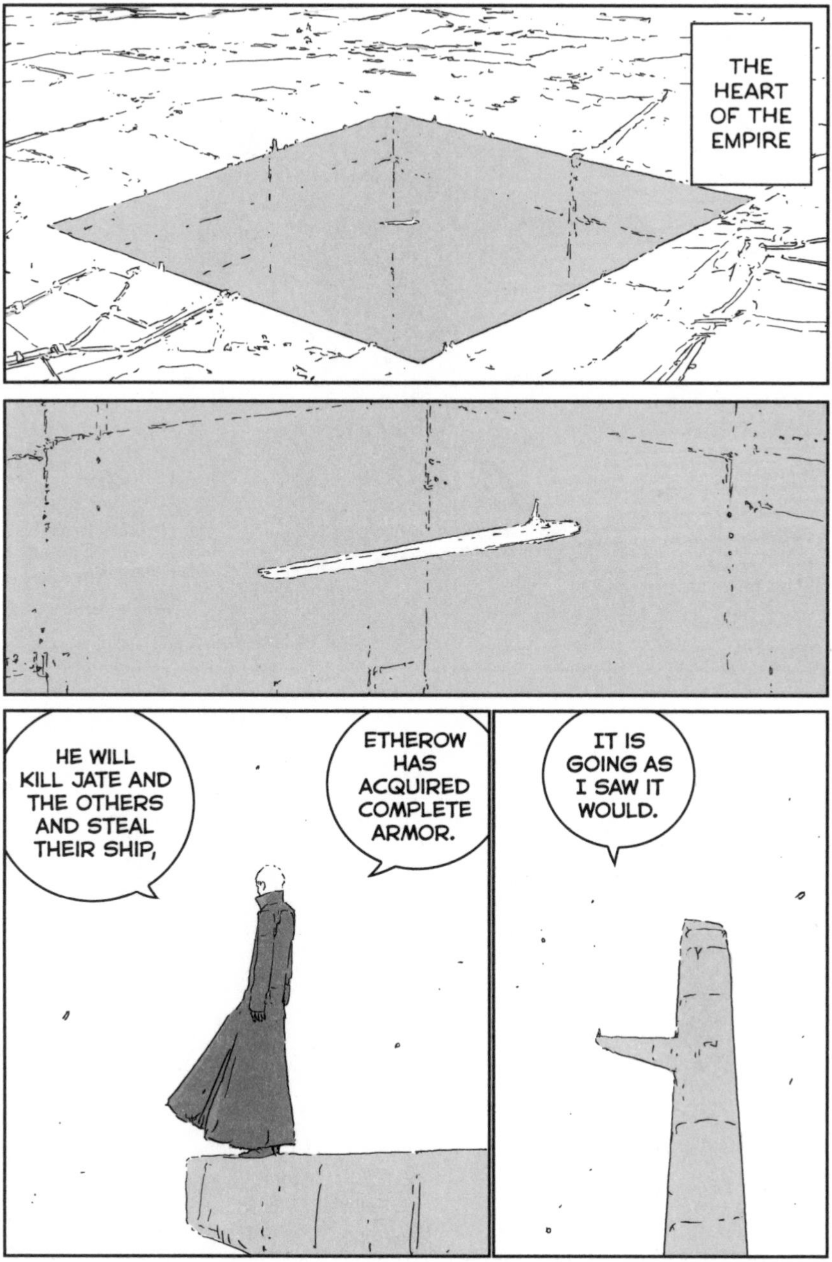
THE HEART OF THE EMPIRE
IT IS GOING AS I SAW IT WOULD.
ETHEROW HAS ACQUIRED COMPLETE ARMOR.
HE WILL KILL JATE AND THE OTHERS AND STEAL THEIR SHIP,

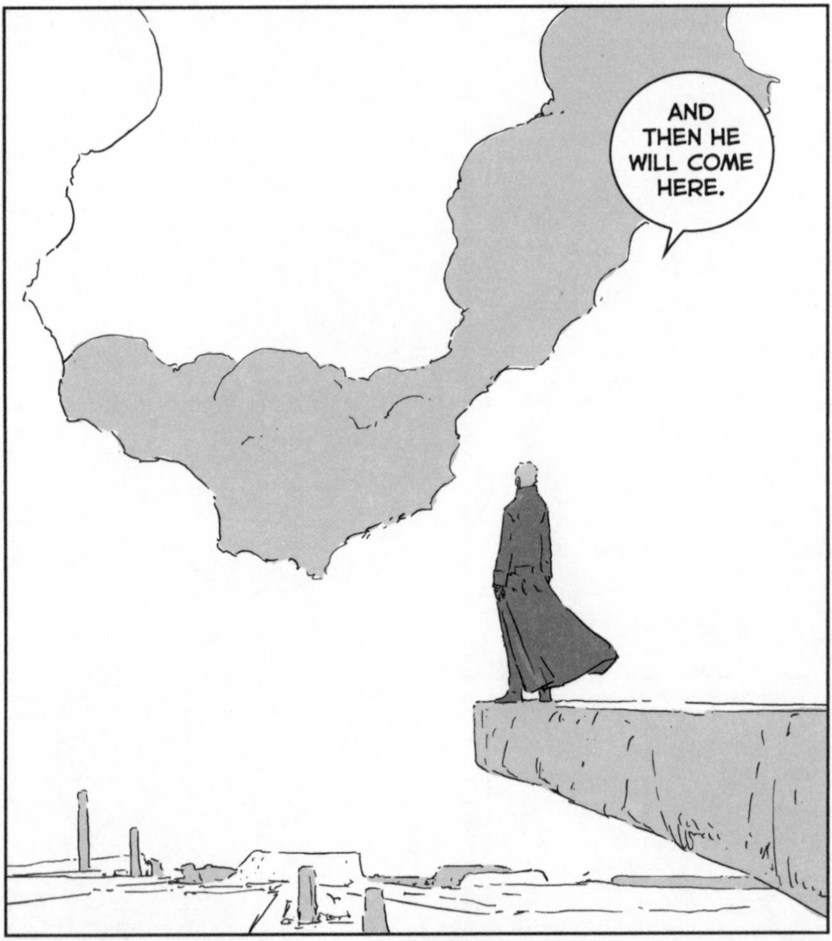
AND THEN HE WILL COME HERE.
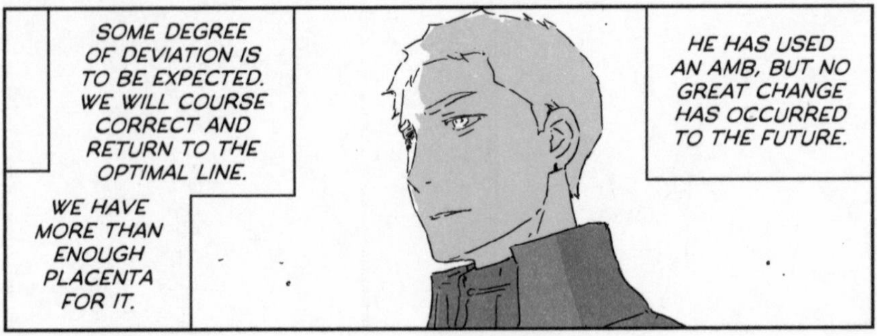
HE HAS USED AN AMB, BUT NO GREAT CHANGE HAS OCCURRED TO THE FUTURE.
SOME DEGREE OF DEVIATION IS TO BE EXPECTED. WE WILL COURSE CORRECT AND RETURN TO THE OPTIMAL LINE.
WE HAVE MORE THAN ENOUGH PLACENTA FOR IT.

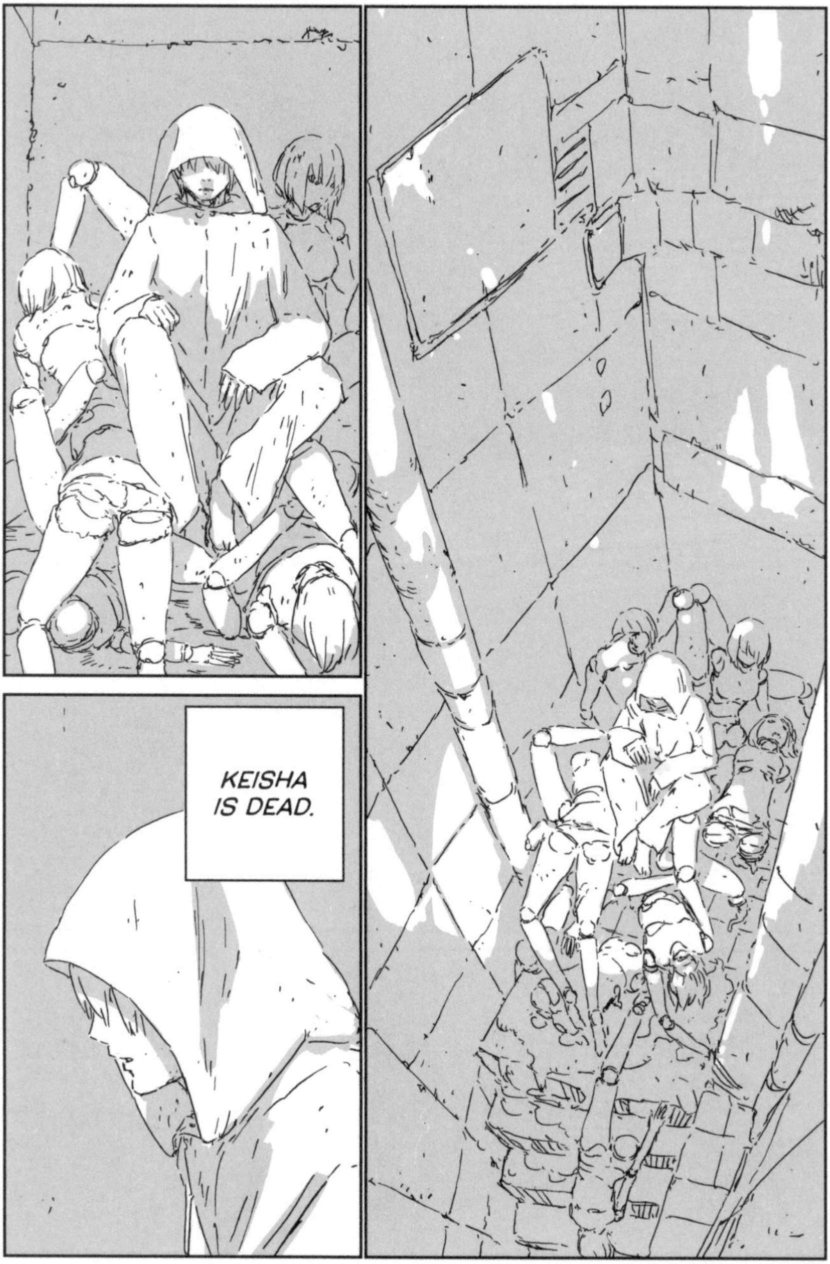
KEISHA IS DEAD.

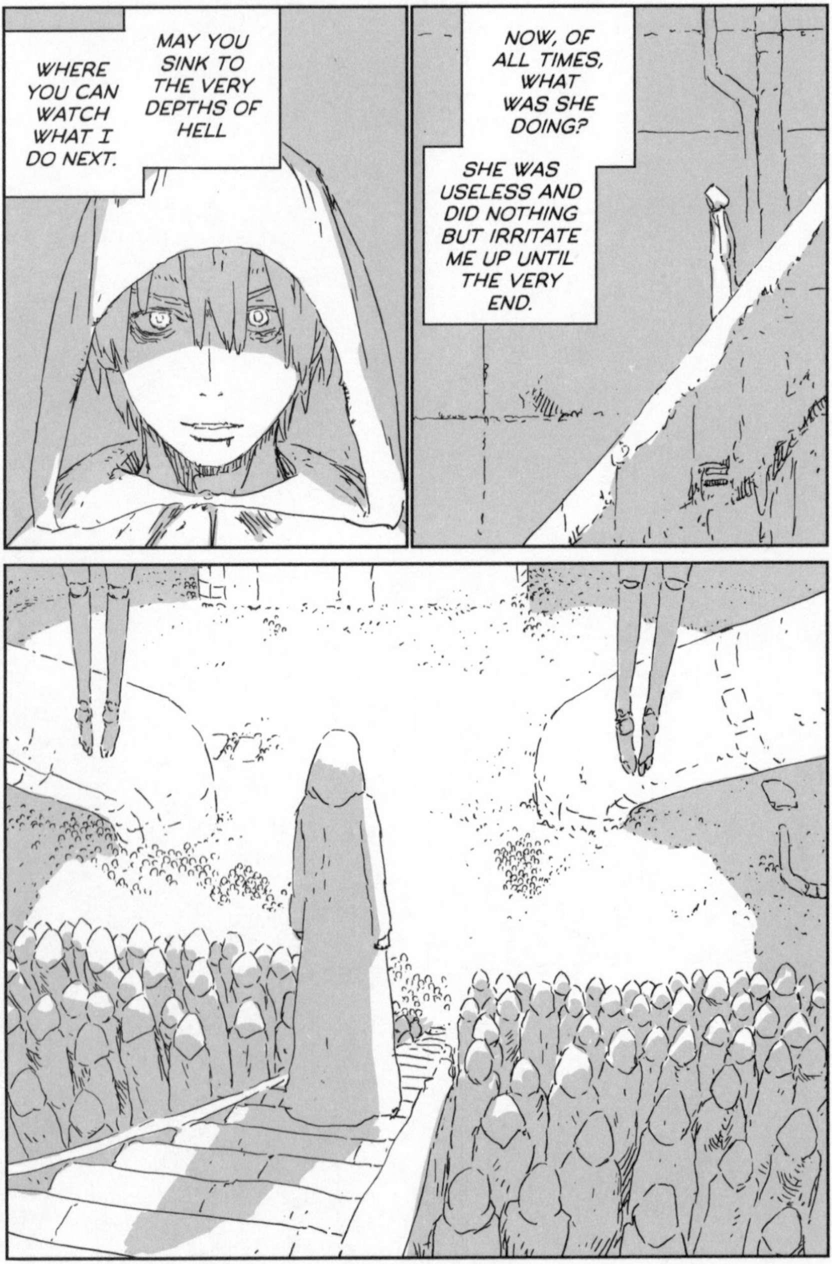
NOW, OF ALL TIMES, WHAT WAS SHE DOING?
SHE WAS USELESS AND DID NOTHING BUT IRRITATE ME UP UNTIL THE VERY END.
MAY YOU SINK TO THE VERY DEPTHS OF HELL
WHERE YOU CAN WATCH WHAT I DO NEXT.

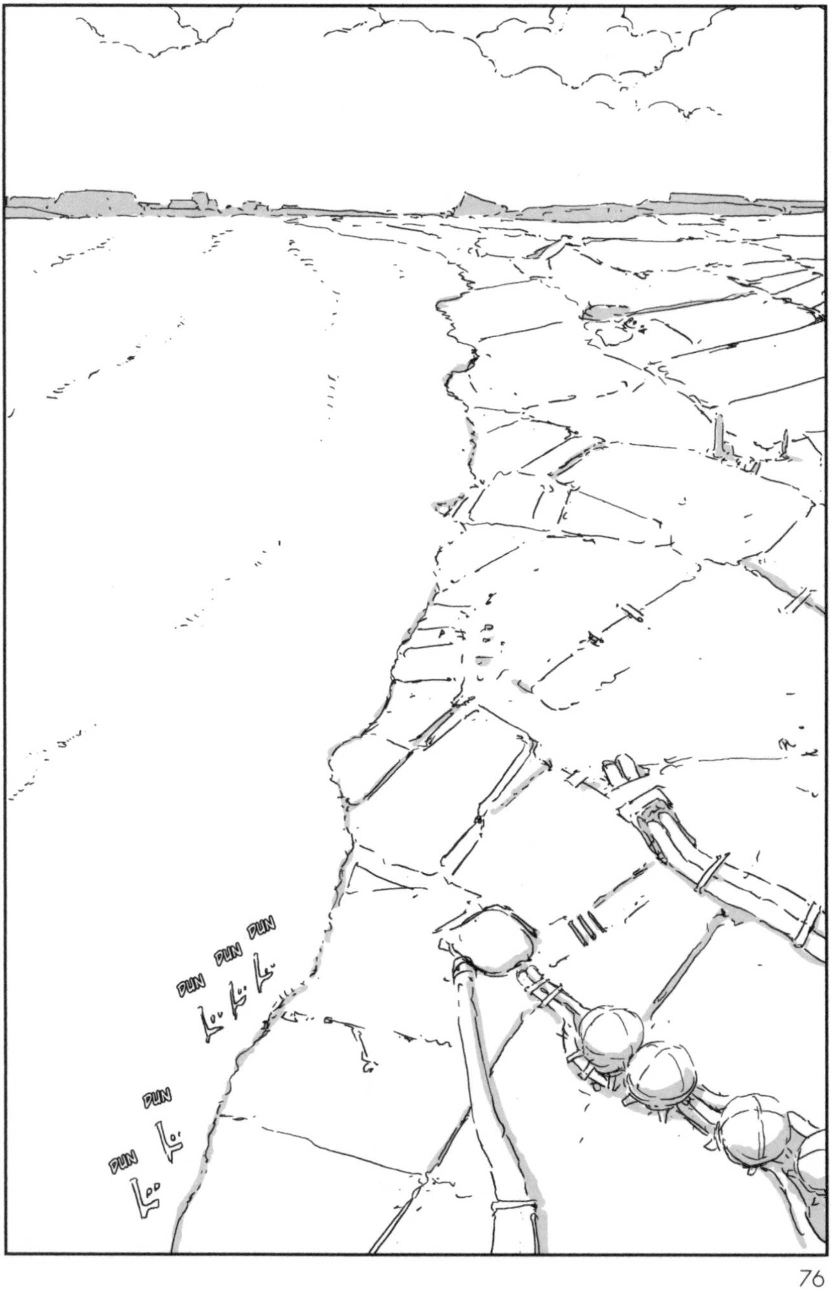
DUN
DUN
DUN
DUN
DUN

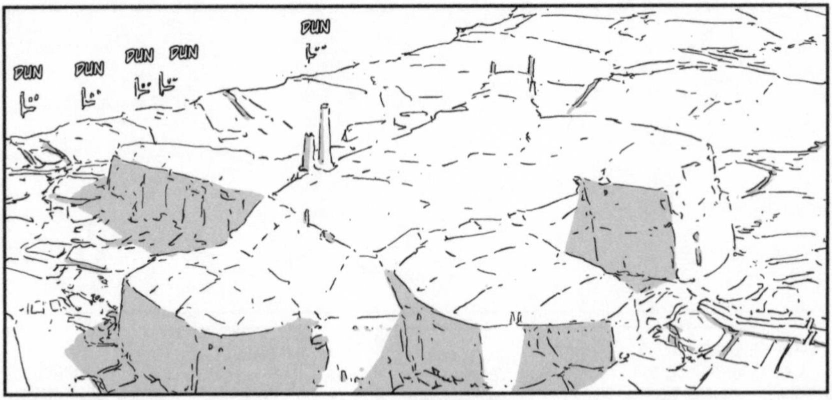
DUN
DUN
DUN
DUN
DUN

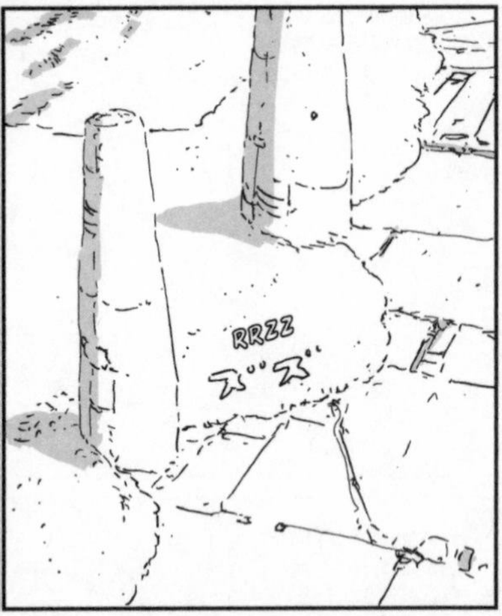
RRZZ

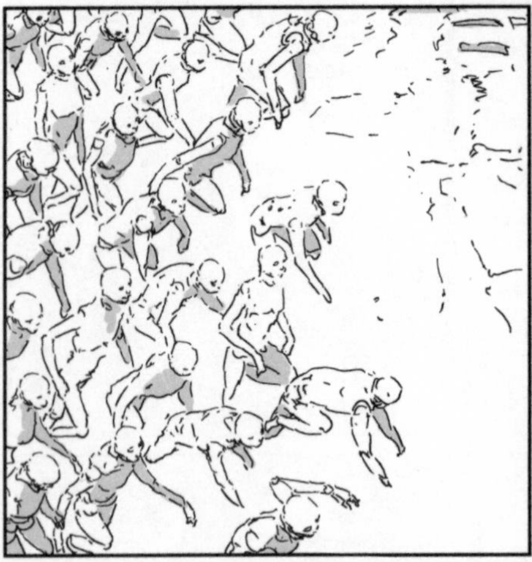

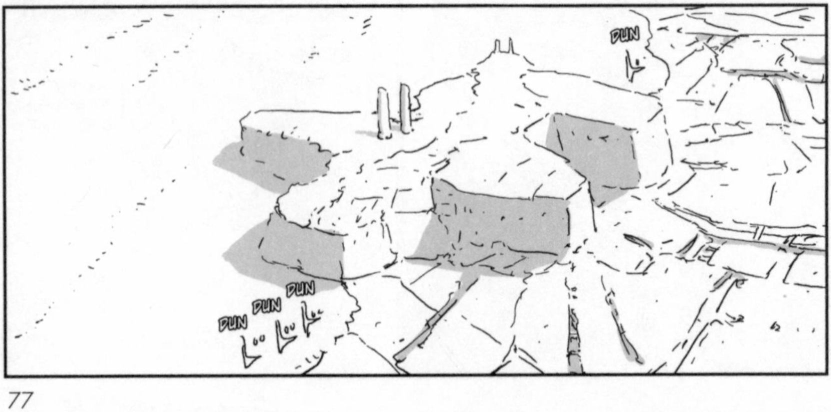
DUN
DUN
DUN
DUN

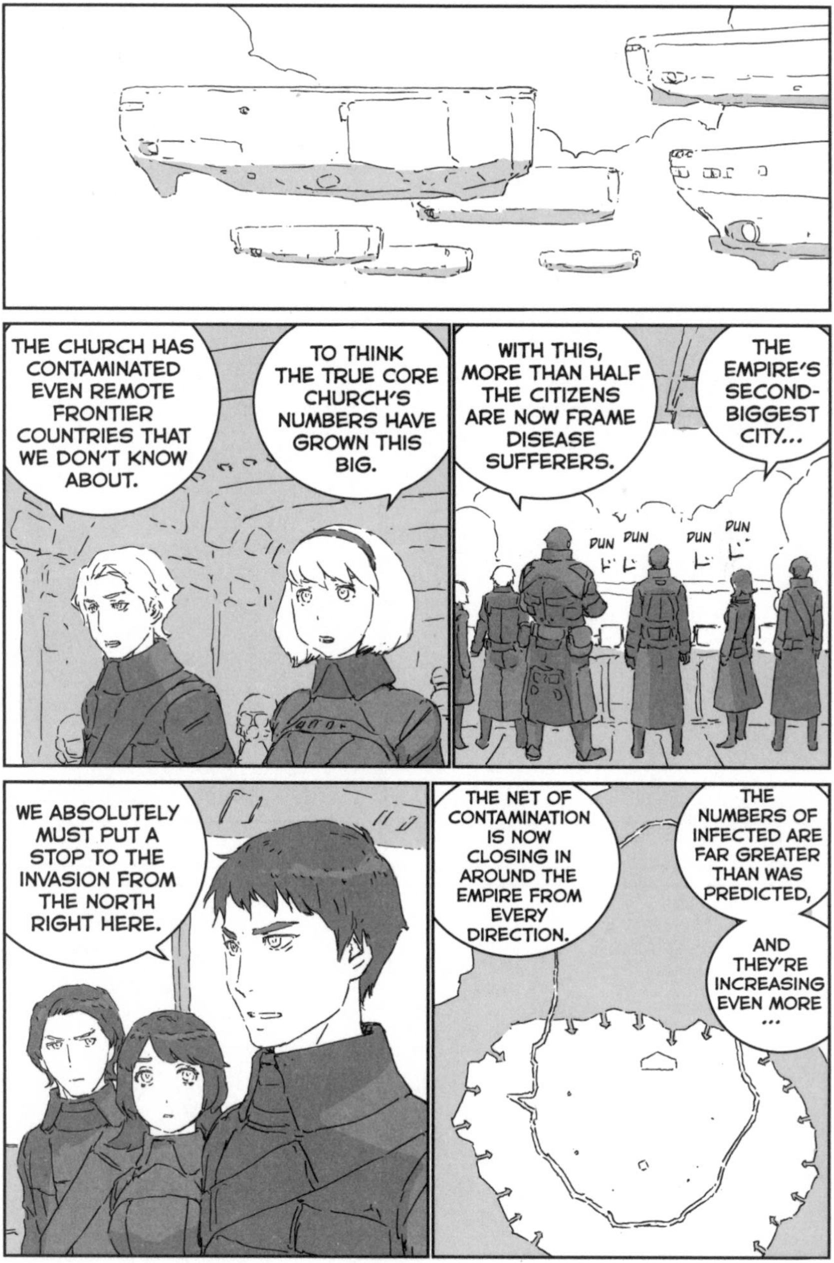
THE EMPIRE'S SECOND-BIGGEST CITY...
WITH THIS, MORE THAN HALF THE CITIZENS ARE NOW FRAME DISEASE SUFFERERS.
DUN DUN
DUN DUN
TO THINK THE TRUE CORE CHURCH'S NUMBERS HAVE GROWN THIS BIG.
THE CHURCH HAS CONTAMINATED EVEN REMOTE FRONTIER COUNTRIES THAT WE DON'T KNOW ABOUT.
THE NUMBERS OF INFECTED ARE FAR GREATER THAN WAS PREDICTED,
AND THEY'RE INCREASING EVEN MORE ...
THE NET OF CONTAMINATION IS NOW CLOSING IN AROUND THE EMPIRE FROM EVERY DIRECTION.
WE ABSOLUTELY MUST PUT A STOP TO THE INVASION FROM THE NORTH RIGHT HERE.

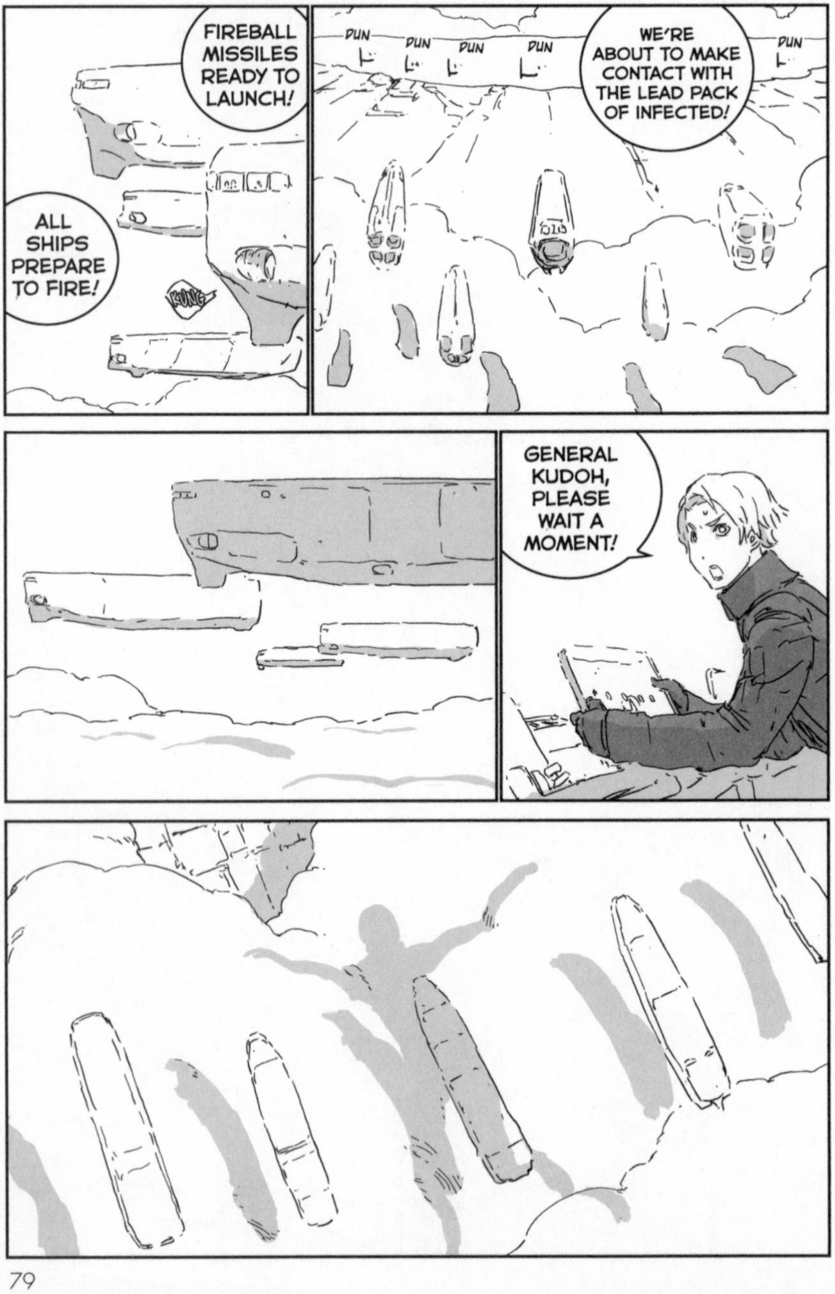
DUN
WE'RE ABOUT TO MAKE CONTACT WITH THE LEAD PACK OF INFECTED!
DUN
DUN
DUN
DUN
FIREBALL MISSILES READY TO LAUNCH!
ALL SHIPS PREPARE TO FIRE!
KUNG
GENERAL KUDOH, PLEASE WAIT A MOMENT!

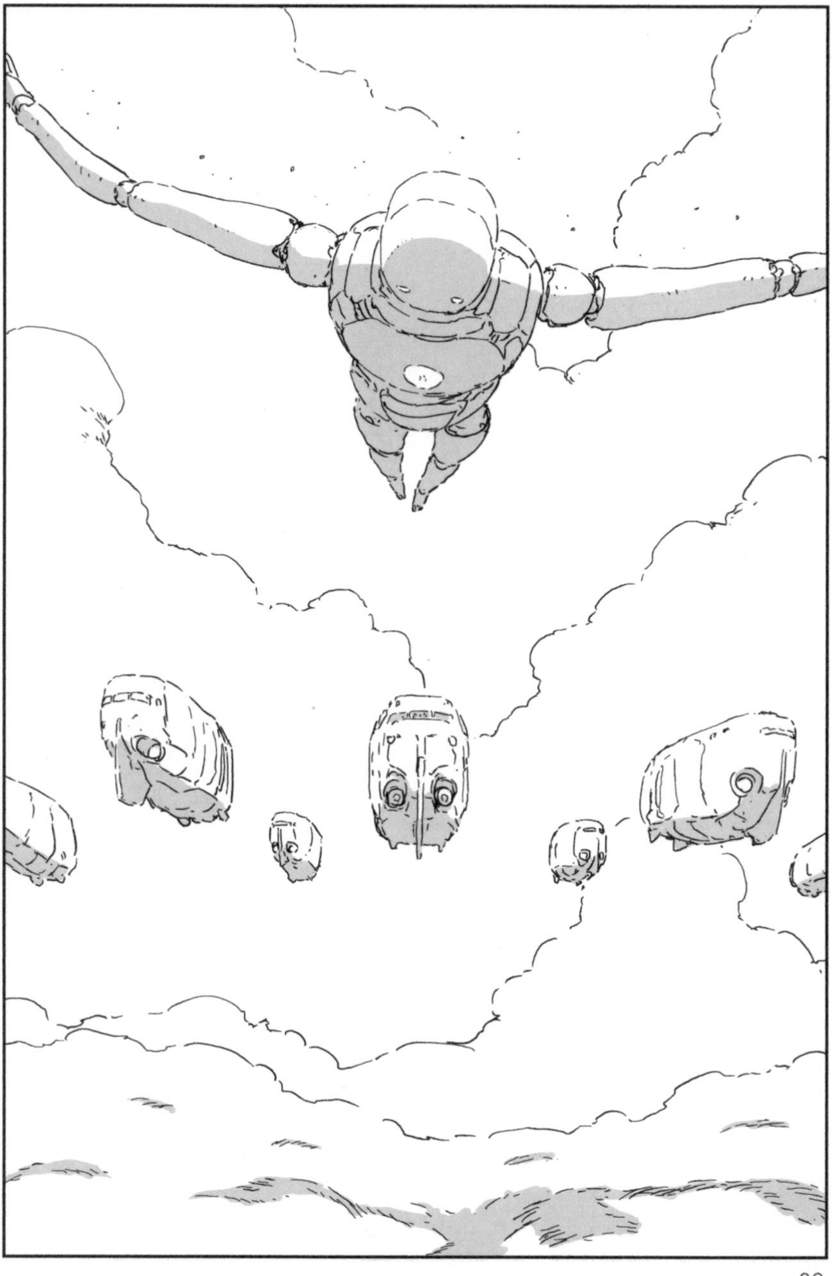

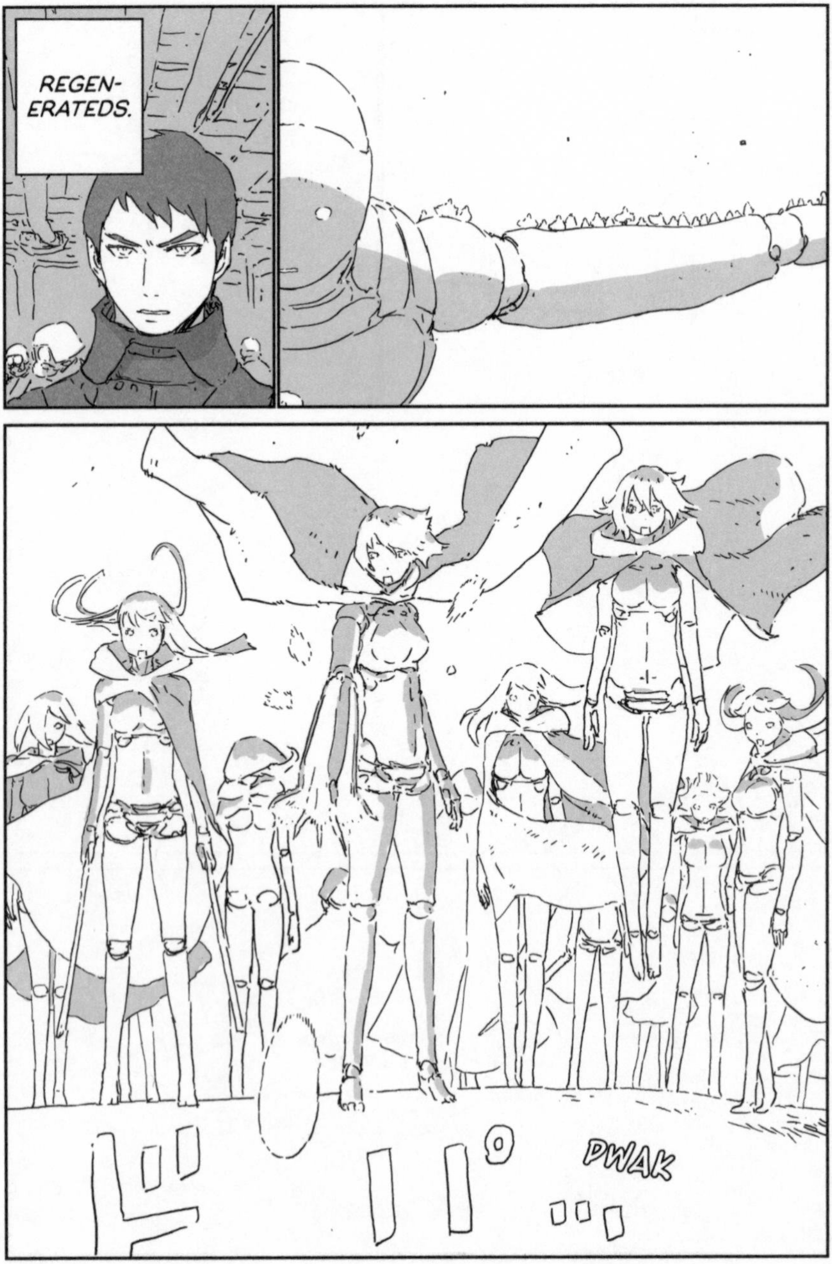
REGEN-ERATEDS.
PWAK

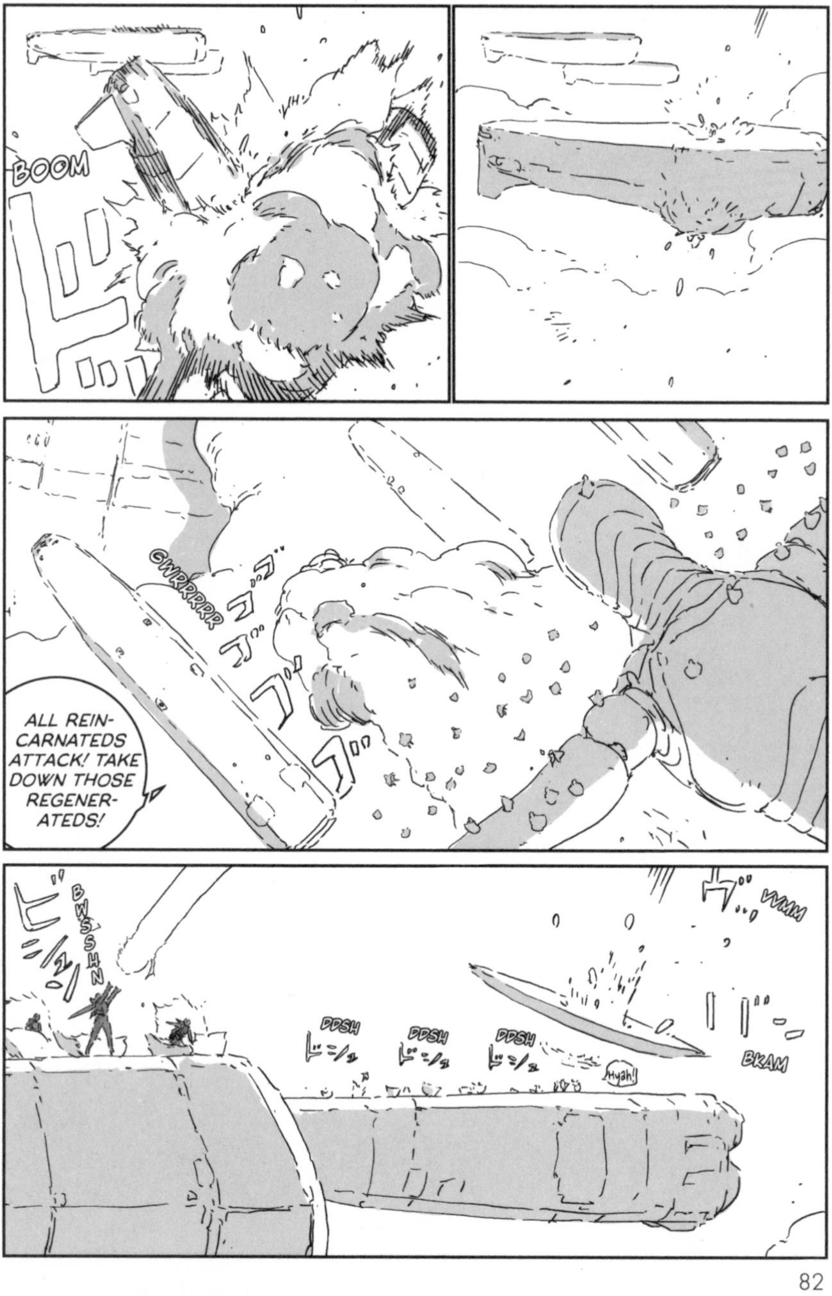
BOOM
GWRRRRR
ALL REIN-CARNATEDS ATTACK! TAKE DOWN THOSE REGENER-ATEDS!
VVMM
BKAM
Hyah!
DDSH
DDSH
DDSH
BWSHN

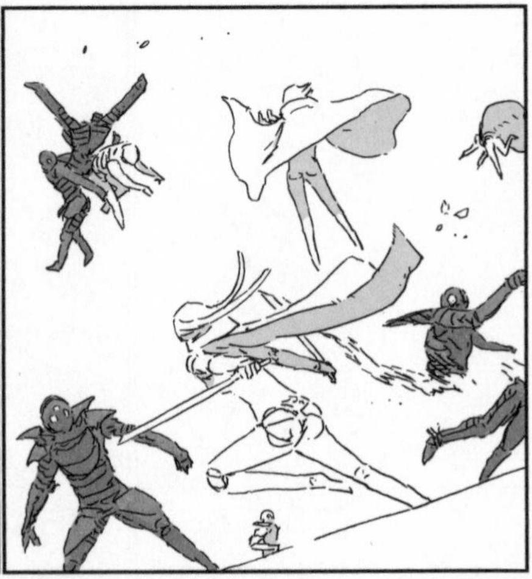
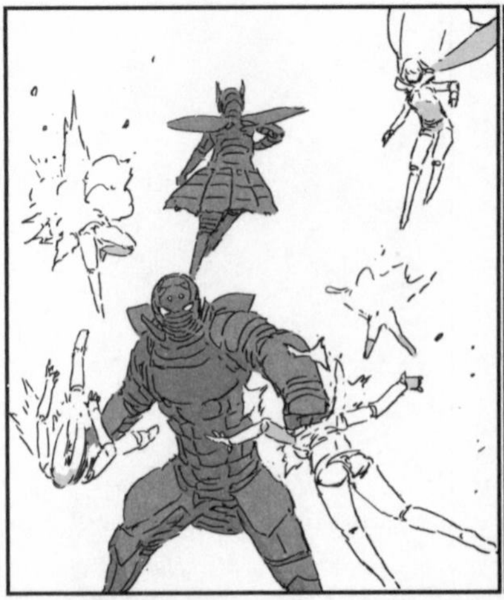
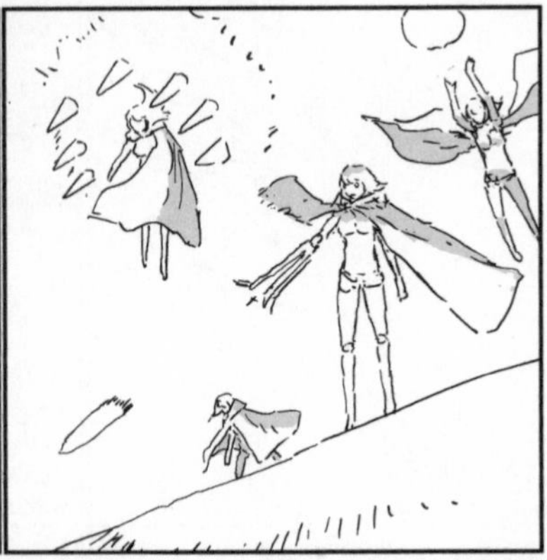
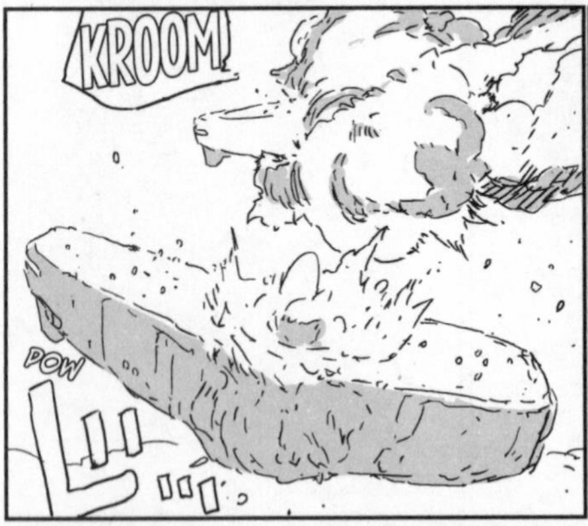
KROOM
POW
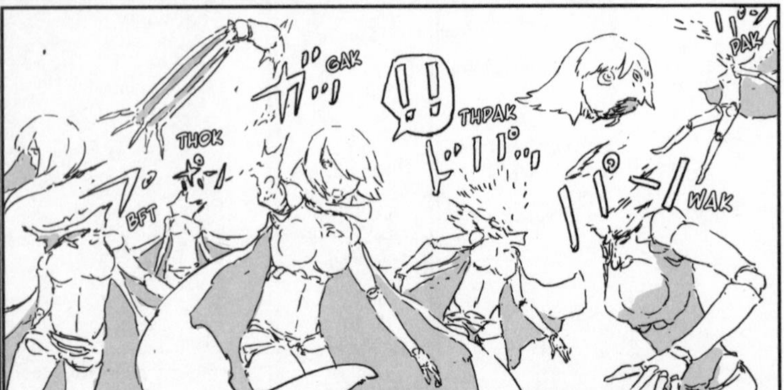
DAK
WAK
THDAK
!!
GAK
THOK
BFT
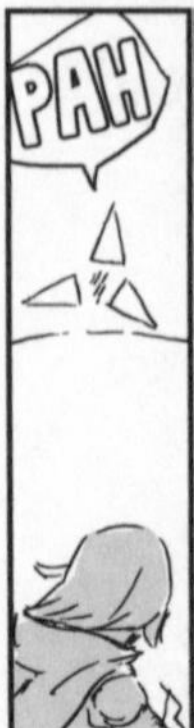
PAH

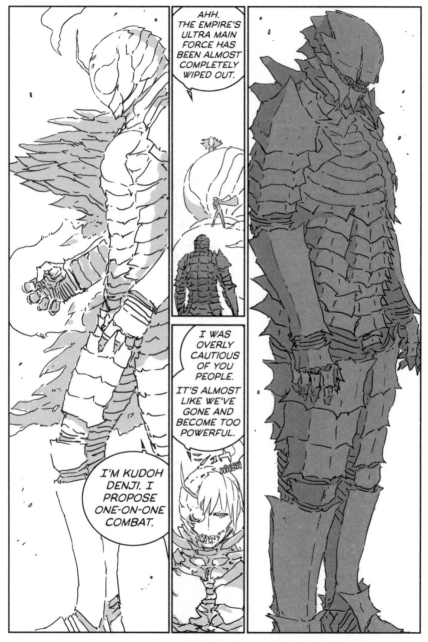

AHH.
THE EMPIRE'S
ULTRA MAIN
FORCE HAS
BEEN ALMOST
COMPLETELY
WIPED OUT.

I WAS
OVERLY
CAUTIOUS
OF YOU
PEOPLE.

IT'S ALMOST
LIKE WE'VE
GONE AND
BECOME TOO
POWERFUL.

WHSH

I'M KUDOH
DENJI. I
PROPOSE
ONE-ON-ONE
COMBAT.

CHAPTER 51 END

APOSIMZ

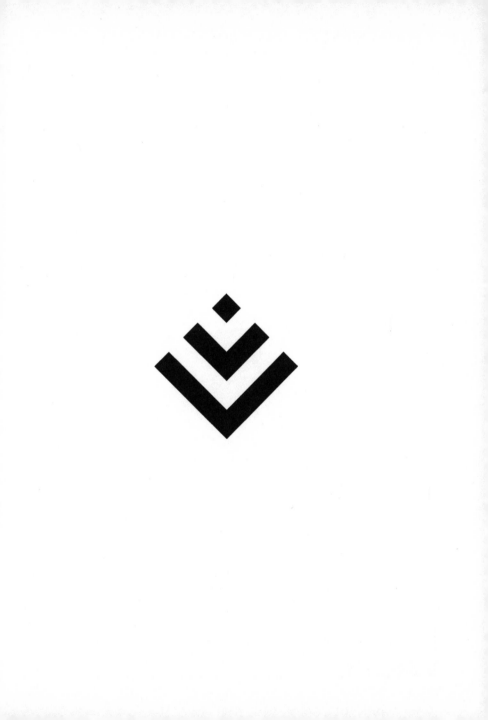

CHAPTER 52

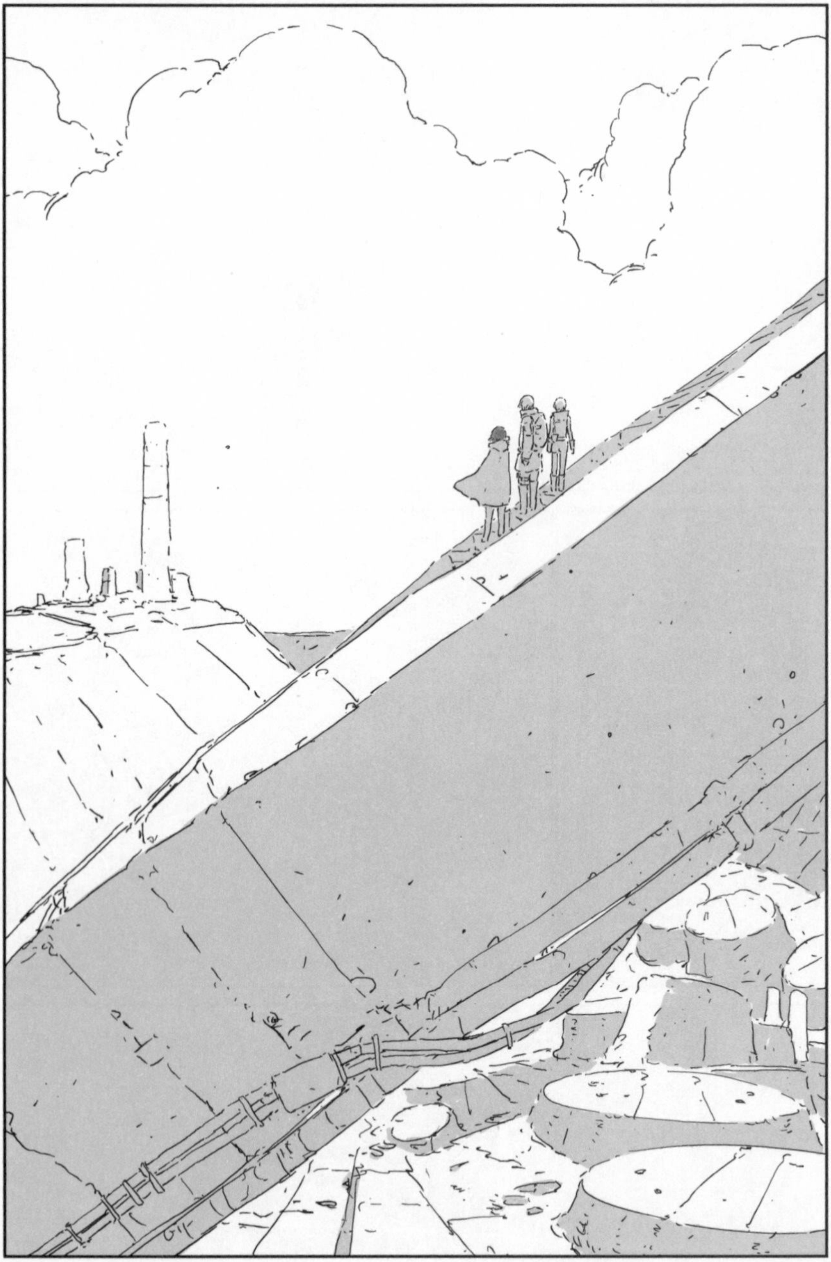

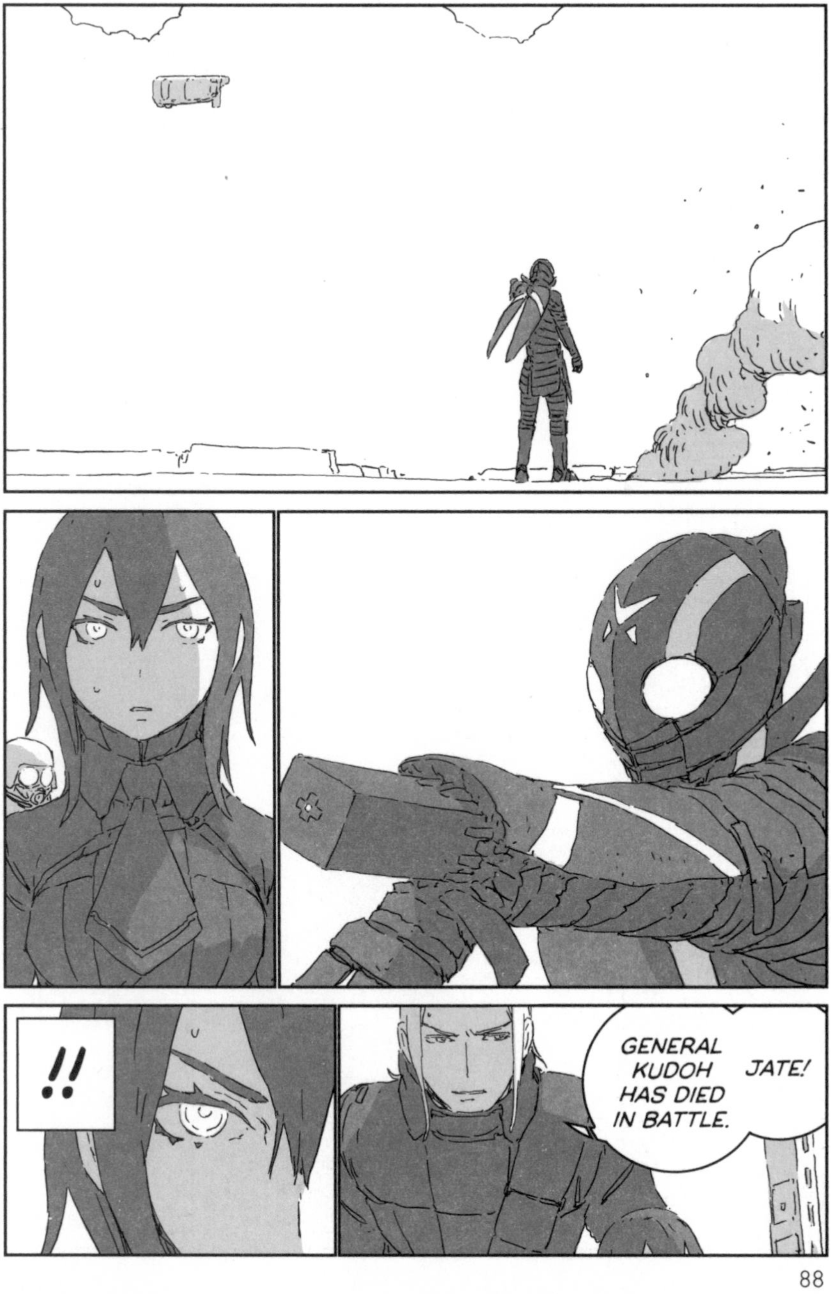
JATE!
GENERAL KUDOH HAS DIED IN BATTLE.
!!

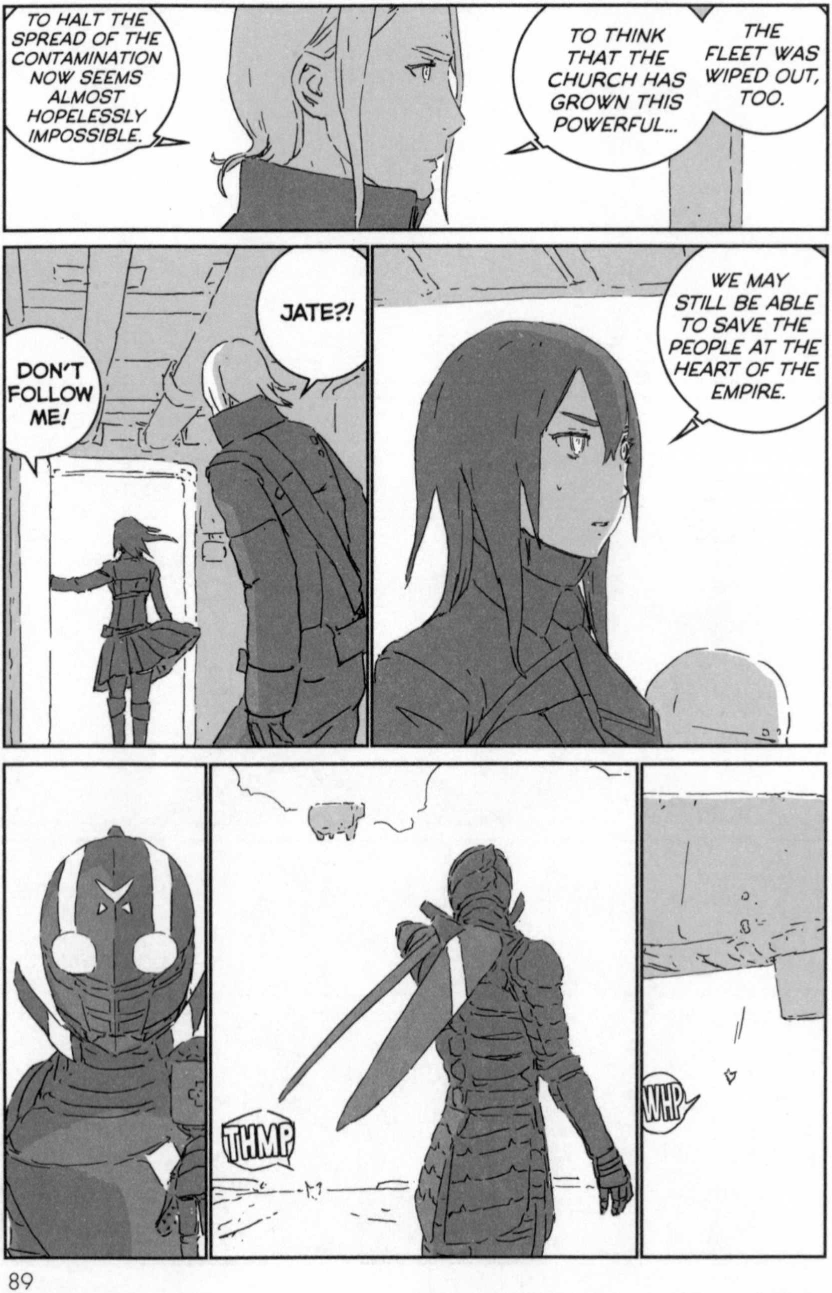
THE FLEET WAS WIPED OUT, TOO.
TO THINK THAT THE CHURCH HAS GROWN THIS POWERFUL...
TO HALT THE SPREAD OF THE CONTAMINATION NOW SEEMS ALMOST HOPELESSLY IMPOSSIBLE.
WE MAY STILL BE ABLE TO SAVE THE PEOPLE AT THE HEART OF THE EMPIRE.
JATE?!
DON'T FOLLOW ME!
WHP
THMP

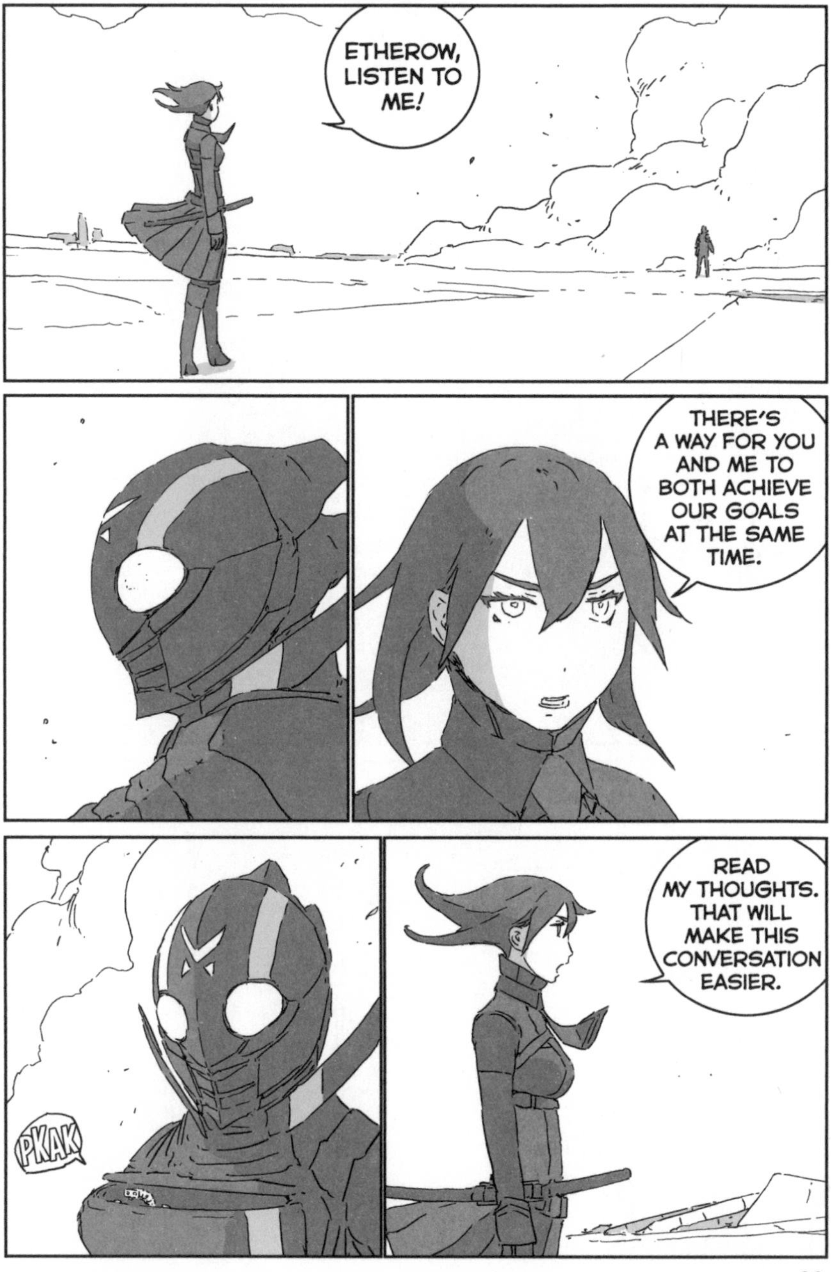
ETHEROW, LISTEN TO ME!
THERE'S A WAY FOR YOU AND ME TO BOTH ACHIEVE OUR GOALS AT THE SAME TIME.
READ MY THOUGHTS. THAT WILL MAKE THIS CONVERSATION EASIER.
PKAK

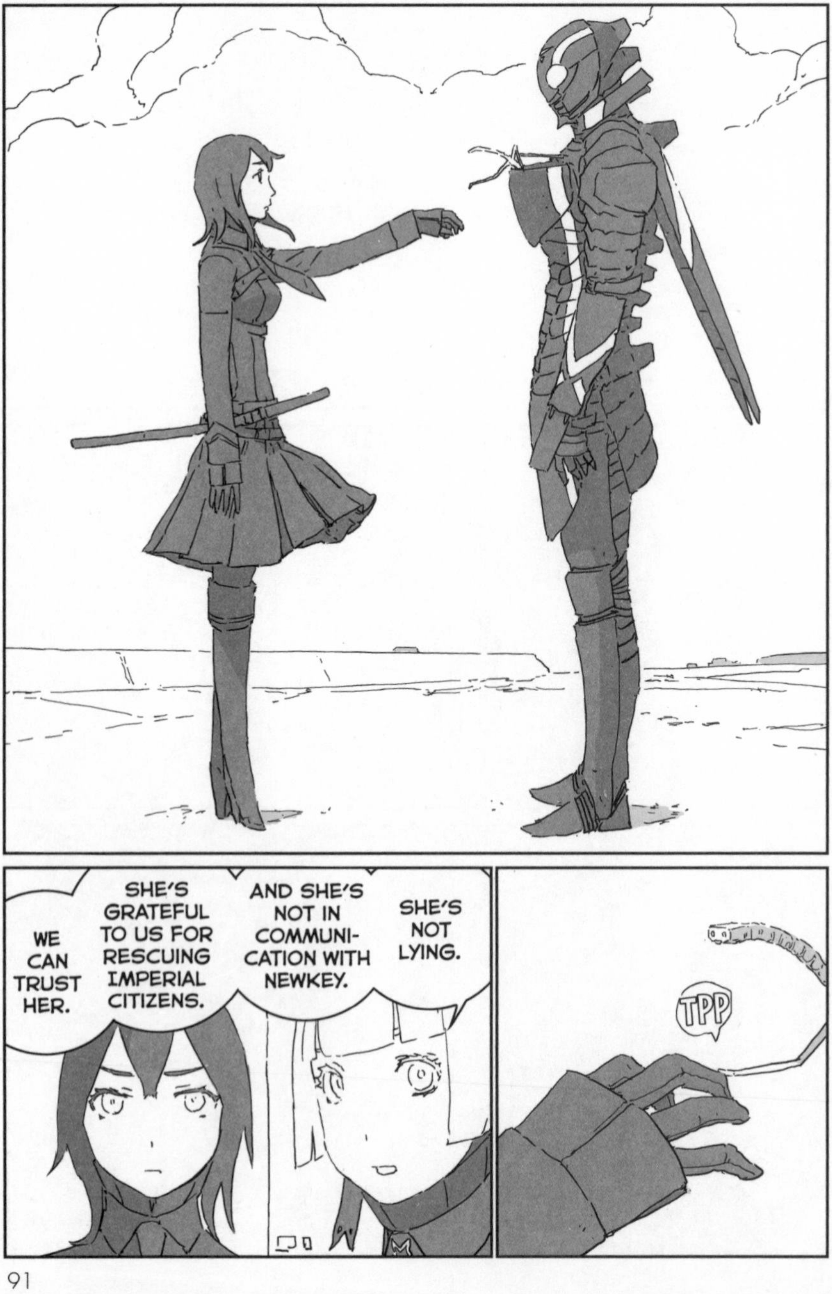
TPP
SHE'S NOT LYING.
AND SHE'S NOT IN COMMUNICATION WITH NEWKEY.
SHE'S GRATEFUL TO US FOR RESCUING IMPERIAL CITIZENS.
WE CAN TRUST HER.

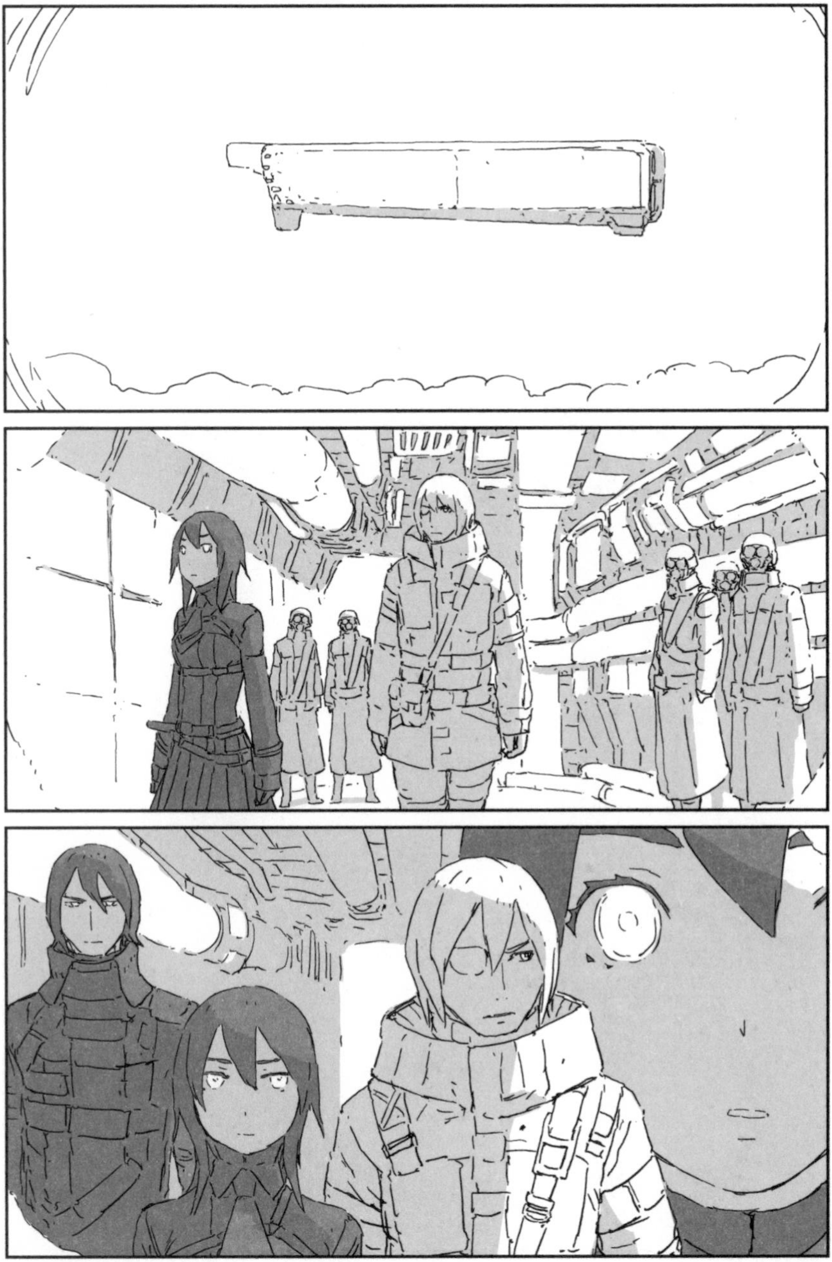

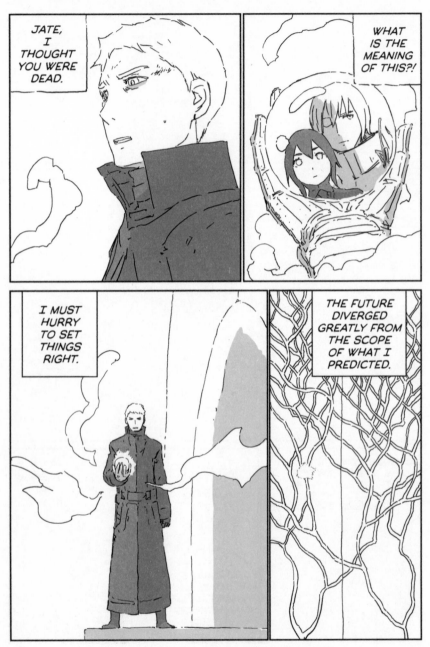

WHAT IS THE MEANING OF THIS?!
JATE, I THOUGHT YOU WERE DEAD.
THE FUTURE DIVERGED GREATLY FROM THE SCOPE OF WHAT I PREDICTED.
I MUST HURRY TO SET THINGS RIGHT.

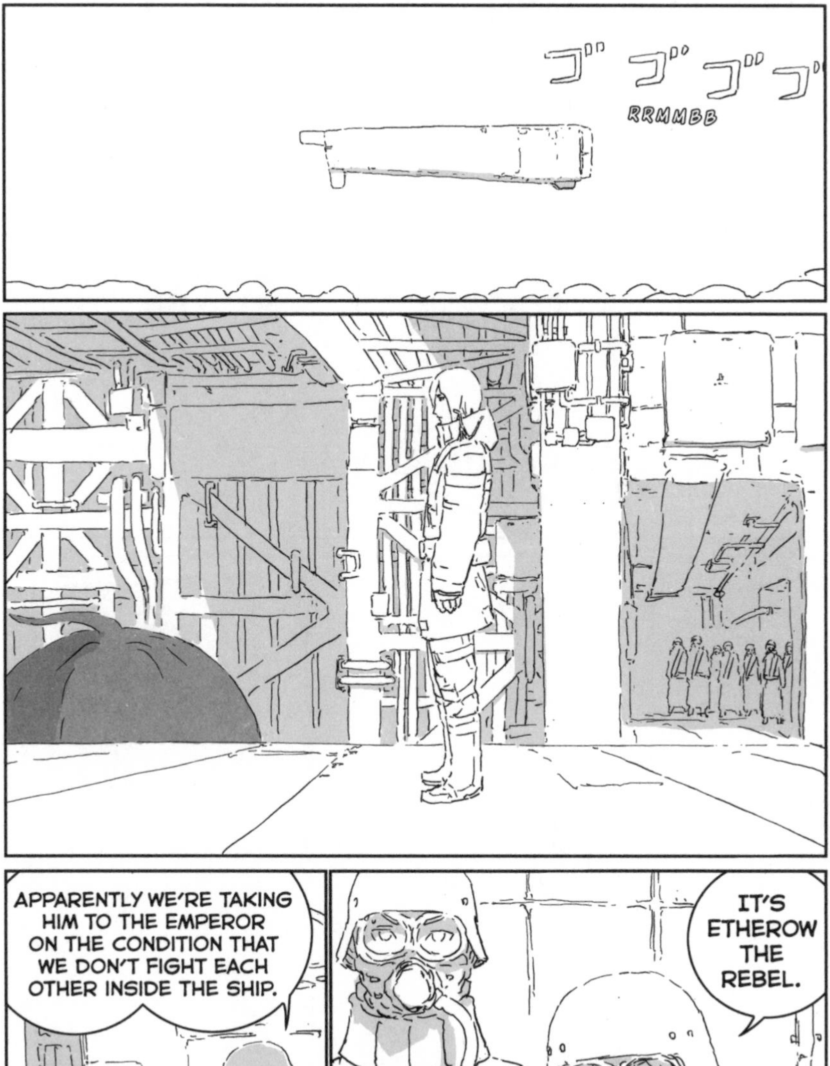
ゴゴゴゴ
RRMMBB
IT'S ETHEROW THE REBEL.
WH-WHAT'S HE DOING JUST RIDING ALONG ON AN IMPERIAL VESSEL?!
APPARENTLY WE'RE TAKING HIM TO THE EMPEROR ON THE CONDITION THAT WE DON'T FIGHT EACH OTHER INSIDE THE SHIP.

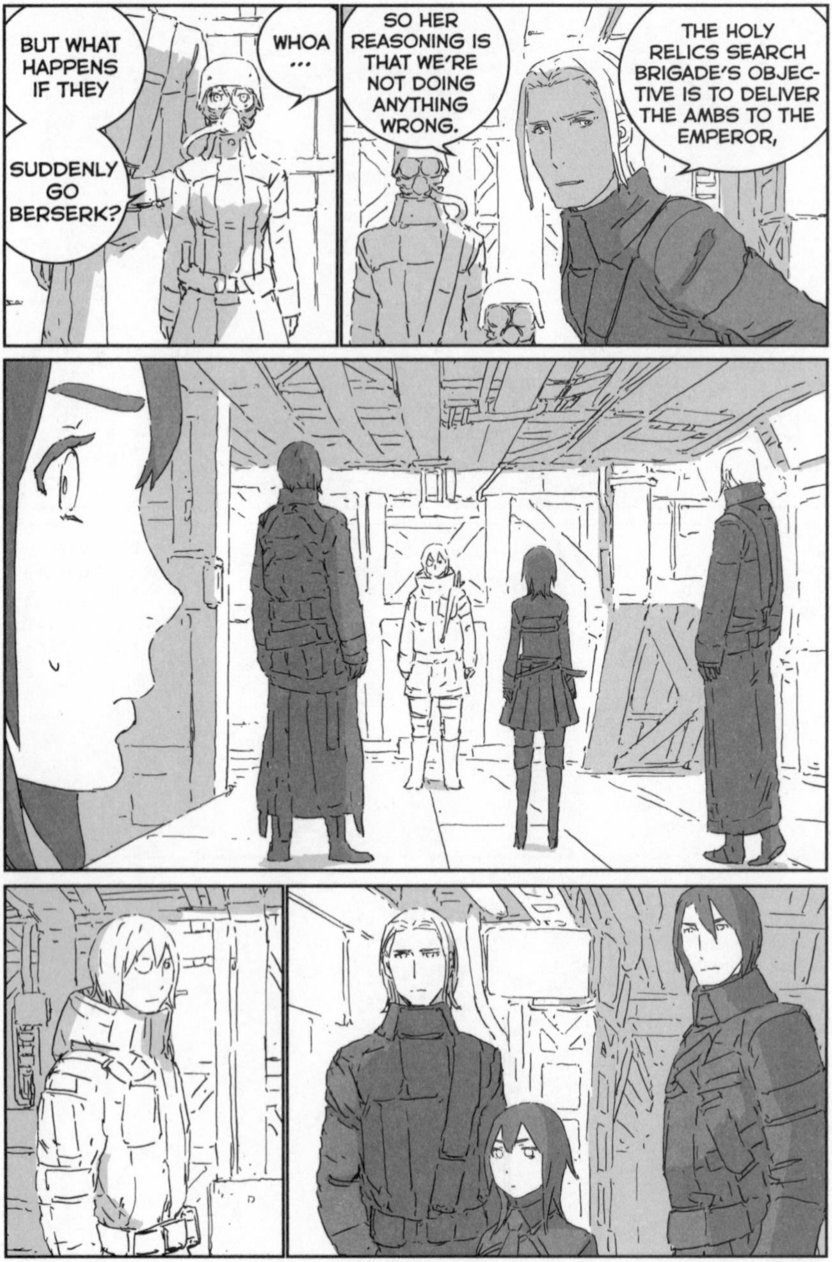
THE HOLY RELICS SEARCH BRIGADE'S OBJECTIVE IS TO DELIVER THE AMBS TO THE EMPEROR,
SO HER REASONING IS THAT WE'RE NOT DOING ANYTHING WRONG.
WHOA ...
BUT WHAT HAPPENS IF THEY
SUDDENLY GO BERSERK?

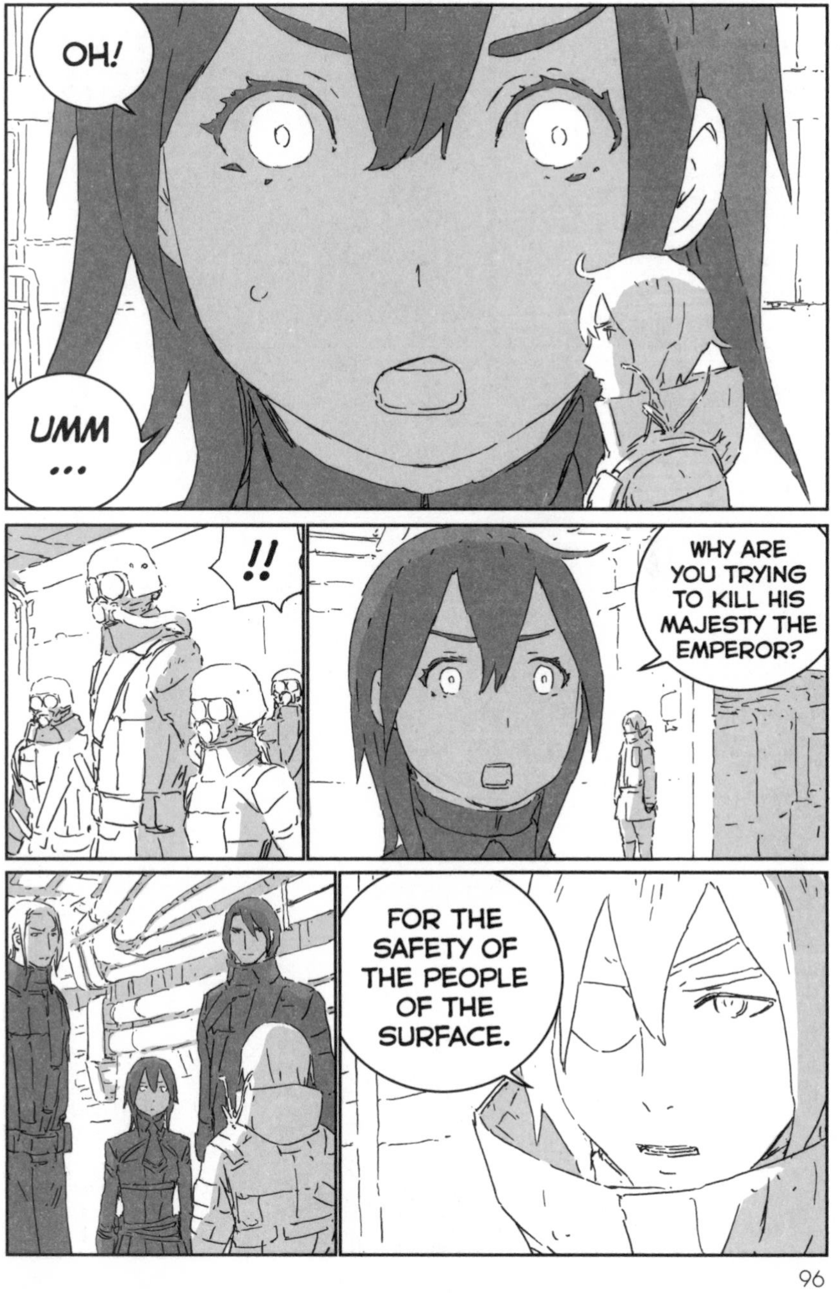
OH!
UMM ...
WHY ARE YOU TRYING TO KILL HIS MAJESTY THE EMPEROR?
!!
FOR THE SAFETY OF THE PEOPLE OF THE SURFACE.

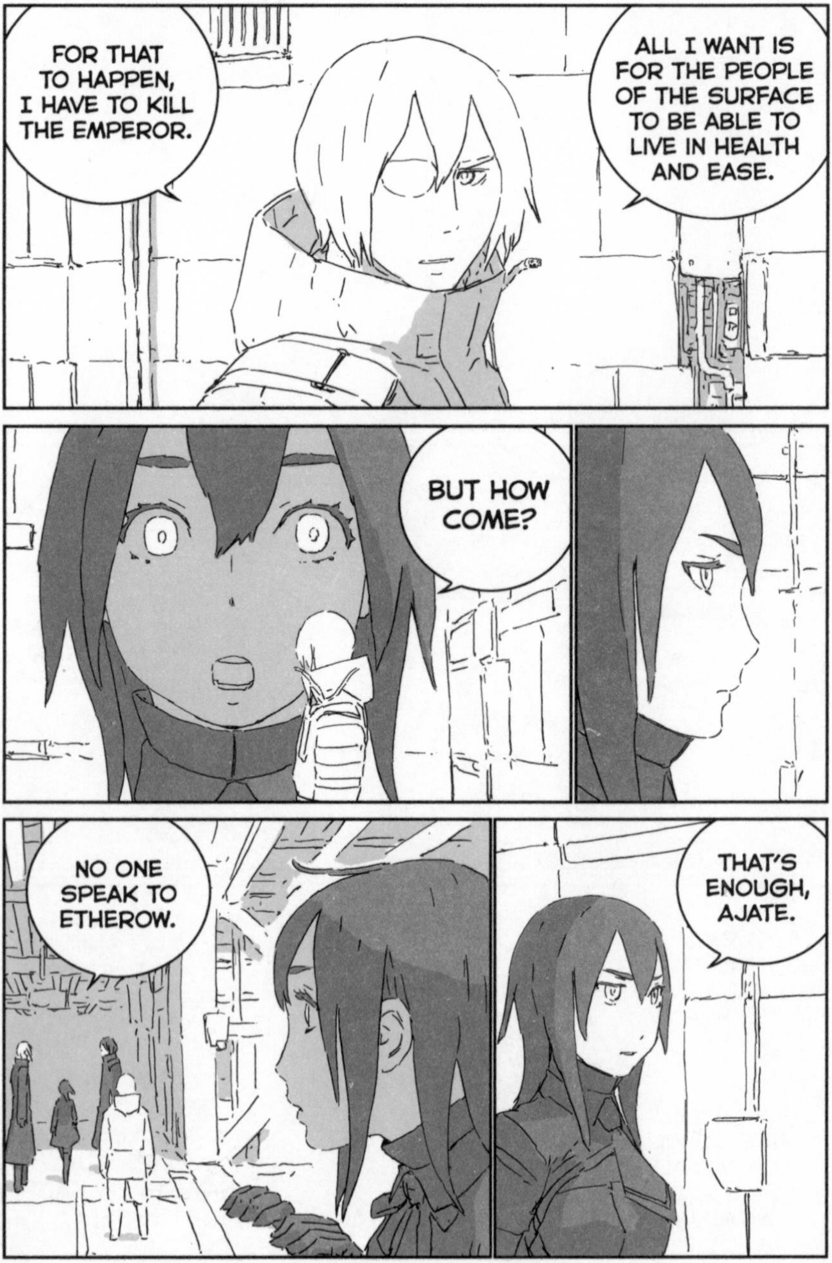
ALL I WANT IS FOR THE PEOPLE OF THE SURFACE TO BE ABLE TO LIVE IN HEALTH AND EASE.
FOR THAT TO HAPPEN, I HAVE TO KILL THE EMPEROR.
BUT HOW COME?
THAT'S ENOUGH, AJATE.
NO ONE SPEAK TO ETHEROW.

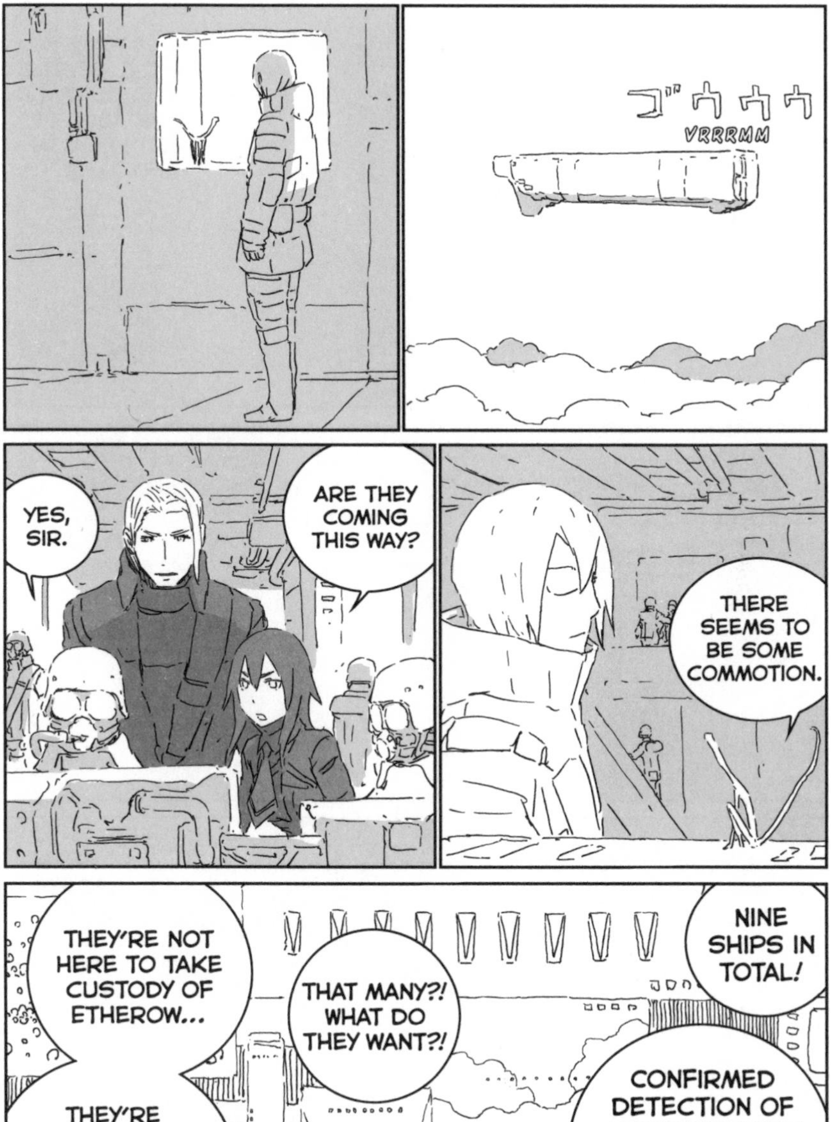
ゴウウウ
VRRRMM
THERE SEEMS TO BE SOME COMMOTION.
ARE THEY COMING THIS WAY?
YES, SIR.
NINE SHIPS IN TOTAL!
CONFIRMED DETECTION OF APPROXIMATELY 100 REINCAR-NATEDS ON EACH VESSEL!
THAT MANY?! WHAT DO THEY WANT?!
THEY'RE NOT HERE TO TAKE CUSTODY OF ETHEROW...
THEY'RE HERE TO KILL HIM AND ALL OF US ALONG WITH HIM.

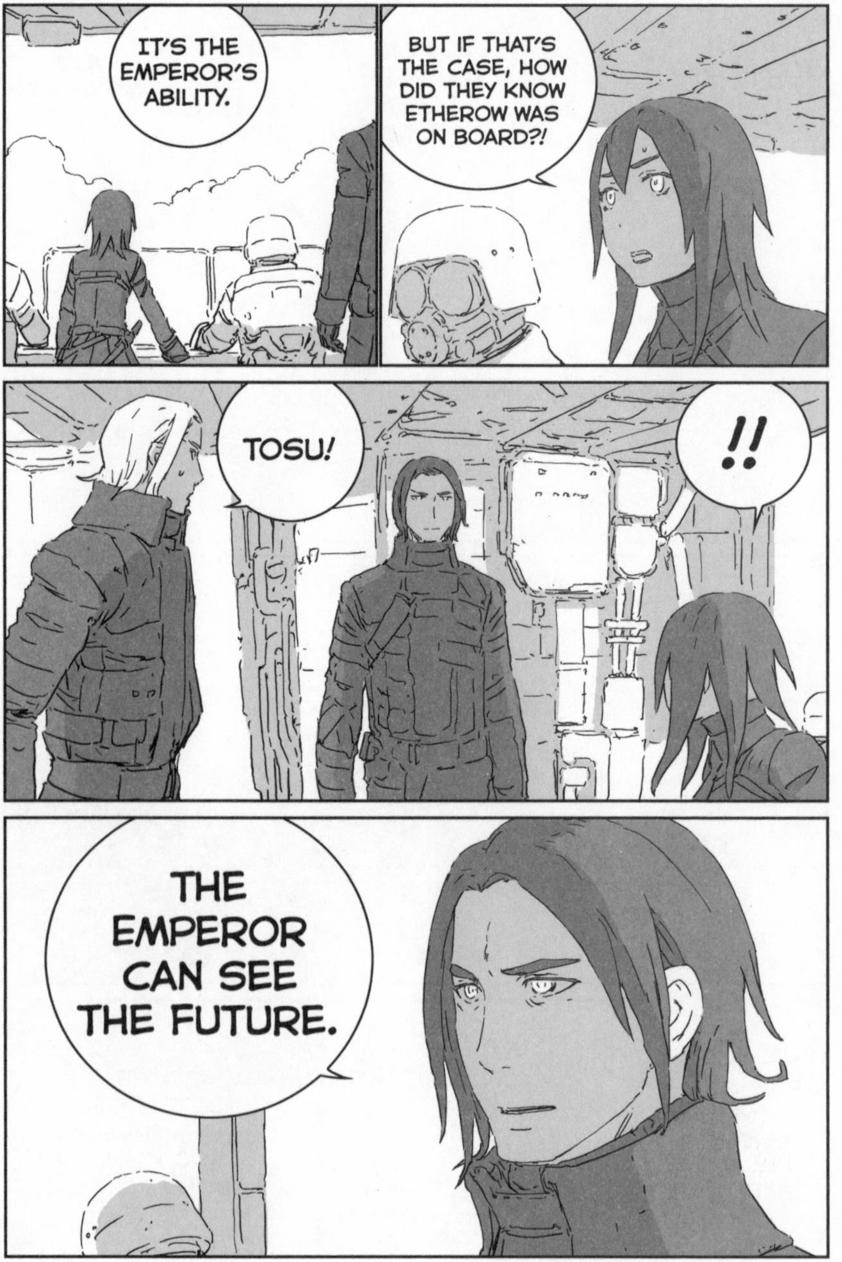
BUT IF THAT'S THE CASE, HOW DID THEY KNOW ETHEROW WAS ON BOARD?!
IT'S THE EMPEROR'S ABILITY.
!!
TOSU!
THE EMPEROR CAN SEE THE FUTURE.

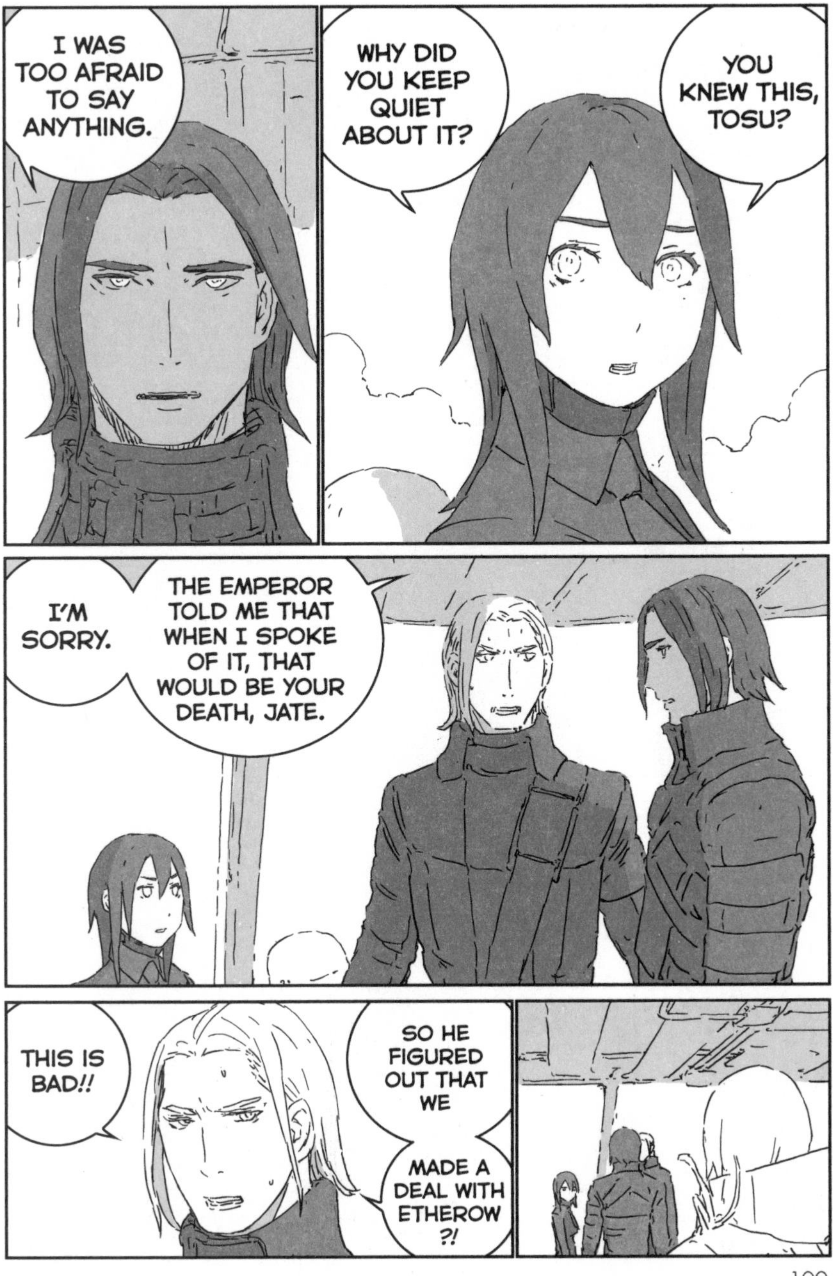
YOU KNEW THIS, TOSU?
WHY DID YOU KEEP QUIET ABOUT IT?
I WAS TOO AFRAID TO SAY ANYTHING.
THE EMPEROR TOLD ME THAT WHEN I SPOKE OF IT, THAT WOULD BE YOUR DEATH, JATE.
I'M SORRY.
SO HE FIGURED OUT THAT WE
MADE A DEAL WITH ETHEROW ?!
THIS IS BAD!!

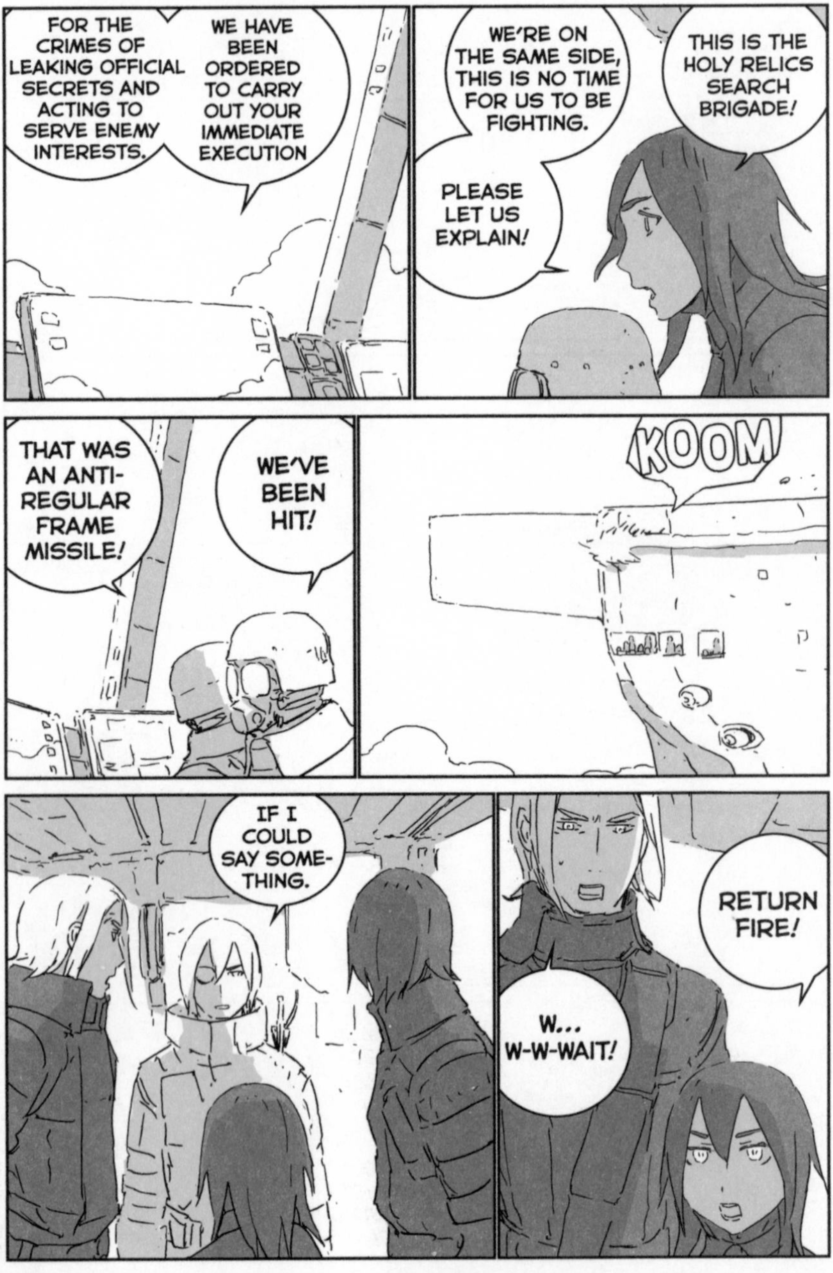
THIS IS THE HOLY RELICS SEARCH BRIGADE!
WE'RE ON THE SAME SIDE, THIS IS NO TIME FOR US TO BE FIGHTING.
PLEASE LET US EXPLAIN!
WE HAVE BEEN ORDERED TO CARRY OUT YOUR IMMEDIATE EXECUTION
FOR THE CRIMES OF LEAKING OFFICIAL SECRETS AND ACTING TO SERVE ENEMY INTERESTS.
KOOM
WE'VE BEEN HIT!
THAT WAS AN ANTI-REGULAR FRAME MISSILE!
RETURN FIRE!
W... W-W-WAIT!
IF I COULD SAY SOME-THING.

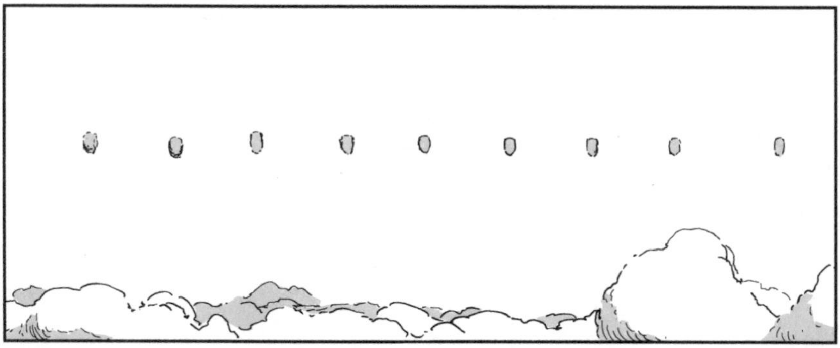

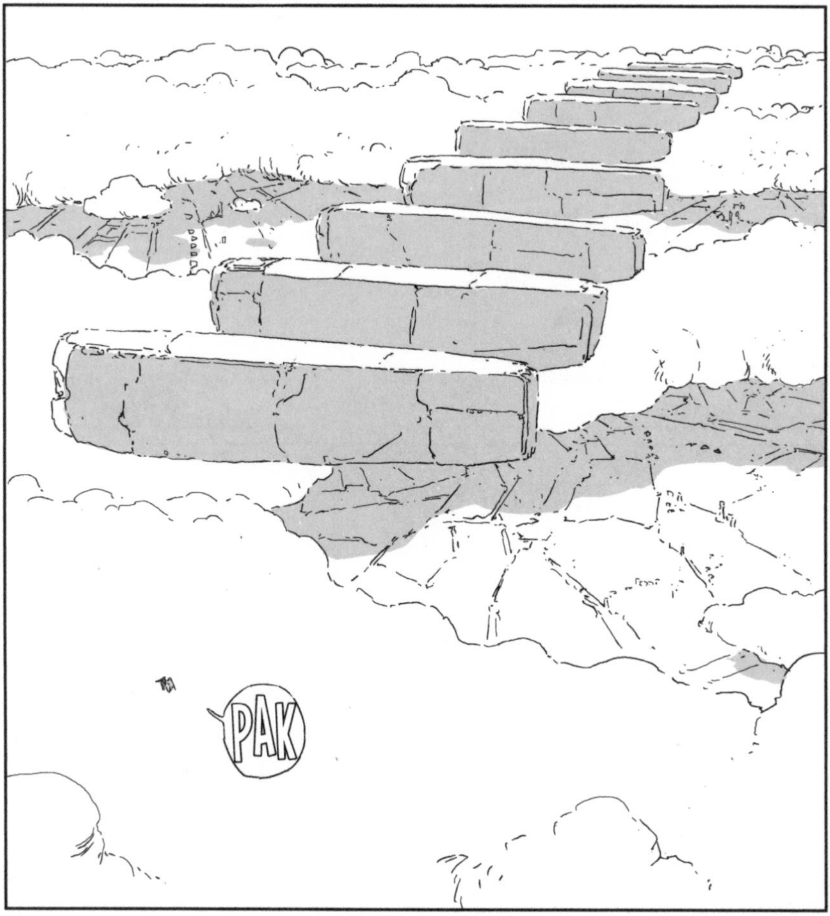
PAK

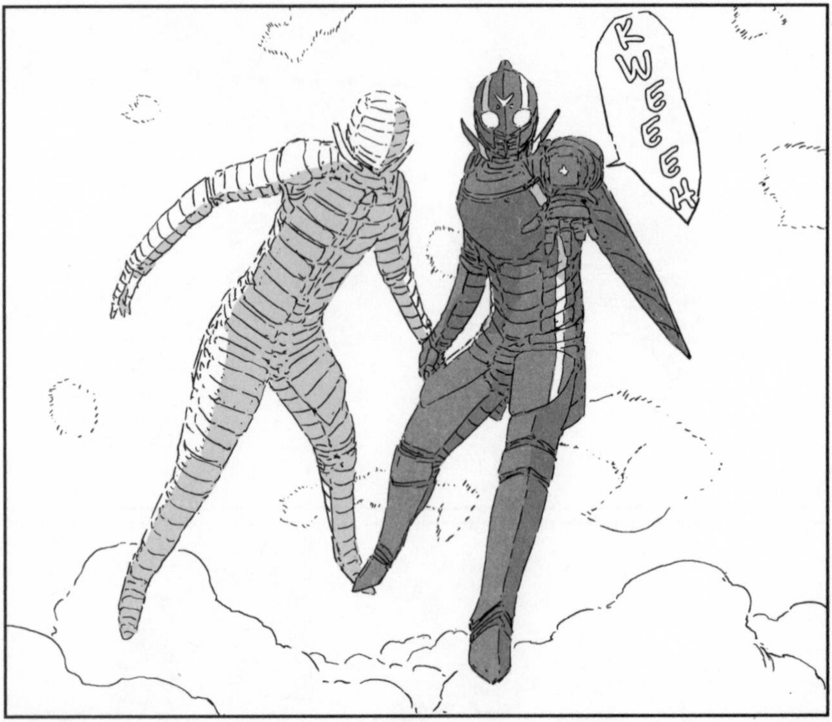
KWEEEH

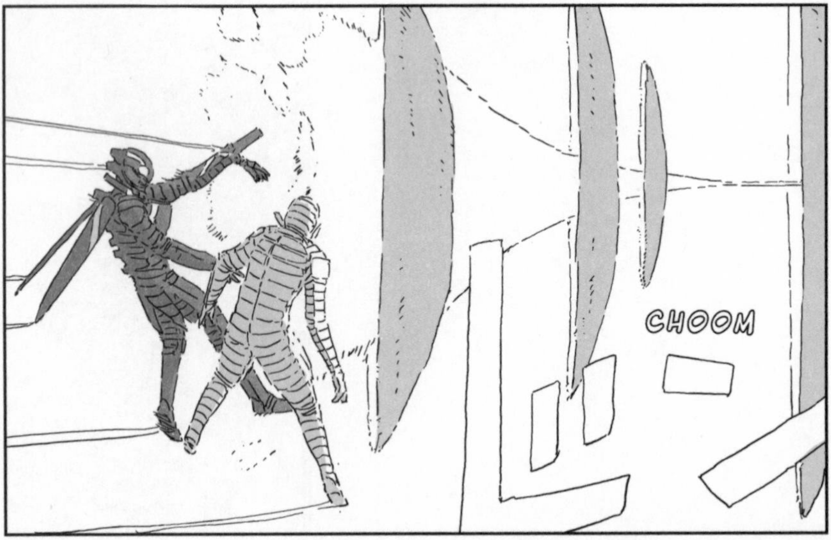
CHOOM

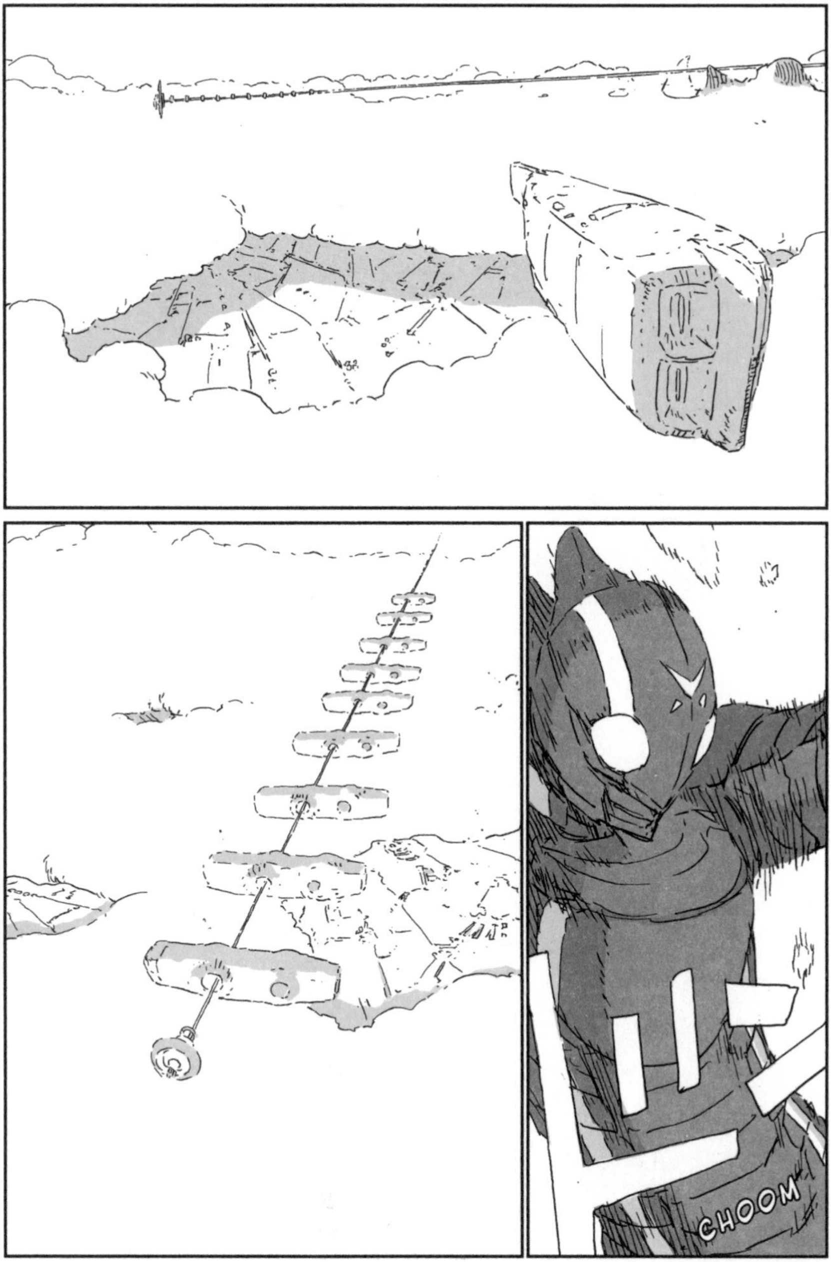
CHOOM

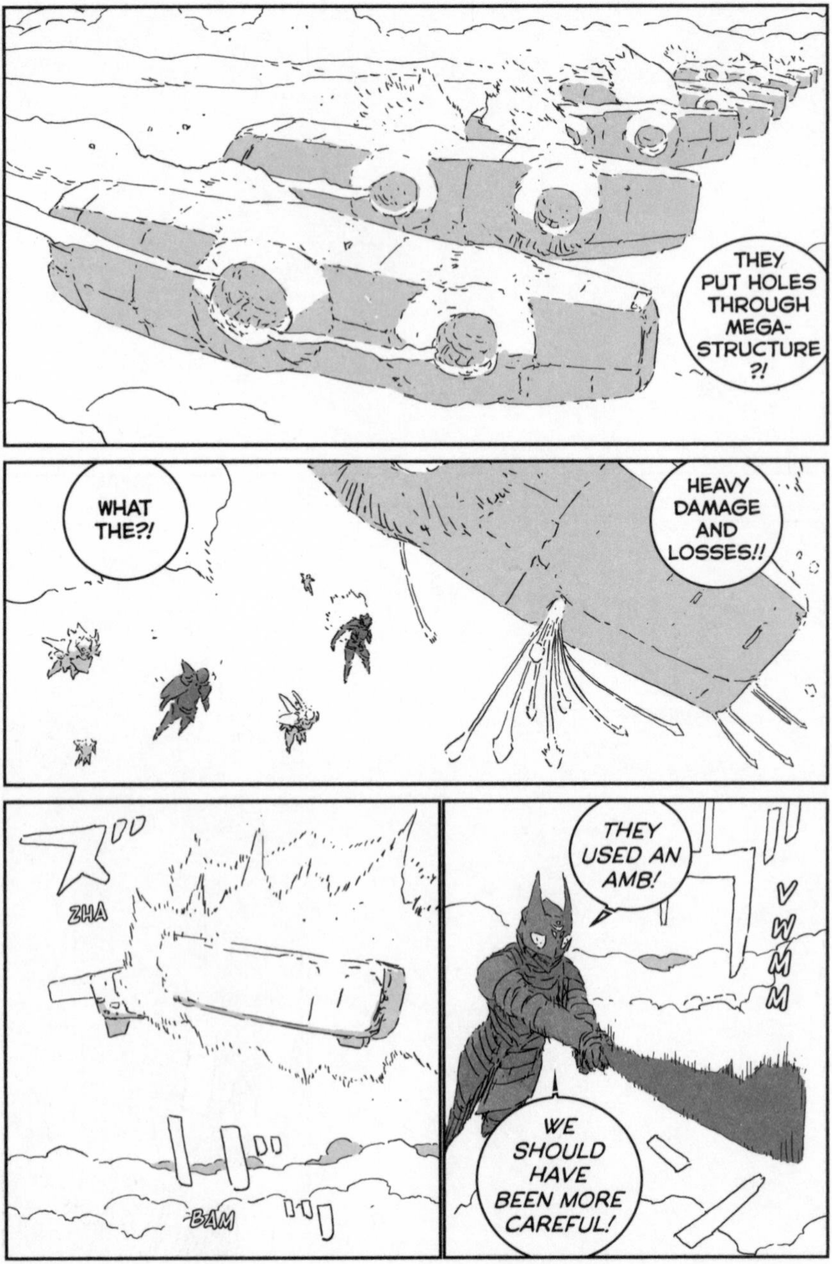
THEY PUT HOLES THROUGH MEGA-STRUCTURE ?!
HEAVY DAMAGE AND LOSSES!!
WHAT THE?!
THEY USED AN AMB!
VWMM
WE SHOULD HAVE BEEN MORE CAREFUL!
ZHA
BAM

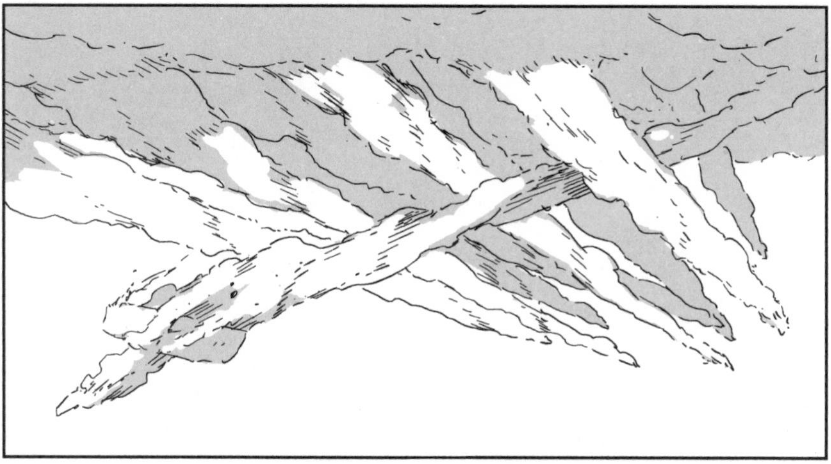

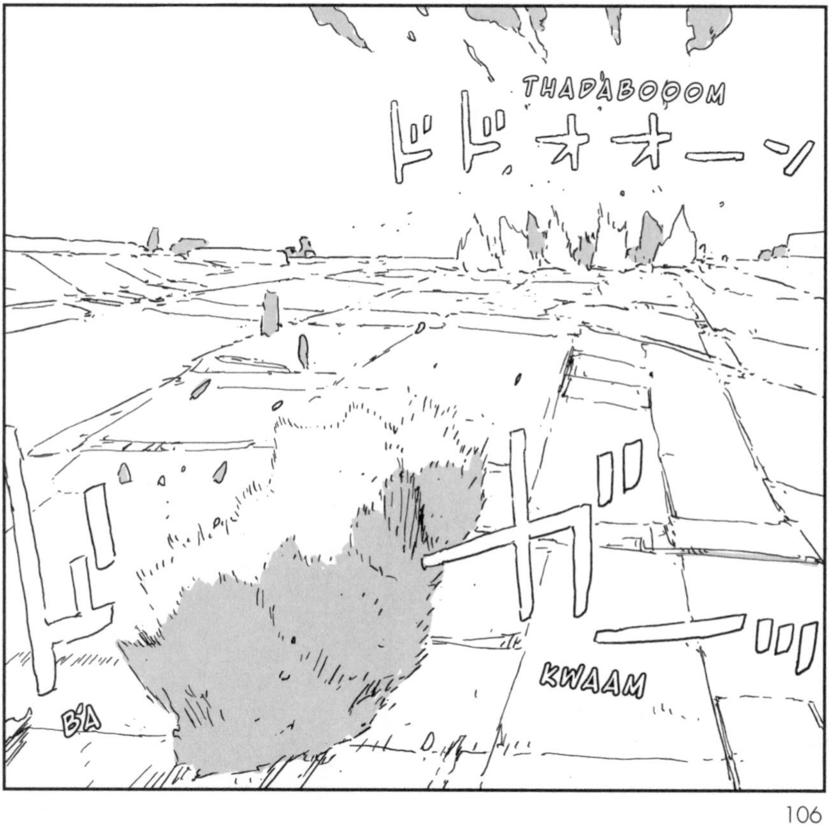
THADABOOOM
ドドオオーン
KWAAM
B'A

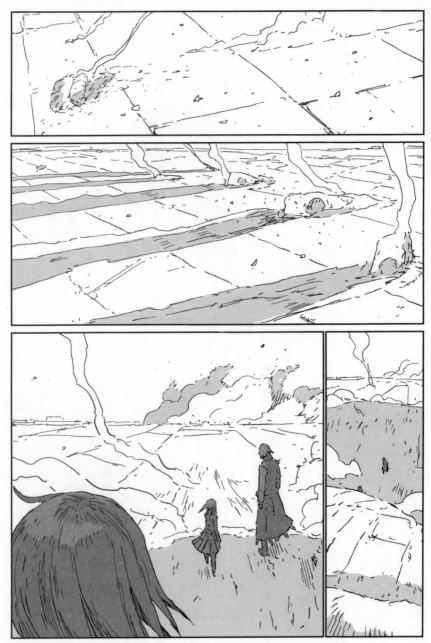

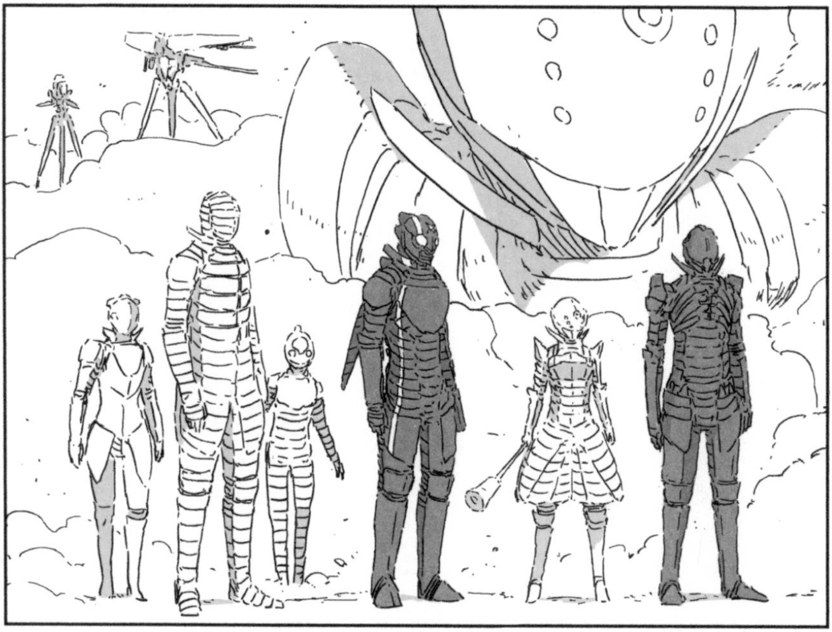

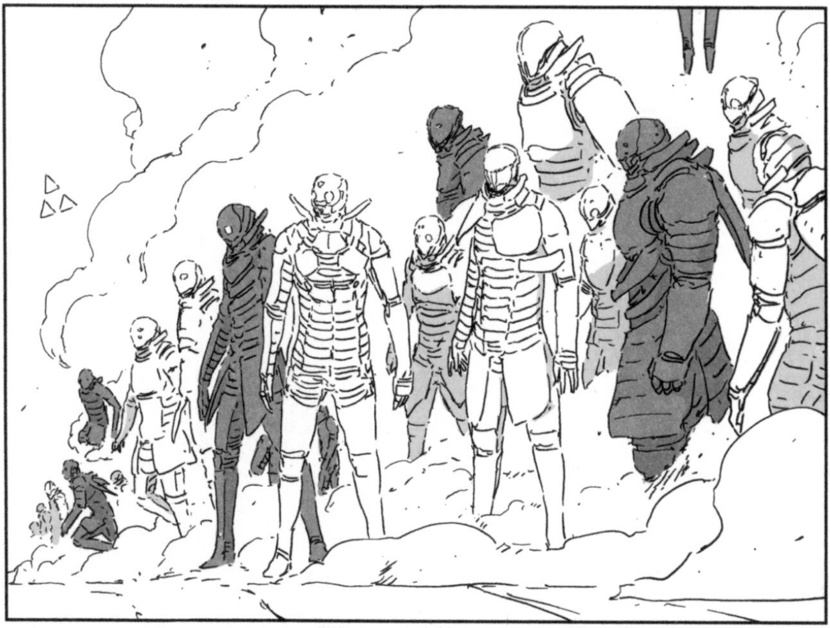

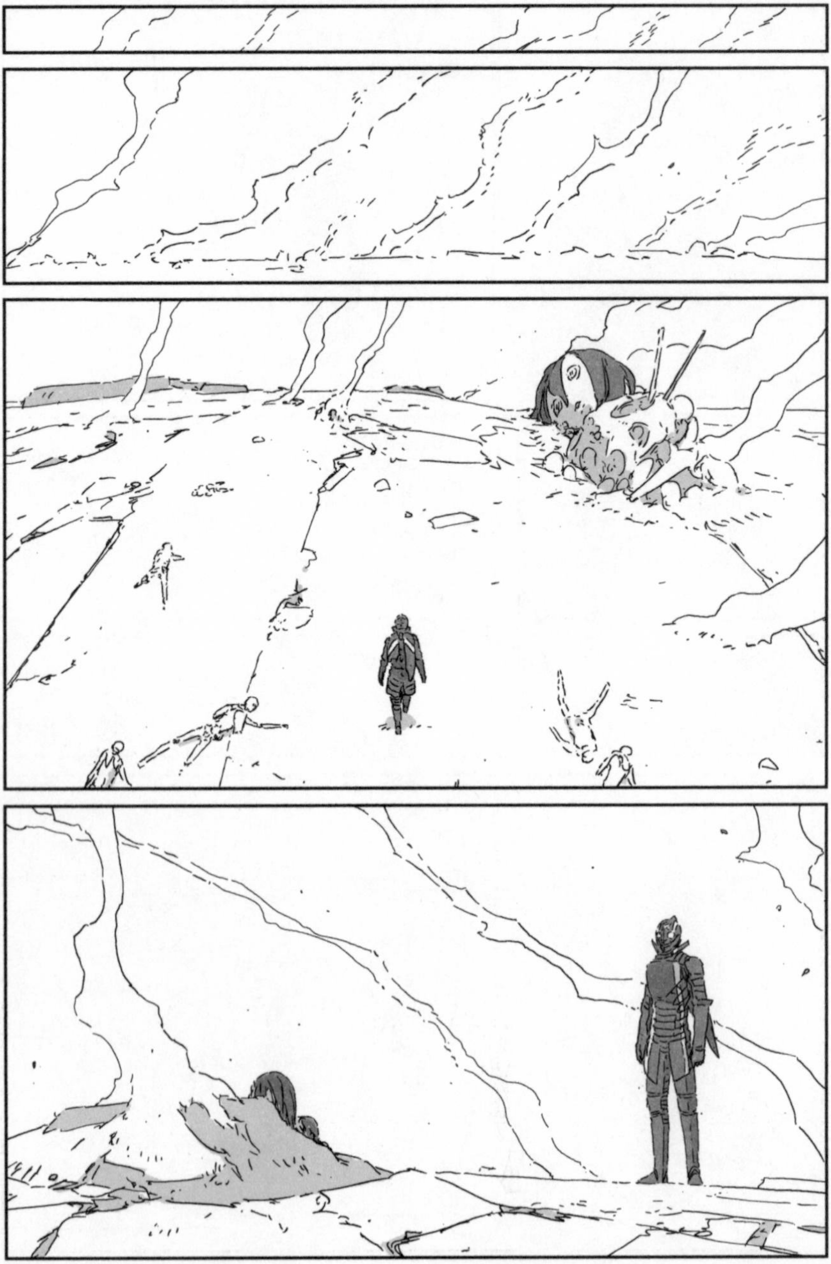

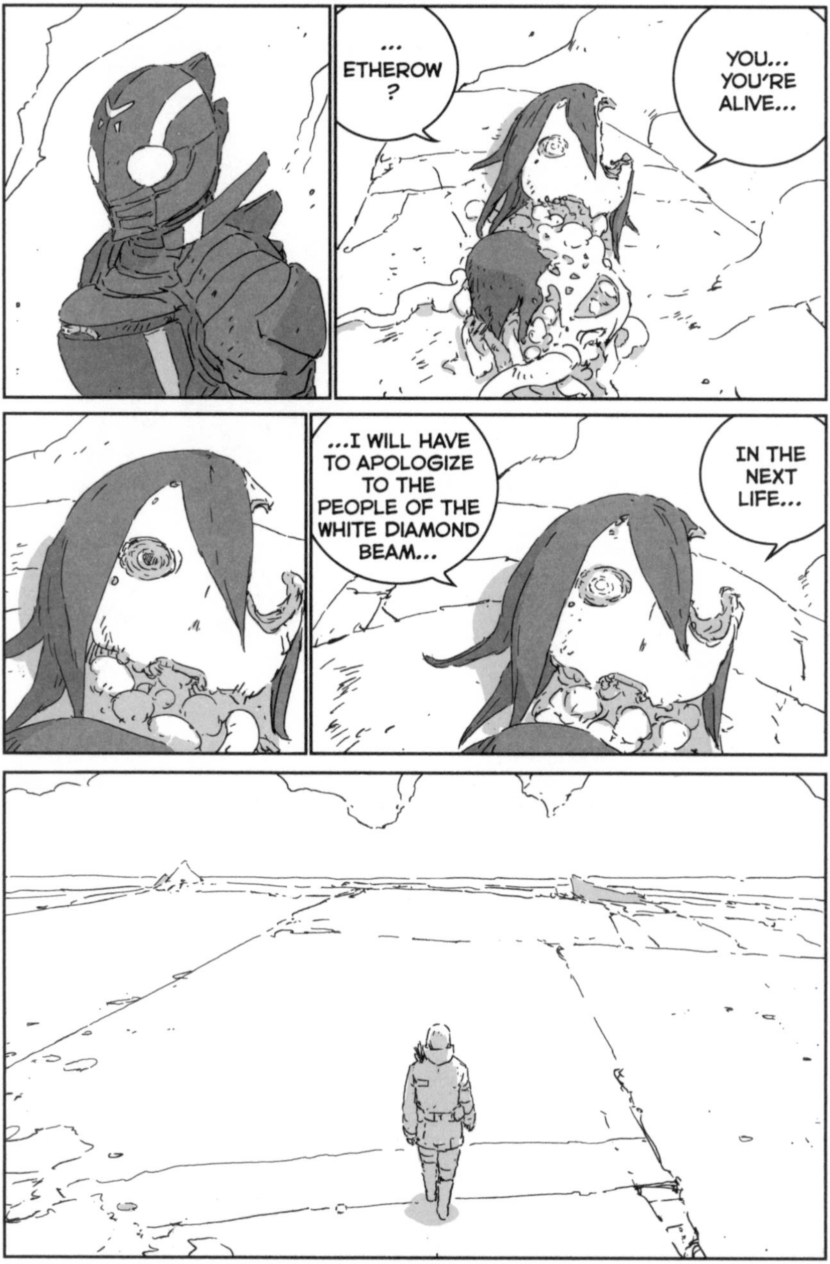
YOU... YOU'RE ALIVE...
... ETHEROW ?
IN THE NEXT LIFE...
...I WILL HAVE TO APOLOGIZE TO THE PEOPLE OF THE WHITE DIAMOND BEAM...

CHAPTER 52 END

APOSIMZ

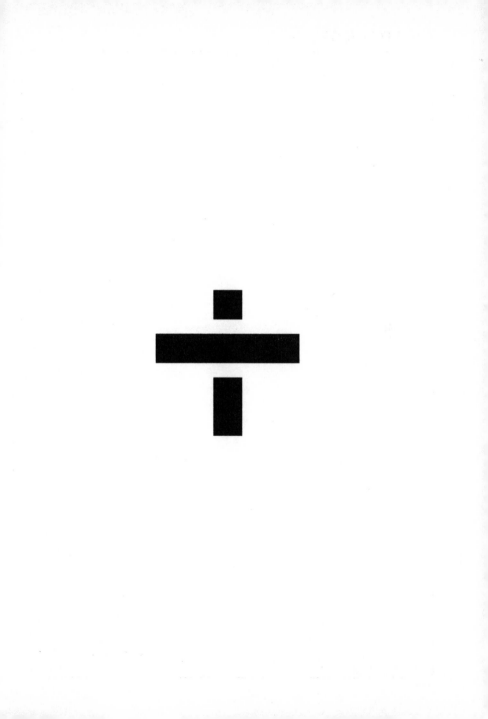

CHAPTER 53

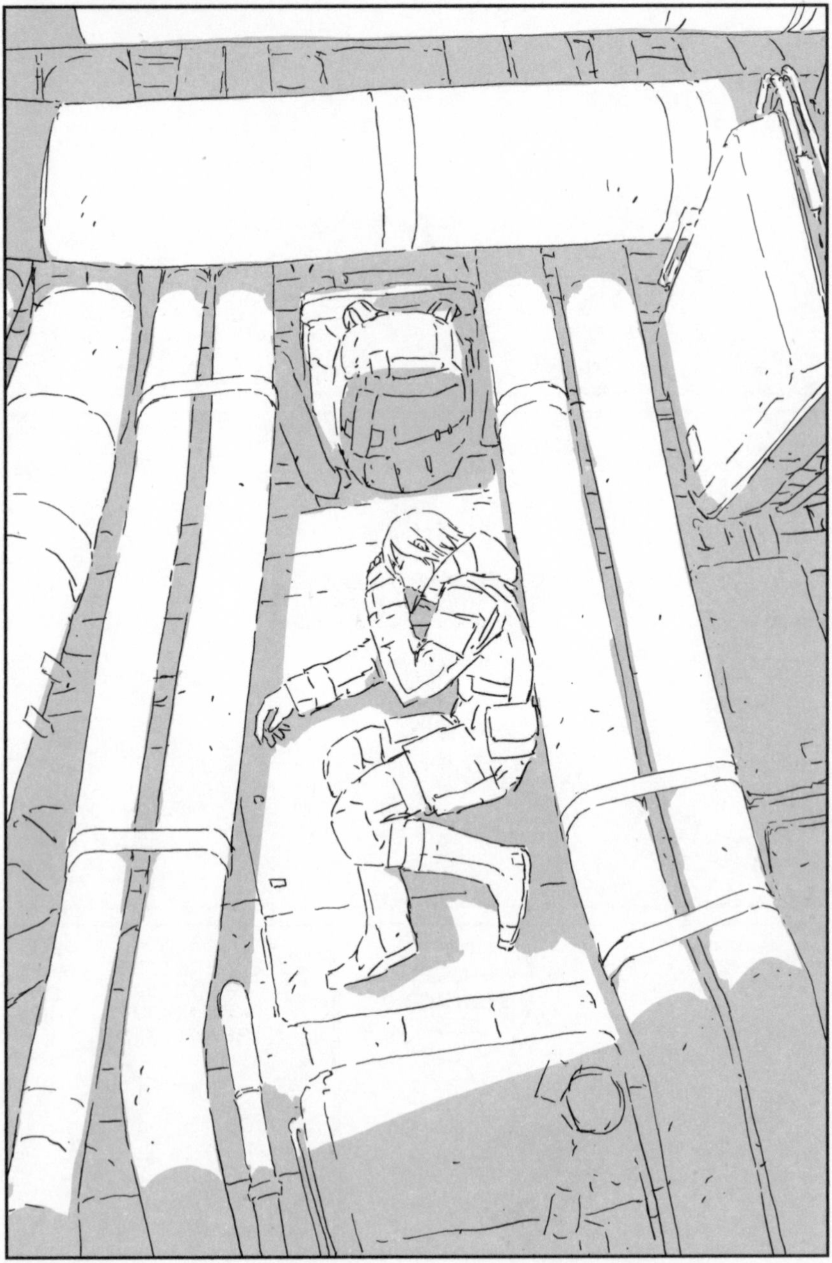

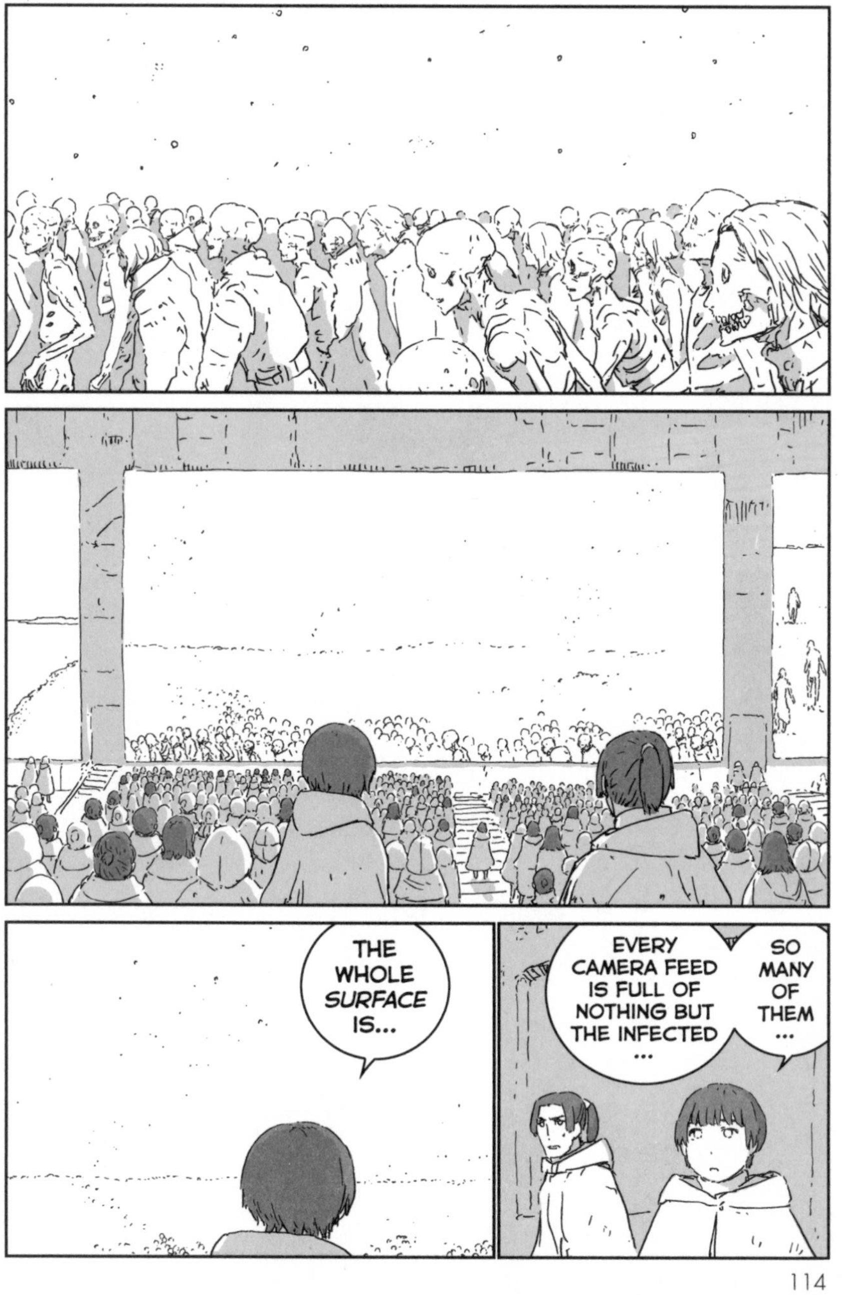
SO MANY OF THEM ...
EVERY CAMERA FEED IS FULL OF NOTHING BUT THE INFECTED ...
THE WHOLE *SURFACE* IS...

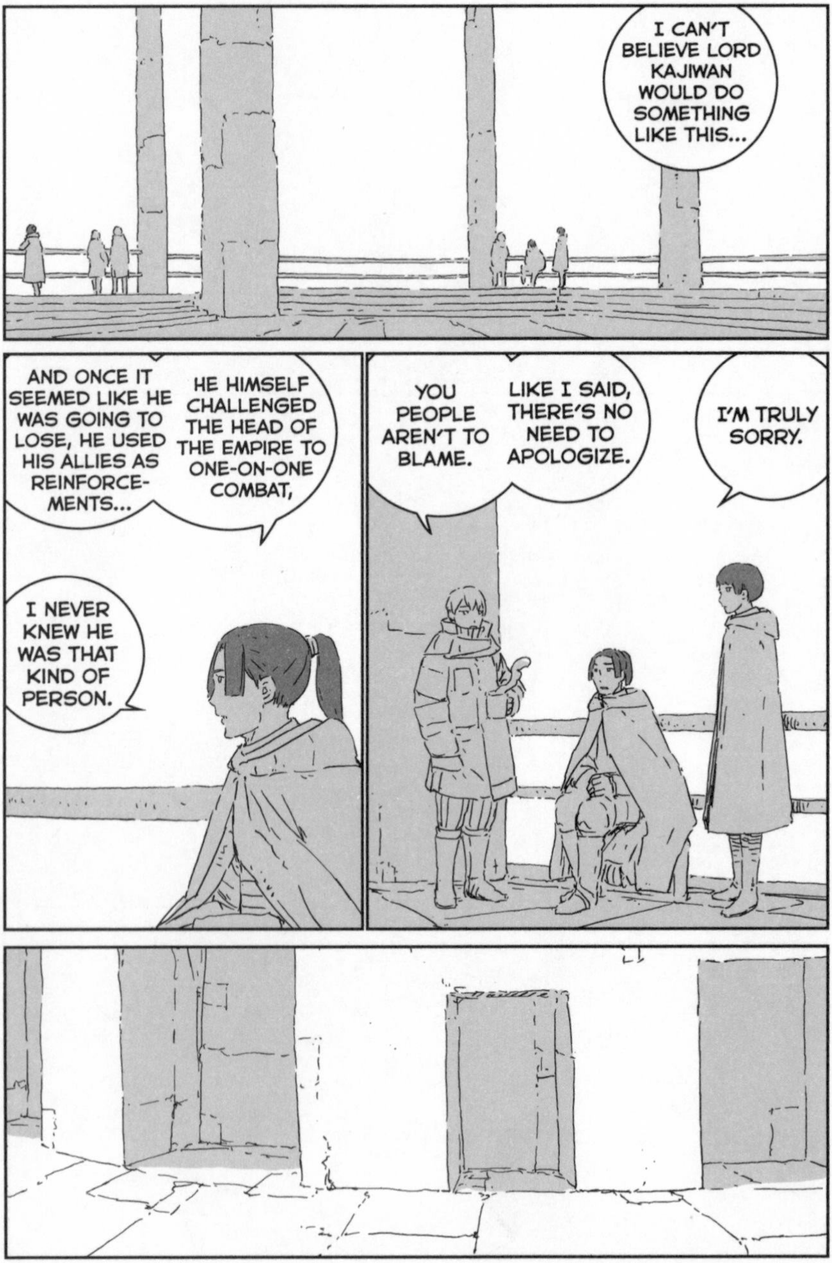
I CAN'T BELIEVE LORD KAJIWAN WOULD DO SOMETHING LIKE THIS...
I'M TRULY SORRY.
LIKE I SAID, THERE'S NO NEED TO APOLOGIZE.
YOU PEOPLE AREN'T TO BLAME.
HE HIMSELF CHALLENGED THE HEAD OF THE EMPIRE TO ONE-ON-ONE COMBAT,
AND ONCE IT SEEMED LIKE HE WAS GOING TO LOSE, HE USED HIS ALLIES AS REINFORCE-MENTS...
I NEVER KNEW HE WAS THAT KIND OF PERSON.

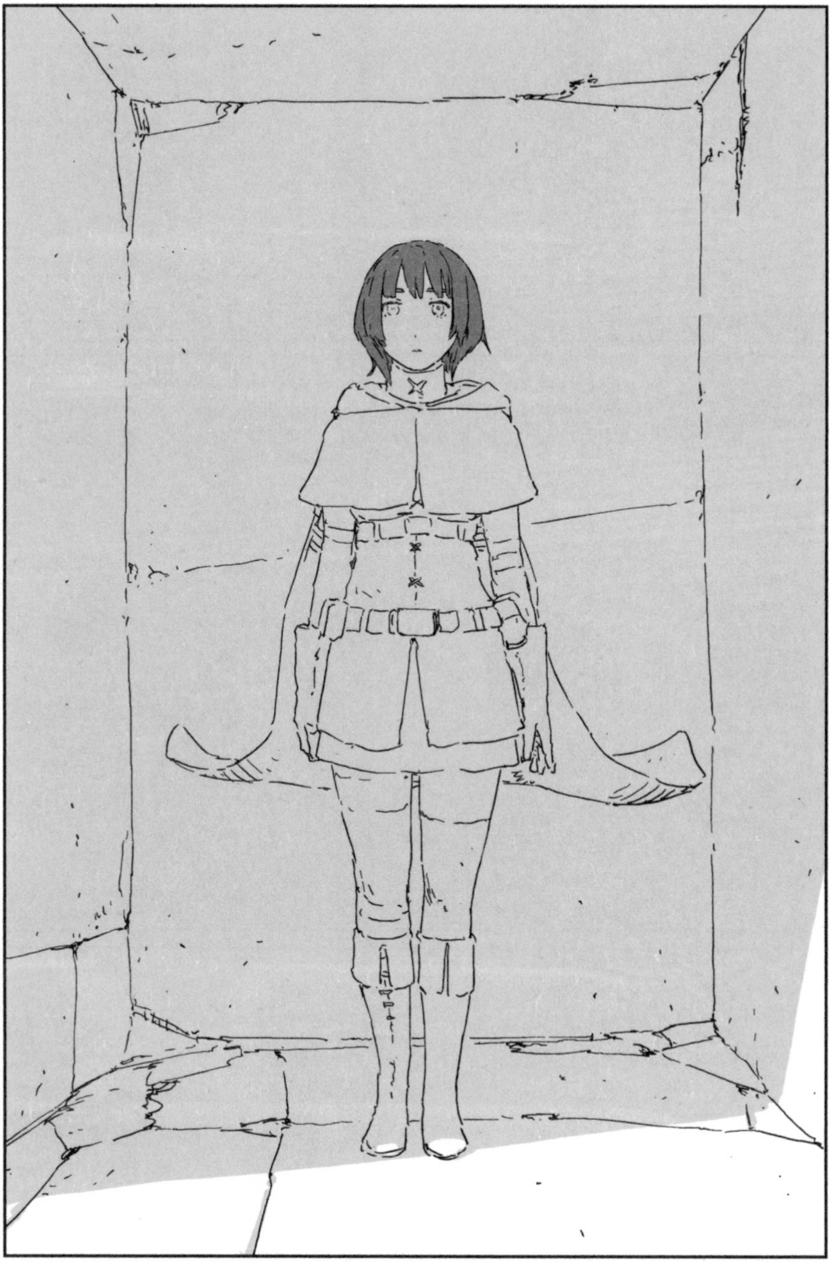

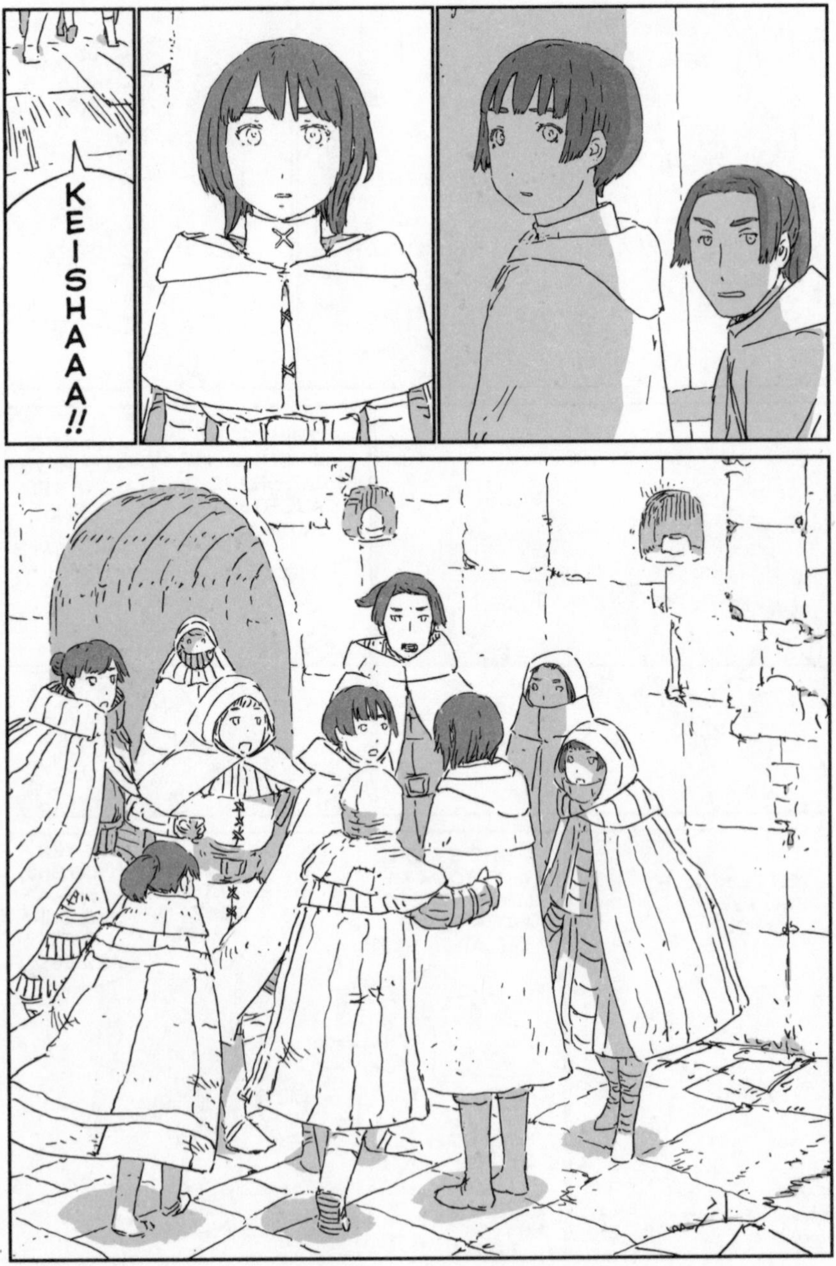
KEISHAAA!!

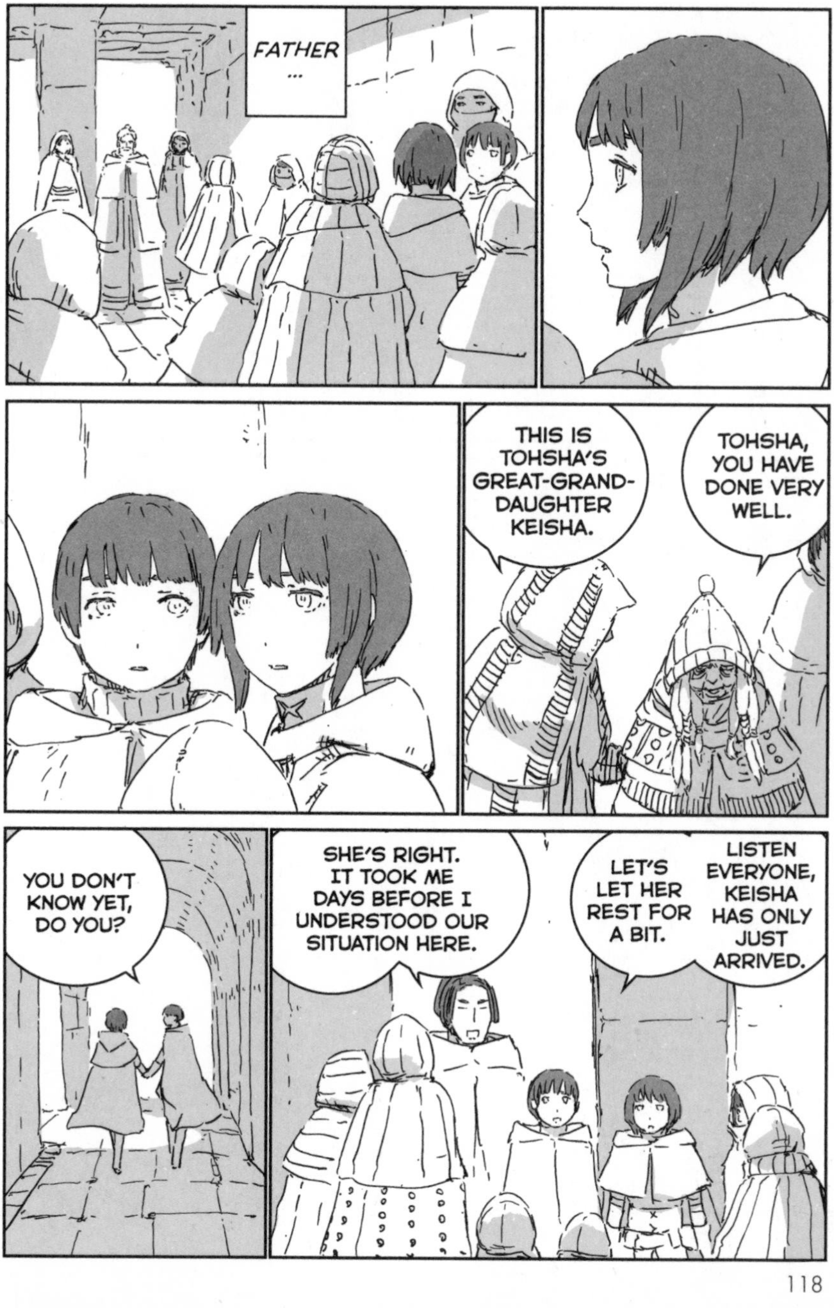
FATHER ...
TOHSHA, YOU HAVE DONE VERY WELL.
THIS IS TOHSHA'S GREAT-GRAND-DAUGHTER KEISHA.
LISTEN EVERYONE, KEISHA HAS ONLY JUST ARRIVED.
LET'S LET HER REST FOR A BIT.
SHE'S RIGHT. IT TOOK ME DAYS BEFORE I UNDERSTOOD OUR SITUATION HERE.
YOU DON'T KNOW YET, DO YOU?

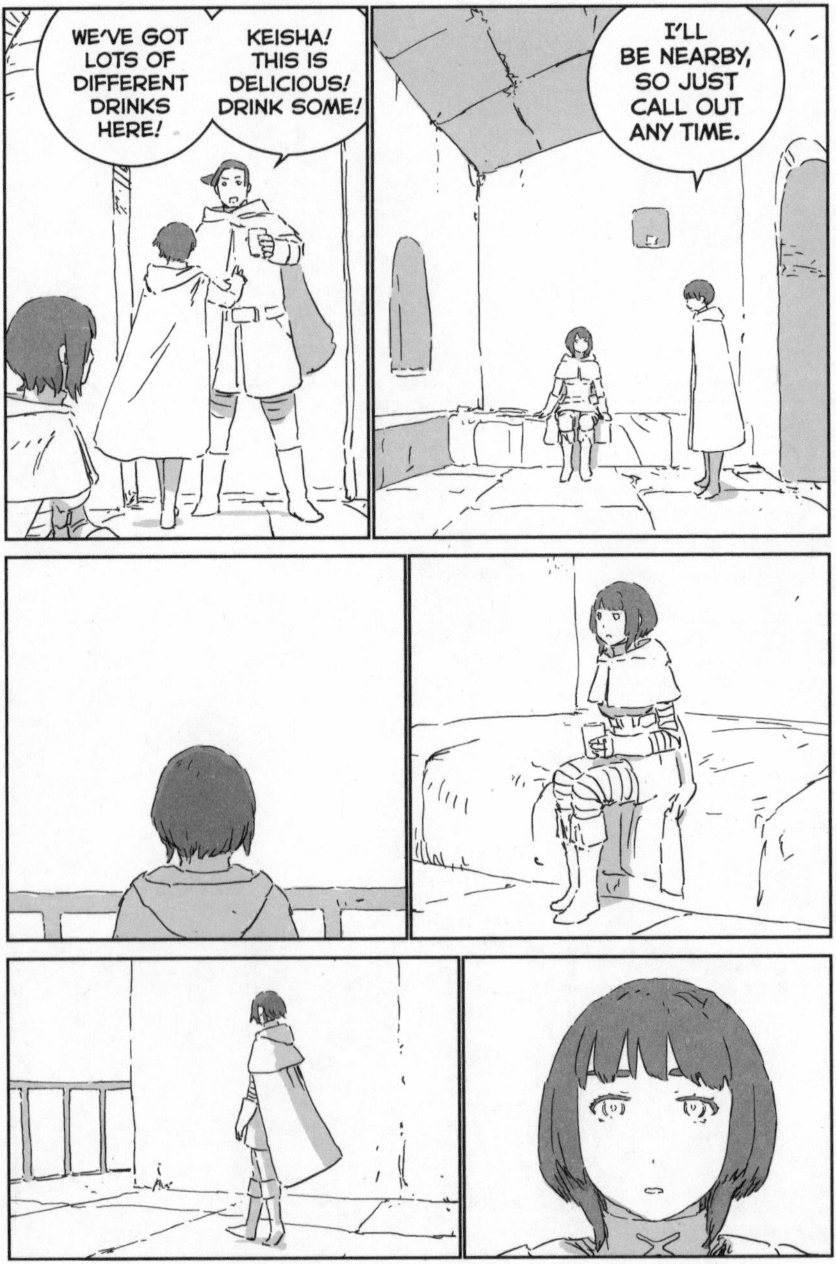
I'LL BE NEARBY, SO JUST CALL OUT ANY TIME.
KEISHA! THIS IS DELICIOUS! DRINK SOME!
WE'VE GOT LOTS OF DIFFERENT DRINKS HERE!

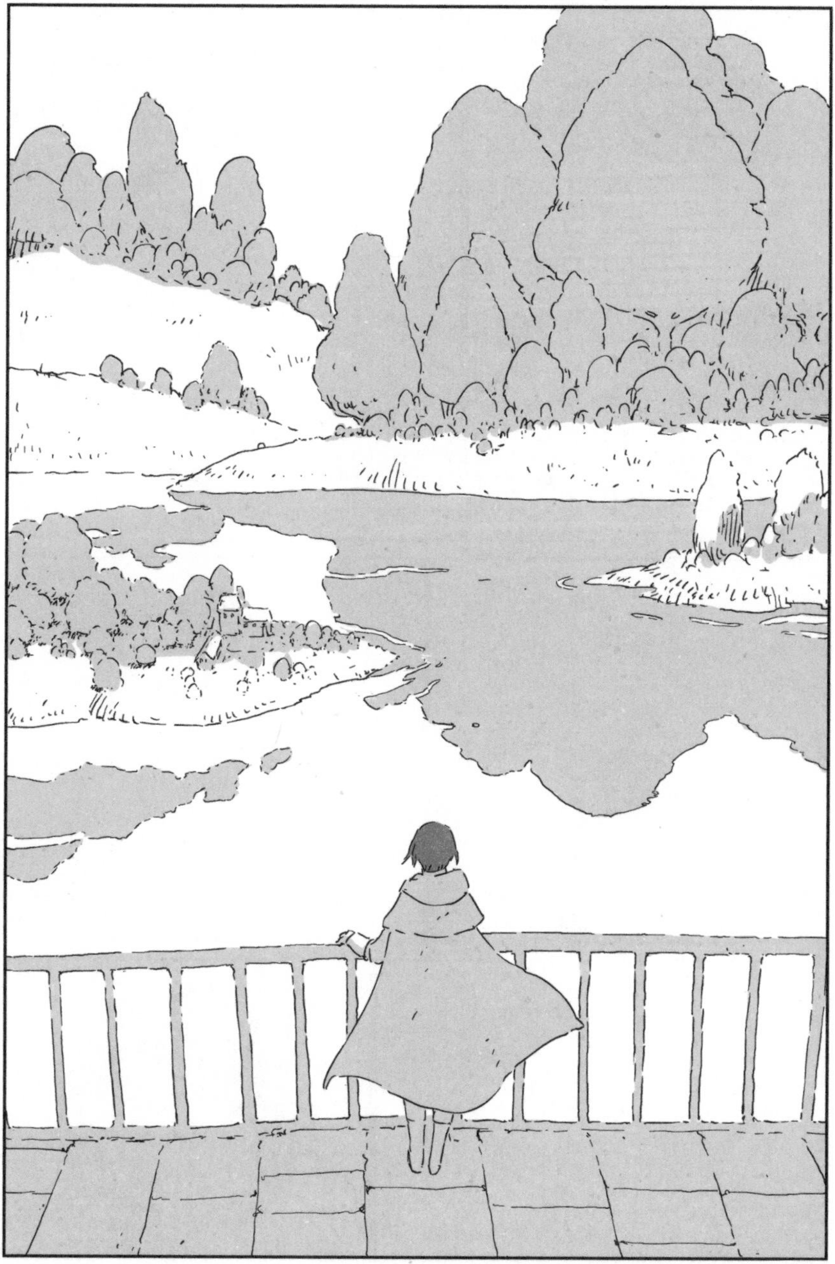

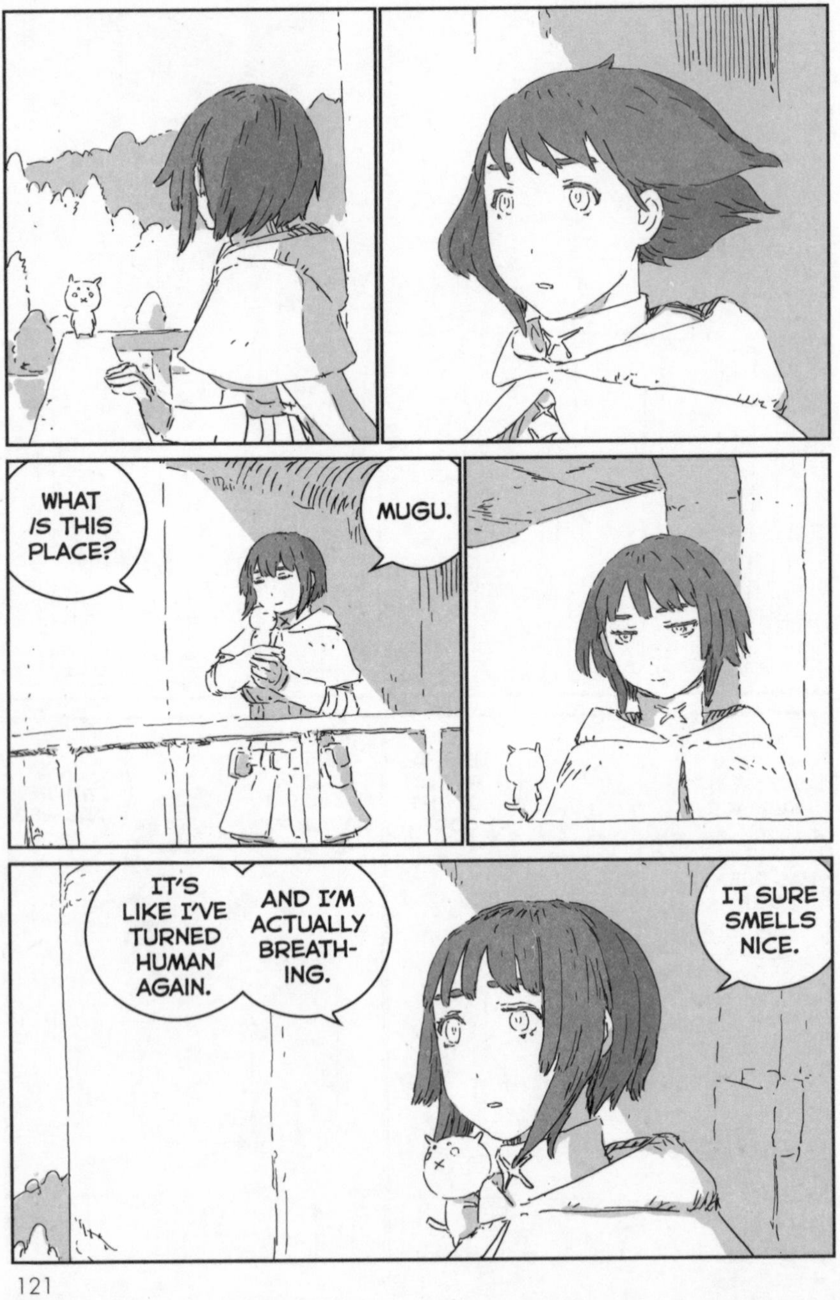
MUGU.
WHAT *IS* THIS PLACE?
IT SURE SMELLS NICE.
AND I'M ACTUALLY BREATH-ING.
IT'S LIKE I'VE TURNED HUMAN AGAIN.

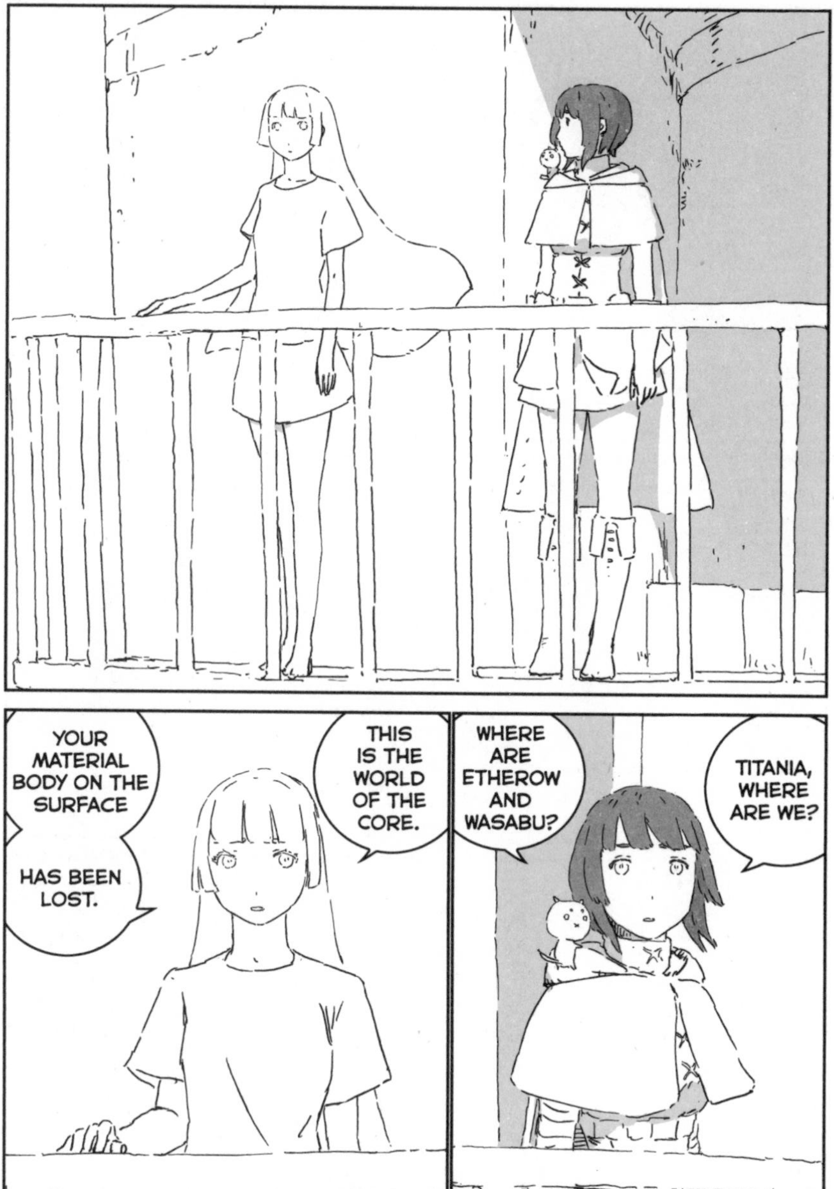
TITANIA, WHERE ARE WE?
WHERE ARE ETHEROW AND WASABU?
THIS IS THE WORLD OF THE CORE.
YOUR MATERIAL BODY ON THE SURFACE
HAS BEEN LOST.

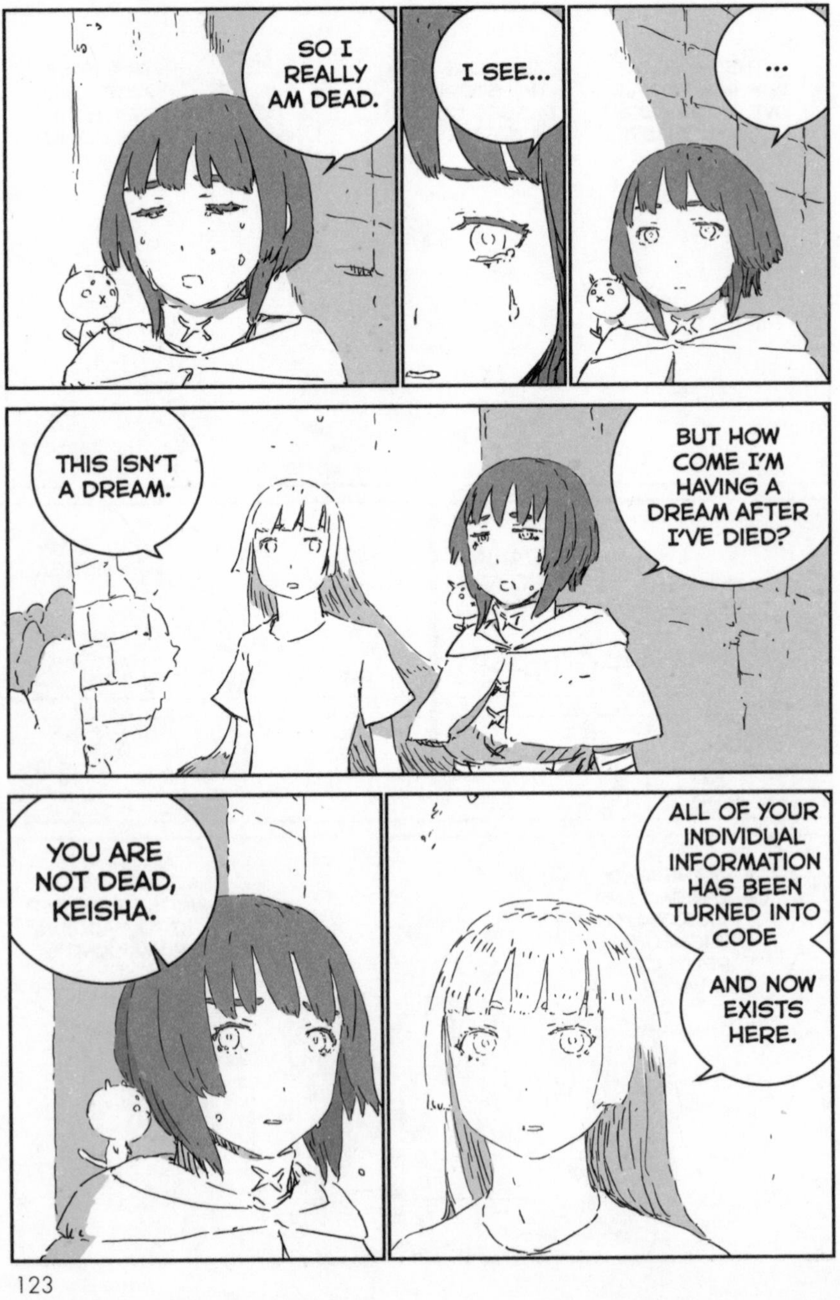
...
I SEE...
SO I REALLY AM DEAD.
BUT HOW COME I'M HAVING A DREAM AFTER I'VE DIED?
THIS ISN'T A DREAM.
ALL OF YOUR INDIVIDUAL INFORMATION HAS BEEN TURNED INTO CODE
AND NOW EXISTS HERE.
YOU ARE NOT DEAD, KEISHA.

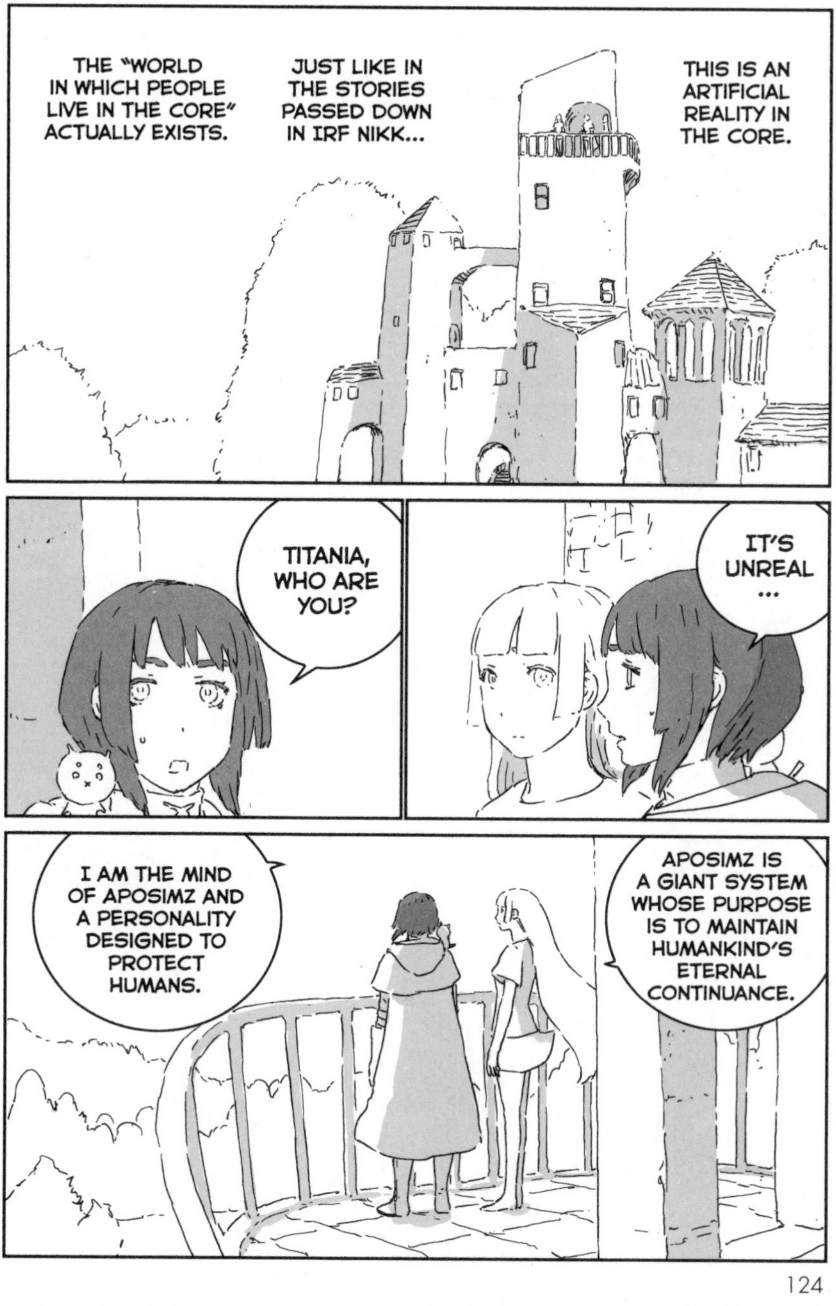
THIS IS AN ARTIFICIAL REALITY IN THE CORE.
JUST LIKE IN THE STORIES PASSED DOWN IN IRF NIKK...
THE "WORLD IN WHICH PEOPLE LIVE IN THE CORE" ACTUALLY EXISTS.
IT'S UNREAL ...
TITANIA, WHO ARE YOU?
APOSIMZ IS A GIANT SYSTEM WHOSE PURPOSE IS TO MAINTAIN HUMANKIND'S ETERNAL CONTINUANCE.
I AM THE MIND OF APOSIMZ AND A PERSONALITY DESIGNED TO PROTECT HUMANS.

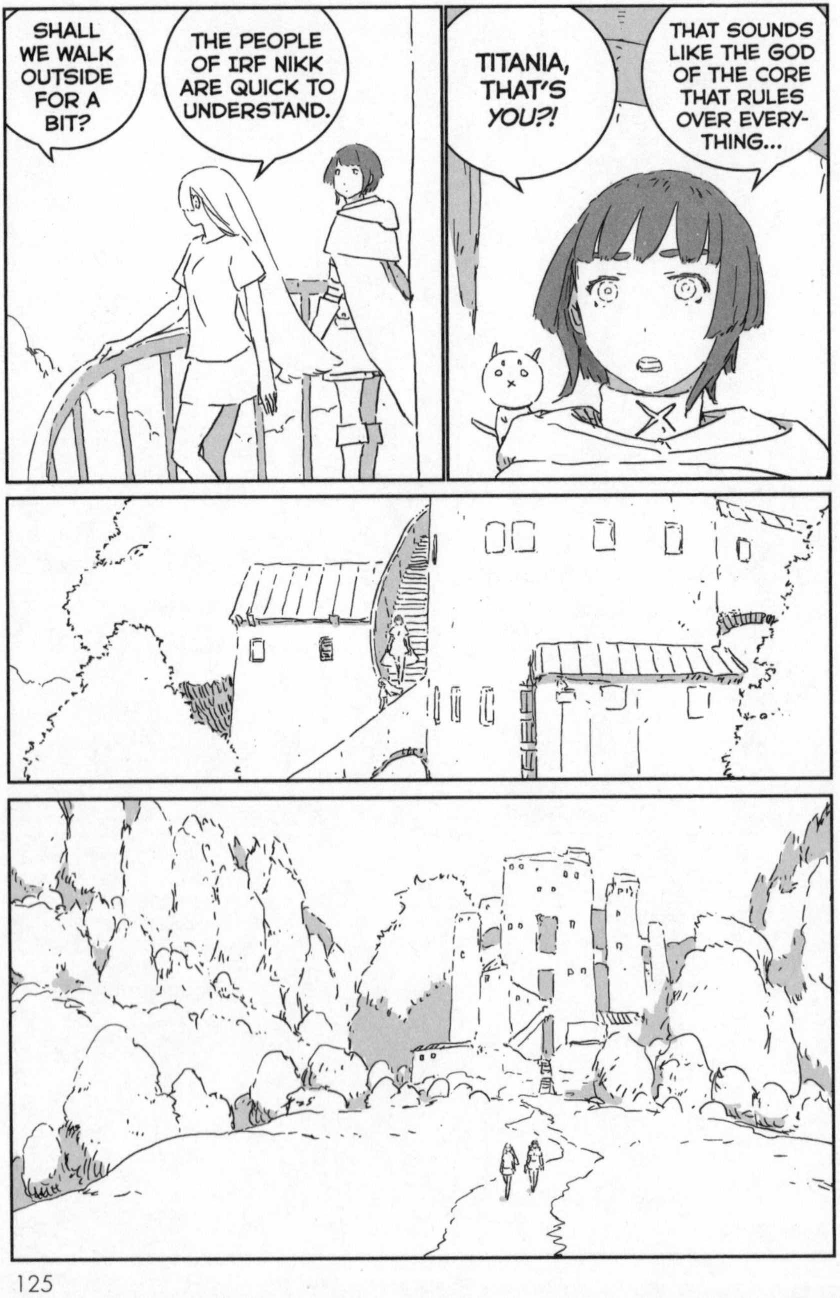
THAT SOUNDS LIKE THE GOD OF THE CORE THAT RULES OVER EVERY-THING...
TITANIA, THAT'S *YOU?!*
THE PEOPLE OF IRF NIKK ARE QUICK TO UNDERSTAND.
SHALL WE WALK OUTSIDE FOR A BIT?

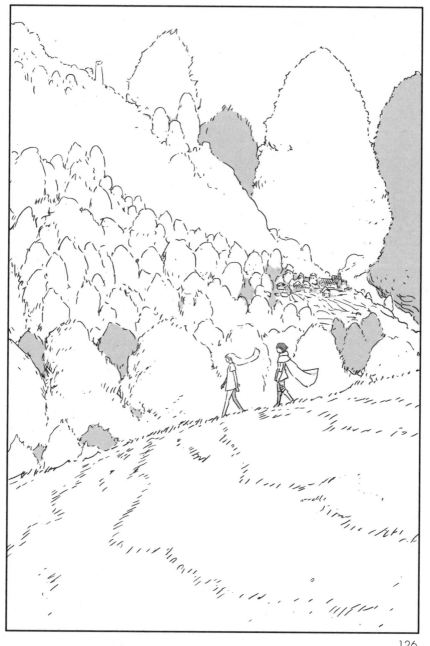

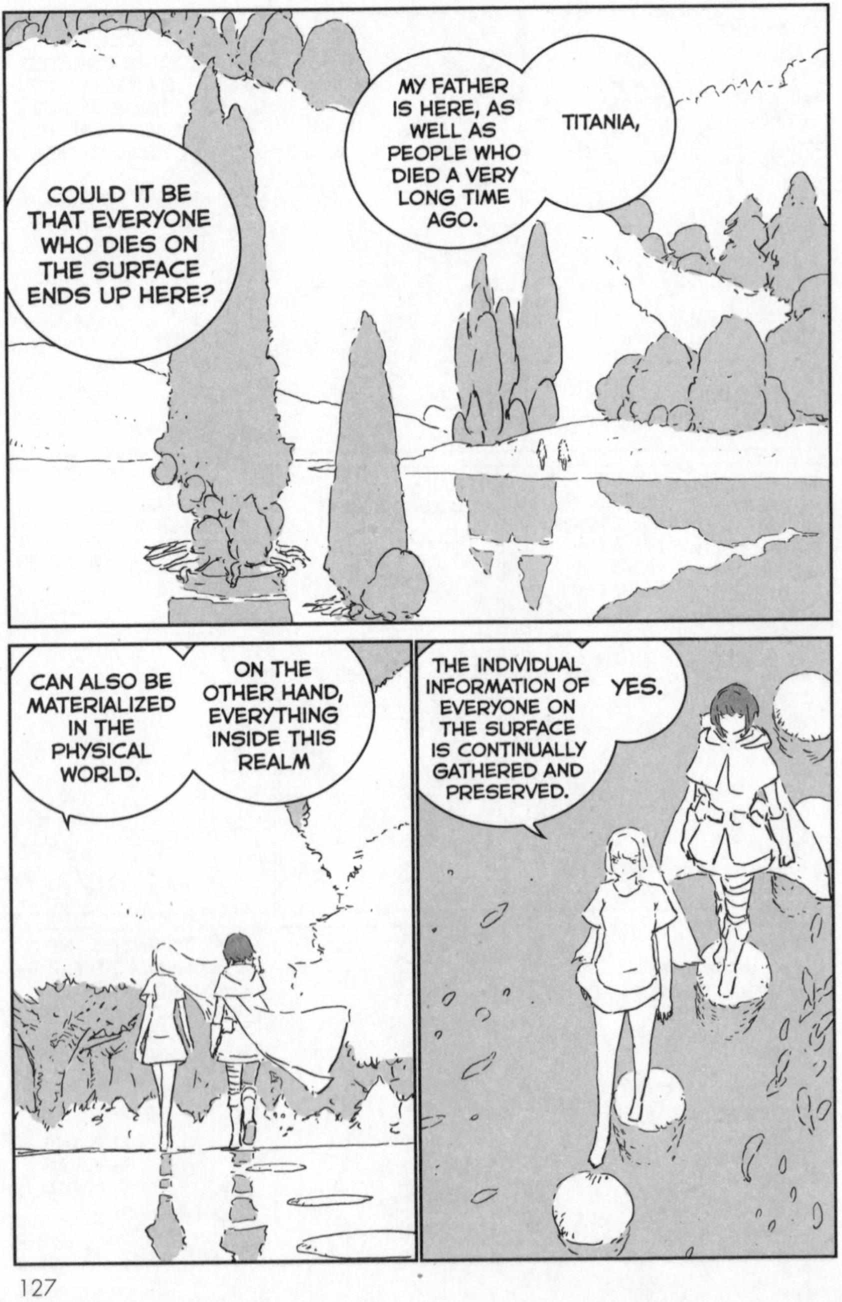
TITANIA, MY FATHER IS HERE, AS WELL AS PEOPLE WHO DIED A VERY LONG TIME AGO.
COULD IT BE THAT EVERYONE WHO DIES ON THE SURFACE ENDS UP HERE?
YES. THE INDIVIDUAL INFORMATION OF EVERYONE ON THE SURFACE IS CONTINUALLY GATHERED AND PRESERVED.
ON THE OTHER HAND, EVERYTHING INSIDE THIS REALM
CAN ALSO BE MATERIALIZED IN THE PHYSICAL WORLD.

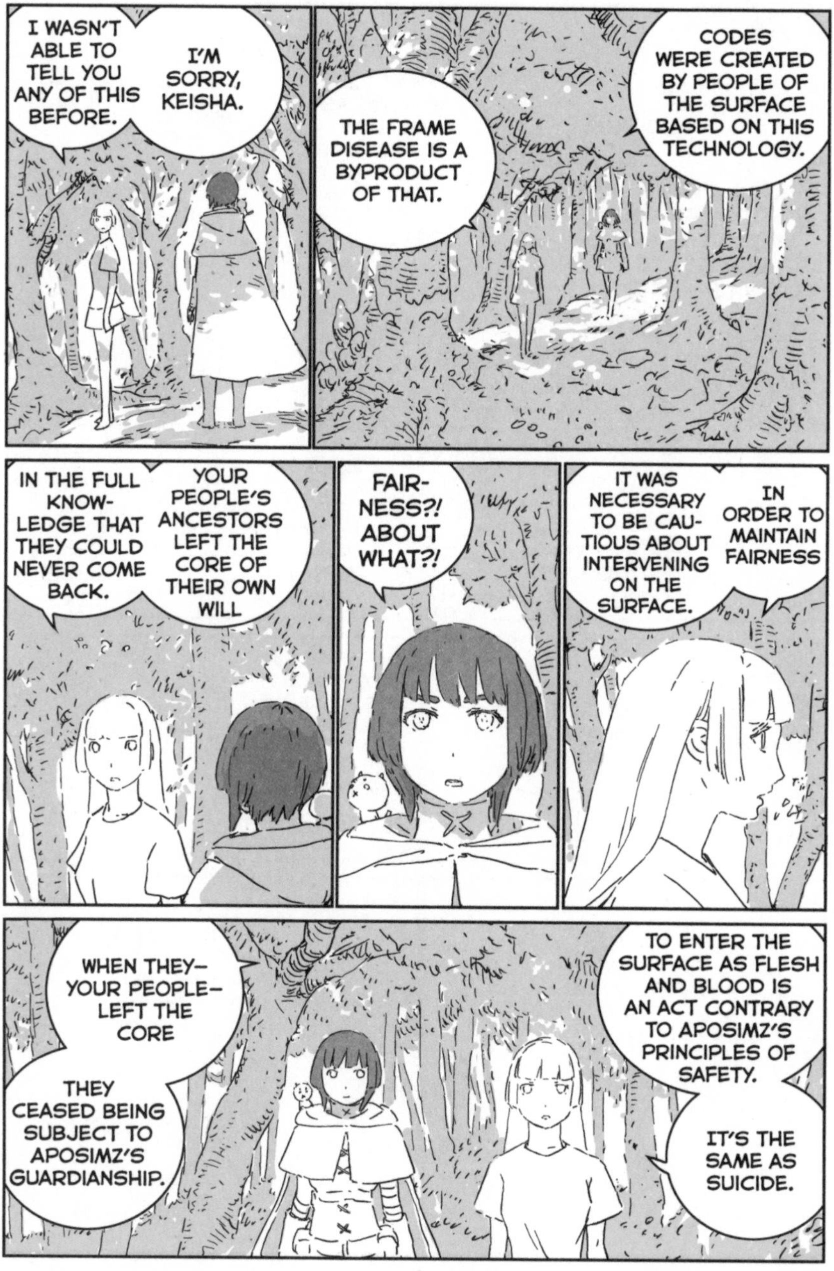
CODES WERE CREATED BY PEOPLE OF THE SURFACE BASED ON THIS TECHNOLOGY.
THE FRAME DISEASE IS A BYPRODUCT OF THAT.
I'M SORRY, KEISHA.
I WASN'T ABLE TO TELL YOU ANY OF THIS BEFORE.
IN ORDER TO MAINTAIN FAIRNESS
IT WAS NECESSARY TO BE CAUTIOUS ABOUT INTERVENING ON THE SURFACE.
FAIRNESS?! ABOUT WHAT?!
YOUR PEOPLE'S ANCESTORS LEFT THE CORE OF THEIR OWN WILL
IN THE FULL KNOWLEDGE THAT THEY COULD NEVER COME BACK.
TO ENTER THE SURFACE AS FLESH AND BLOOD IS AN ACT CONTRARY TO APOSIMZ'S PRINCIPLES OF SAFETY.
IT'S THE SAME AS SUICIDE.
WHEN THEY—YOUR PEOPLE—LEFT THE CORE
THEY CEASED BEING SUBJECT TO APOSIMZ'S GUARDIANSHIP.

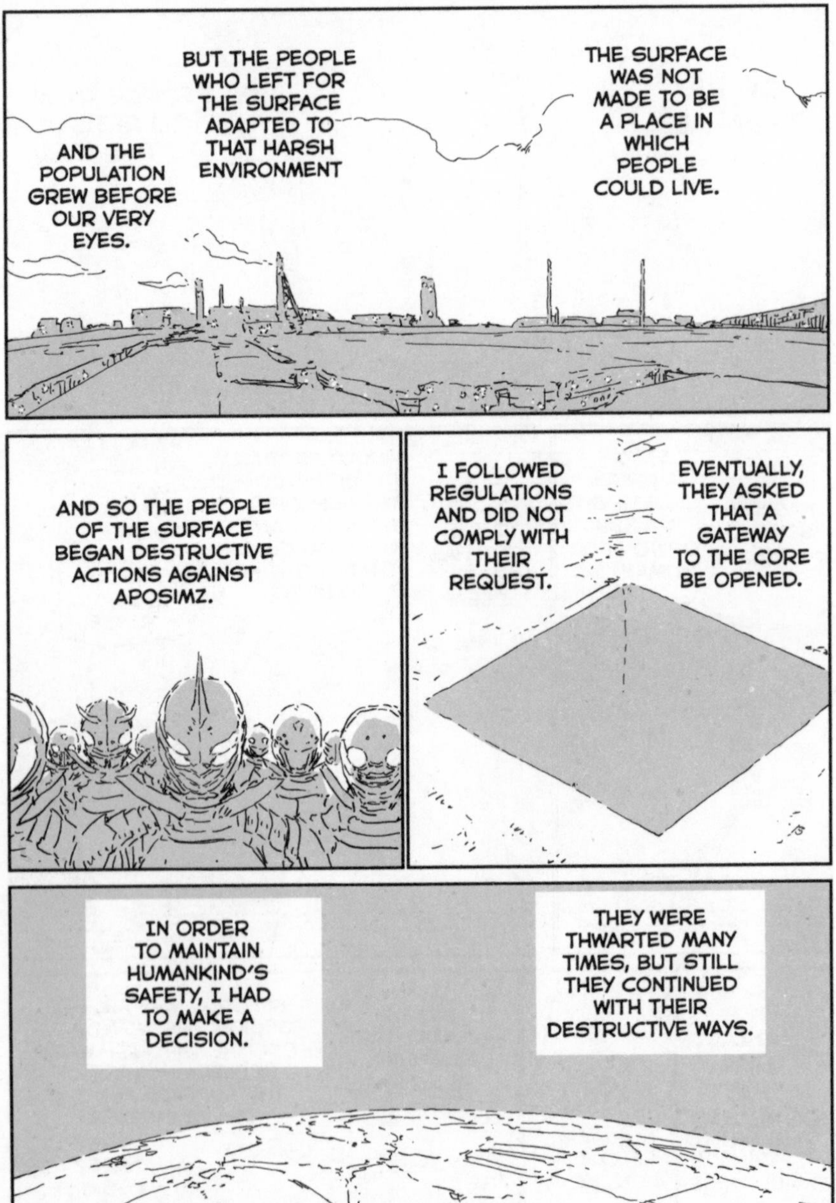
THE SURFACE WAS NOT MADE TO BE A PLACE IN WHICH PEOPLE COULD LIVE.
BUT THE PEOPLE WHO LEFT FOR THE SURFACE ADAPTED TO THAT HARSH ENVIRONMENT
AND THE POPULATION GREW BEFORE OUR VERY EYES.
EVENTUALLY, THEY ASKED THAT A GATEWAY TO THE CORE BE OPENED.
I FOLLOWED REGULATIONS AND DID NOT COMPLY WITH THEIR REQUEST.
AND SO THE PEOPLE OF THE SURFACE BEGAN DESTRUCTIVE ACTIONS AGAINST APOSIMZ.
THEY WERE THWARTED MANY TIMES, BUT STILL THEY CONTINUED WITH THEIR DESTRUCTIVE WAYS.
IN ORDER TO MAINTAIN HUMANKIND'S SAFETY, I HAD TO MAKE A DECISION.

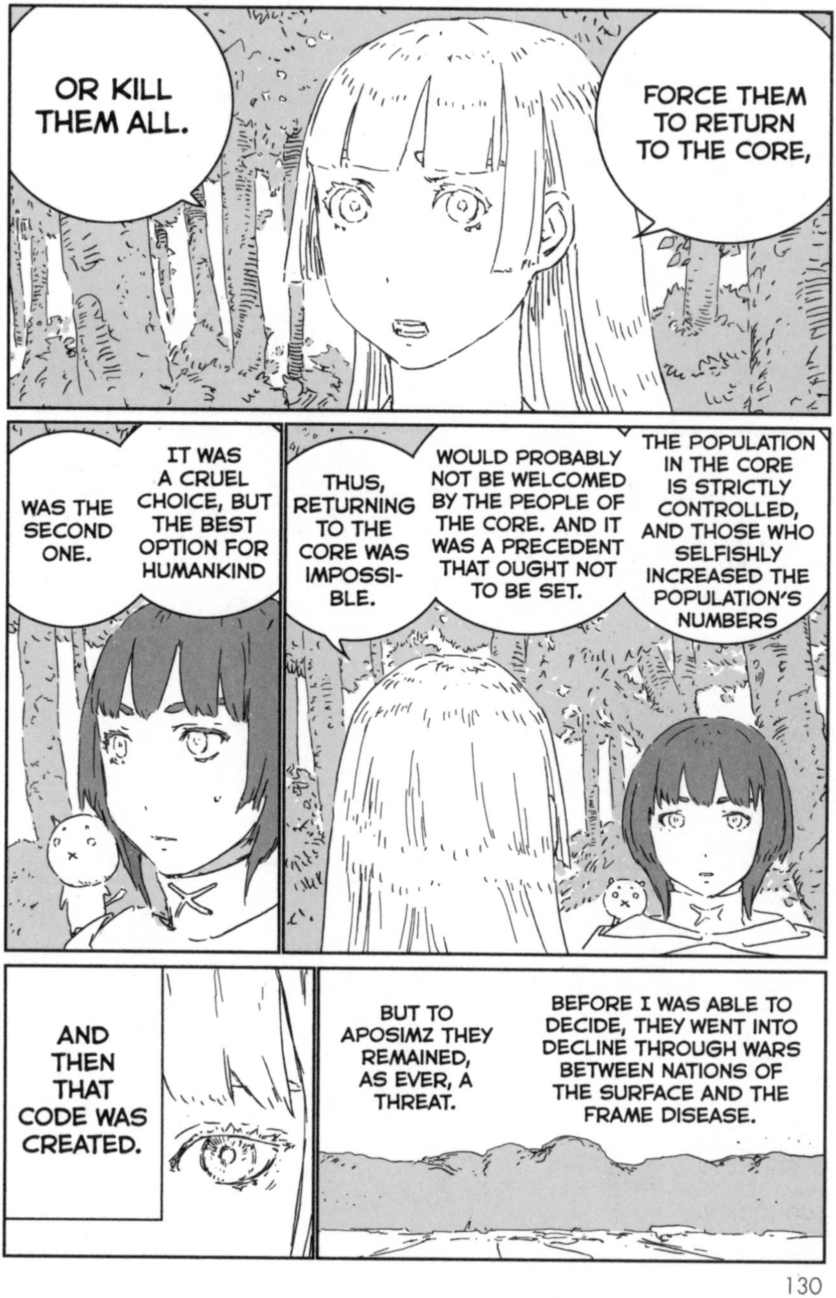
FORCE THEM TO RETURN TO THE CORE,
OR KILL THEM ALL.
THE POPULATION IN THE CORE IS STRICTLY CONTROLLED, AND THOSE WHO SELFISHLY INCREASED THE POPULATION'S NUMBERS
WOULD PROBABLY NOT BE WELCOMED BY THE PEOPLE OF THE CORE. AND IT WAS A PRECEDENT THAT OUGHT NOT TO BE SET.
THUS, RETURNING TO THE CORE WAS IMPOSSI-BLE.
IT WAS A CRUEL CHOICE, BUT THE BEST OPTION FOR HUMANKIND
WAS THE SECOND ONE.
BEFORE I WAS ABLE TO DECIDE, THEY WENT INTO DECLINE THROUGH WARS BETWEEN NATIONS OF THE SURFACE AND THE FRAME DISEASE.
BUT TO APOSIMZ THEY REMAINED, AS EVER, A THREAT.
AND THEN THAT CODE WAS CREATED.

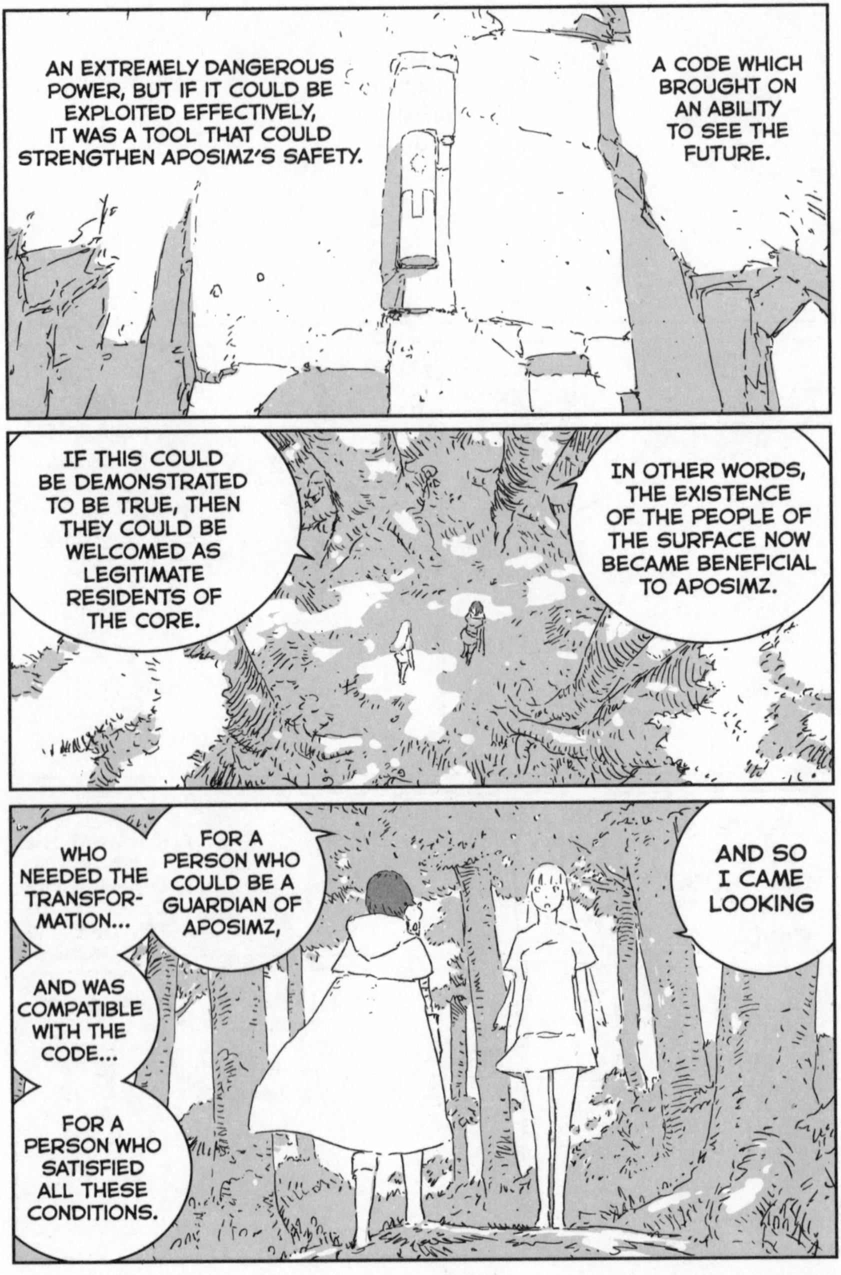
A CODE WHICH BROUGHT ON AN ABILITY TO SEE THE FUTURE.
AN EXTREMELY DANGEROUS POWER, BUT IF IT COULD BE EXPLOITED EFFECTIVELY, IT WAS A TOOL THAT COULD STRENGTHEN APOSIMZ'S SAFETY.
IN OTHER WORDS, THE EXISTENCE OF THE PEOPLE OF THE SURFACE NOW BECAME BENEFICIAL TO APOSIMZ.
IF THIS COULD BE DEMONSTRATED TO BE TRUE, THEN THEY COULD BE WELCOMED AS LEGITIMATE RESIDENTS OF THE CORE.
AND SO I CAME LOOKING
FOR A PERSON WHO COULD BE A GUARDIAN OF APOSIMZ,
WHO NEEDED THE TRANSFORMATION...
AND WAS COMPATIBLE WITH THE CODE...
FOR A PERSON WHO SATISFIED ALL THESE CONDITIONS.

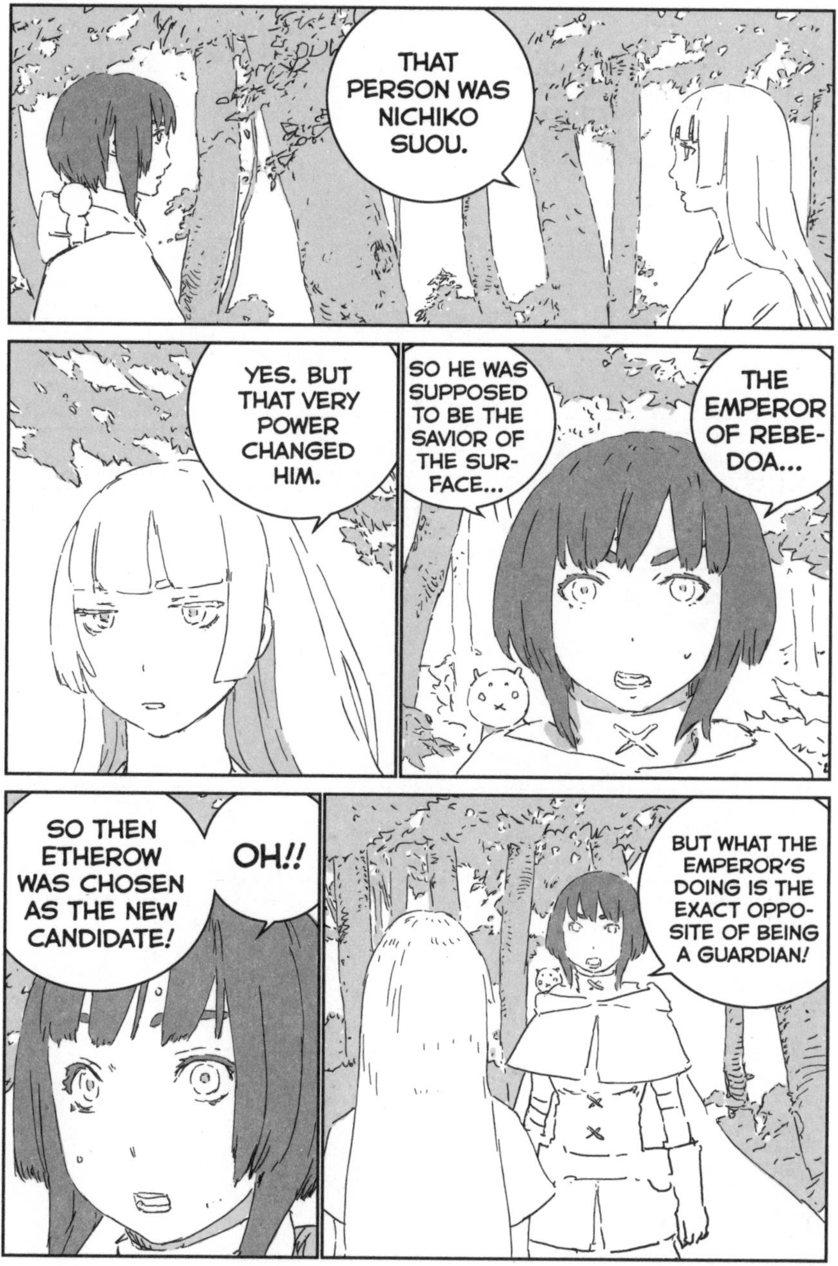
THAT PERSON WAS NICHIKO SUOU.
THE EMPEROR OF REBE-DOA...
SO HE WAS SUPPOSED TO BE THE SAVIOR OF THE SUR-FACE...
YES. BUT THAT VERY POWER CHANGED HIM.
BUT WHAT THE EMPEROR'S DOING IS THE EXACT OPPO-SITE OF BEING A GUARDIAN!
OH!!
SO THEN ETHEROW WAS CHOSEN AS THE NEW CANDIDATE!

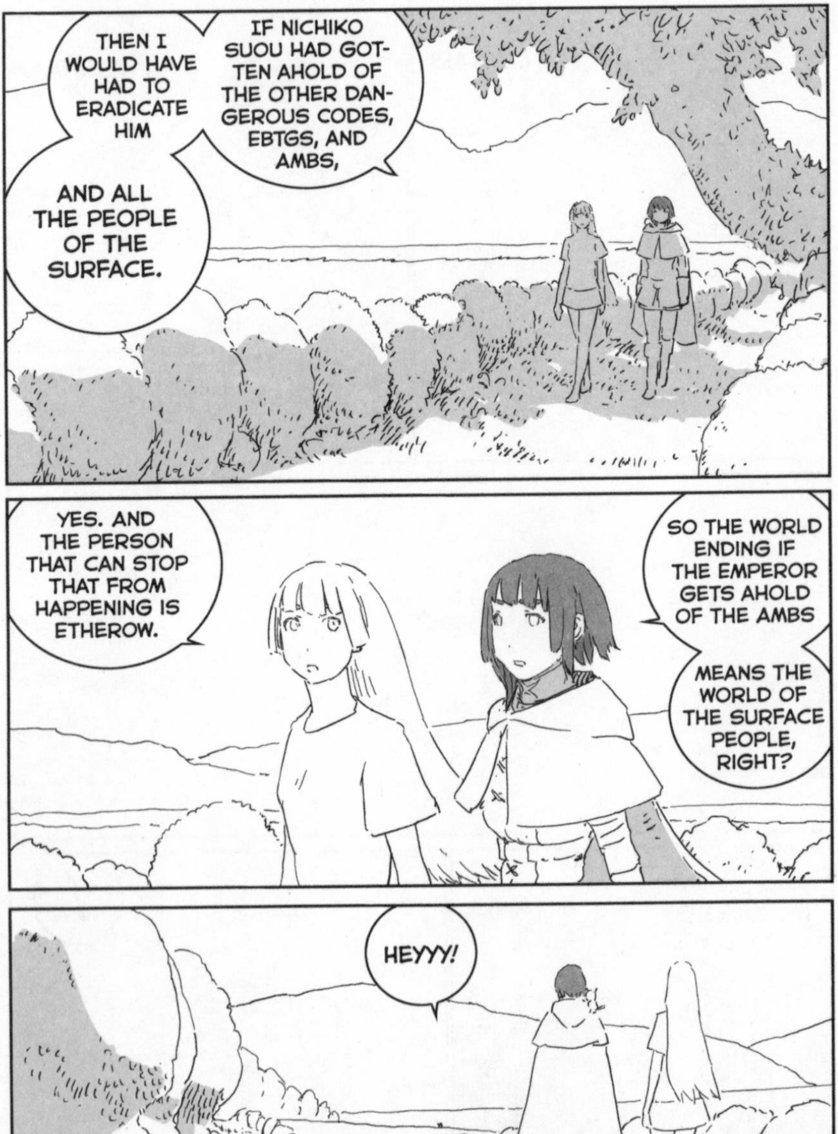
IF NICHIKO SUOU HAD GOTTEN AHOLD OF THE OTHER DANGEROUS CODES, EBTGS, AND AMBS,
THEN I WOULD HAVE HAD TO ERADICATE HIM
AND ALL THE PEOPLE OF THE SURFACE.
SO THE WORLD ENDING IF THE EMPEROR GETS AHOLD OF THE AMBS
MEANS THE WORLD OF THE SURFACE PEOPLE, RIGHT?
YES. AND THE PERSON THAT CAN STOP THAT FROM HAPPENING IS ETHEROW.
HEYYY!

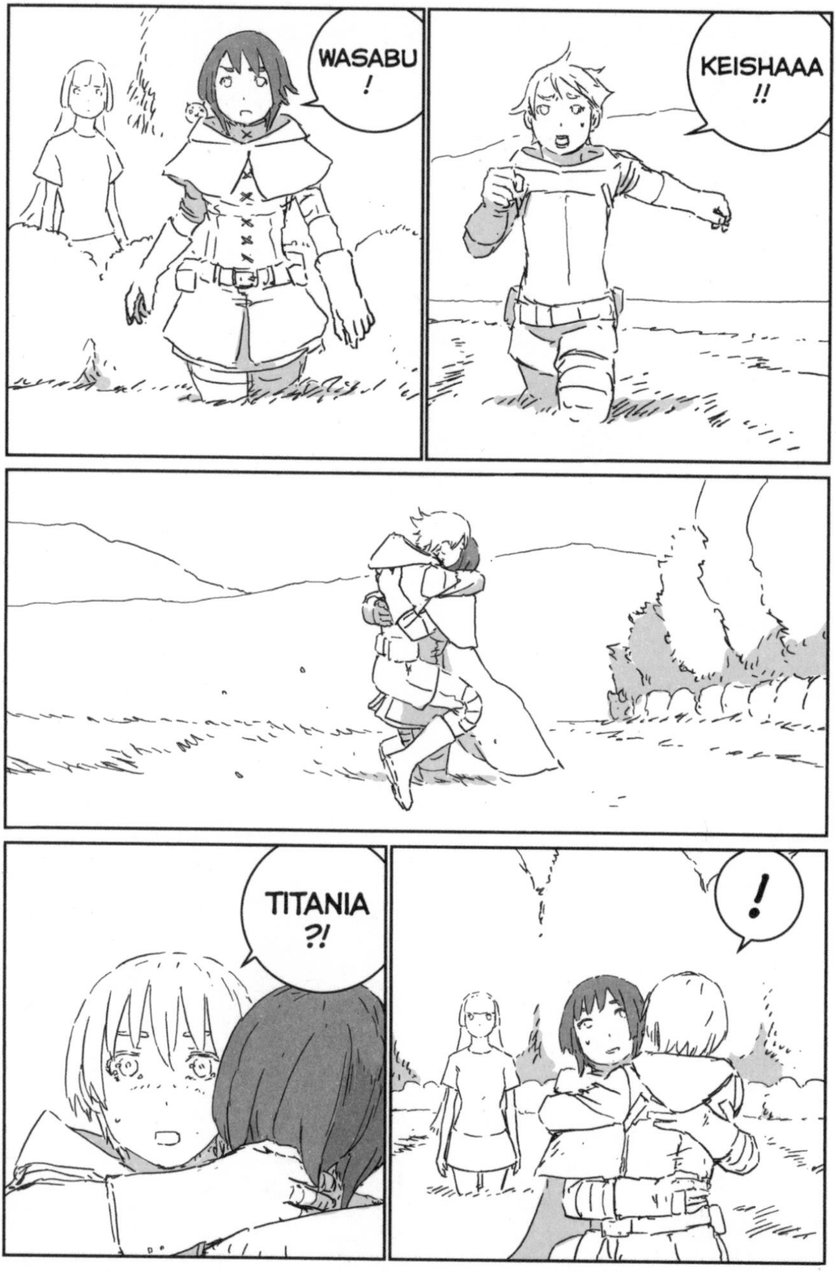
KEISHAAA !!
WASABU !
!
TITANIA ?!

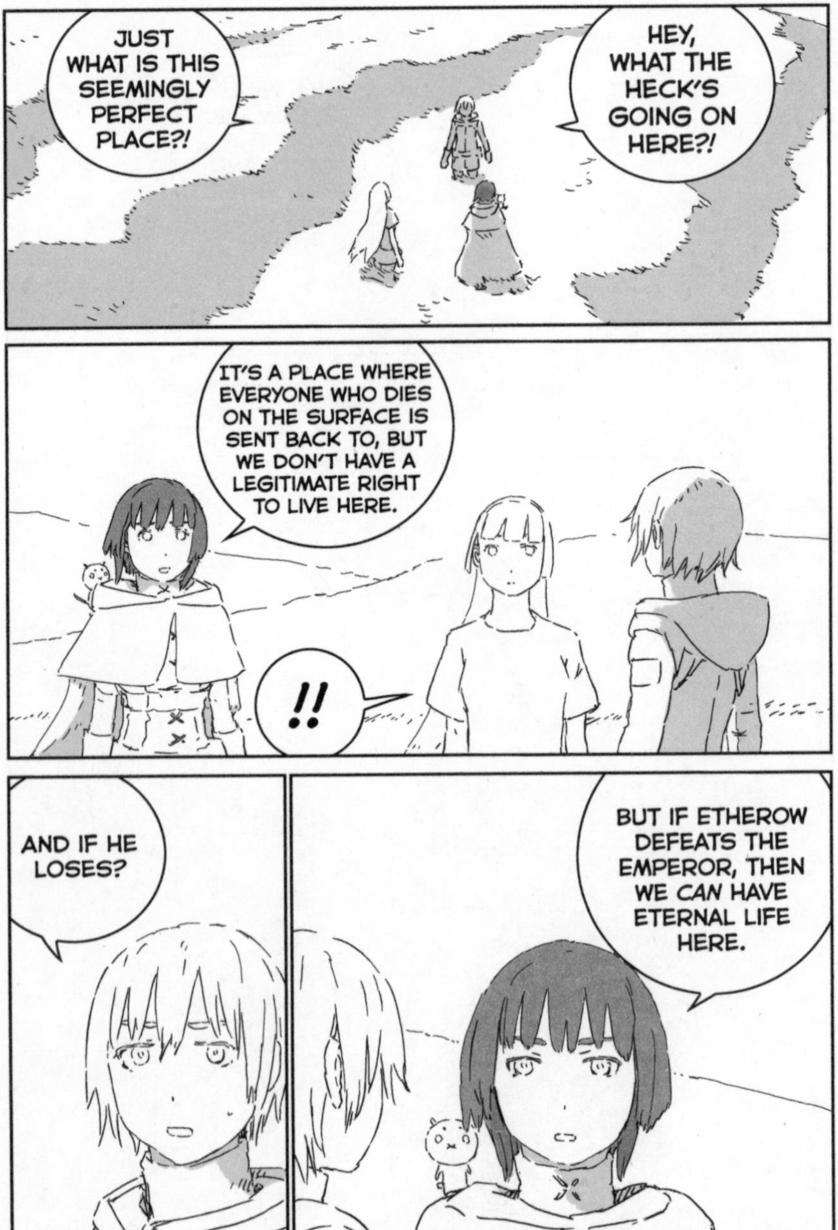
HEY, WHAT THE HECK'S GOING ON HERE?!
JUST WHAT IS THIS SEEMINGLY PERFECT PLACE?!
IT'S A PLACE WHERE EVERYONE WHO DIES ON THE SURFACE IS SENT BACK TO, BUT WE DON'T HAVE A LEGITIMATE RIGHT TO LIVE HERE.
!!
BUT IF ETHEROW DEFEATS THE EMPEROR, THEN WE *CAN* HAVE ETERNAL LIFE HERE.
AND IF HE LOSES?

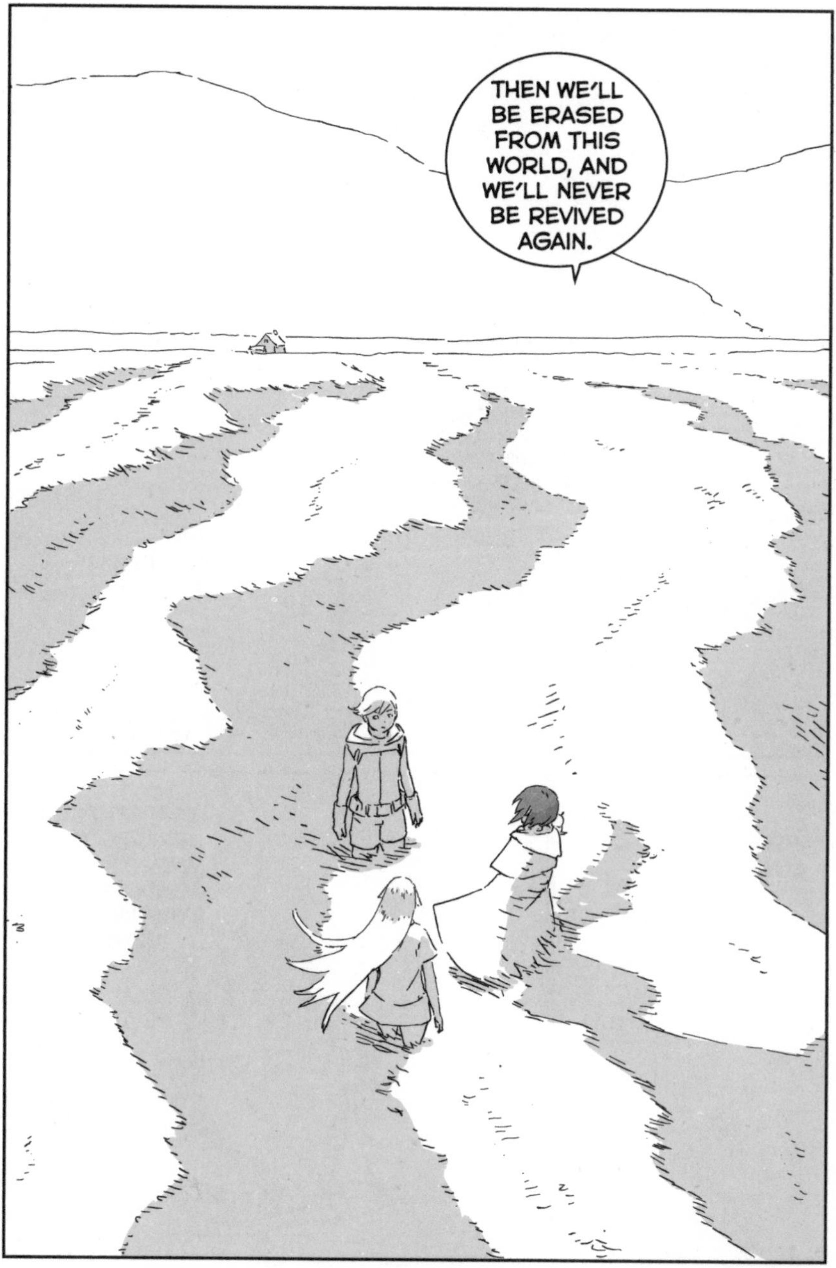
THEN WE'LL BE ERASED FROM THIS WORLD, AND WE'LL NEVER BE REVIVED AGAIN.

CHAPTER 53 END

APOSIMZ

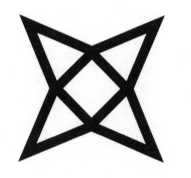

CHAPTER 54

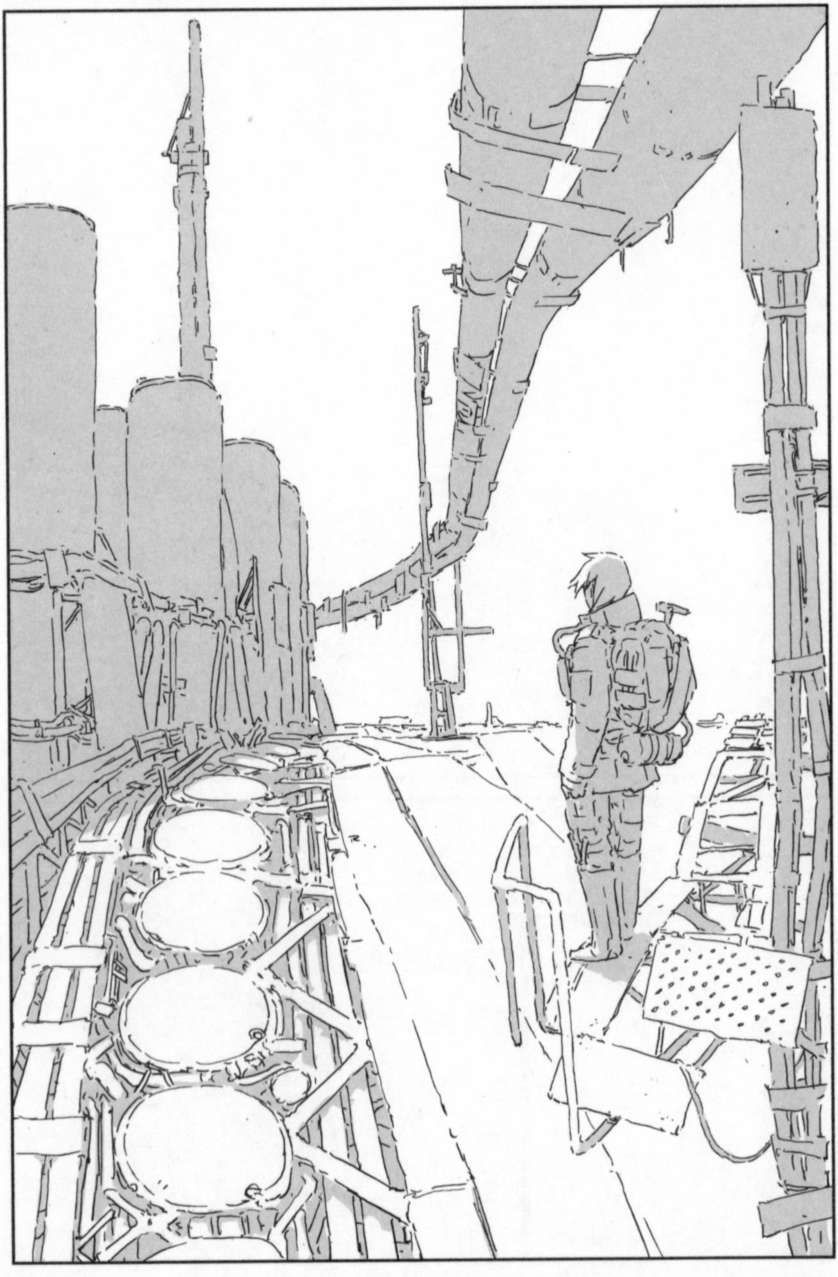

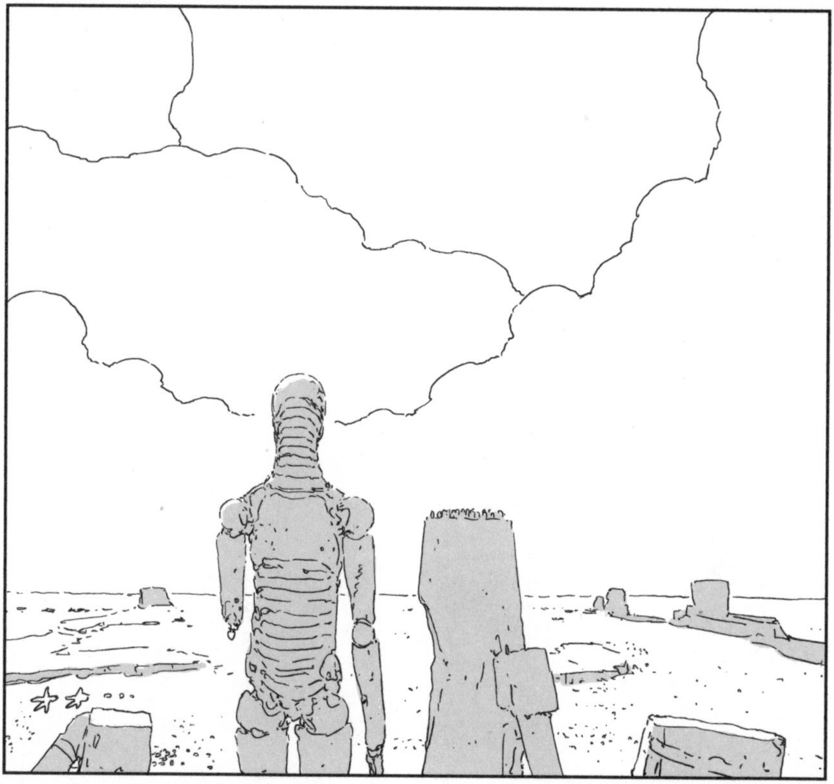

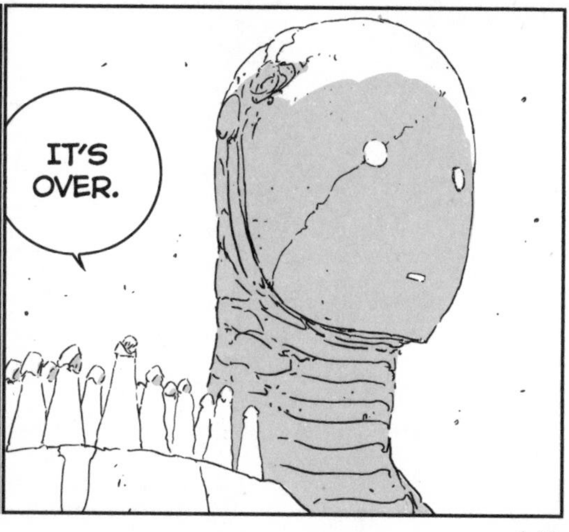
IT'S OVER.

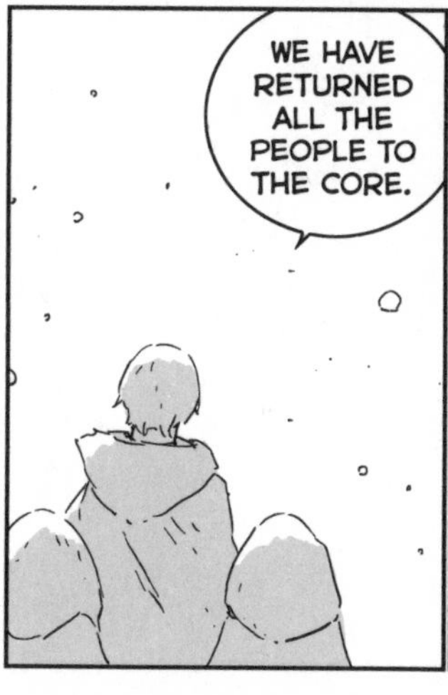
WE HAVE RETURNED ALL THE PEOPLE TO THE CORE.

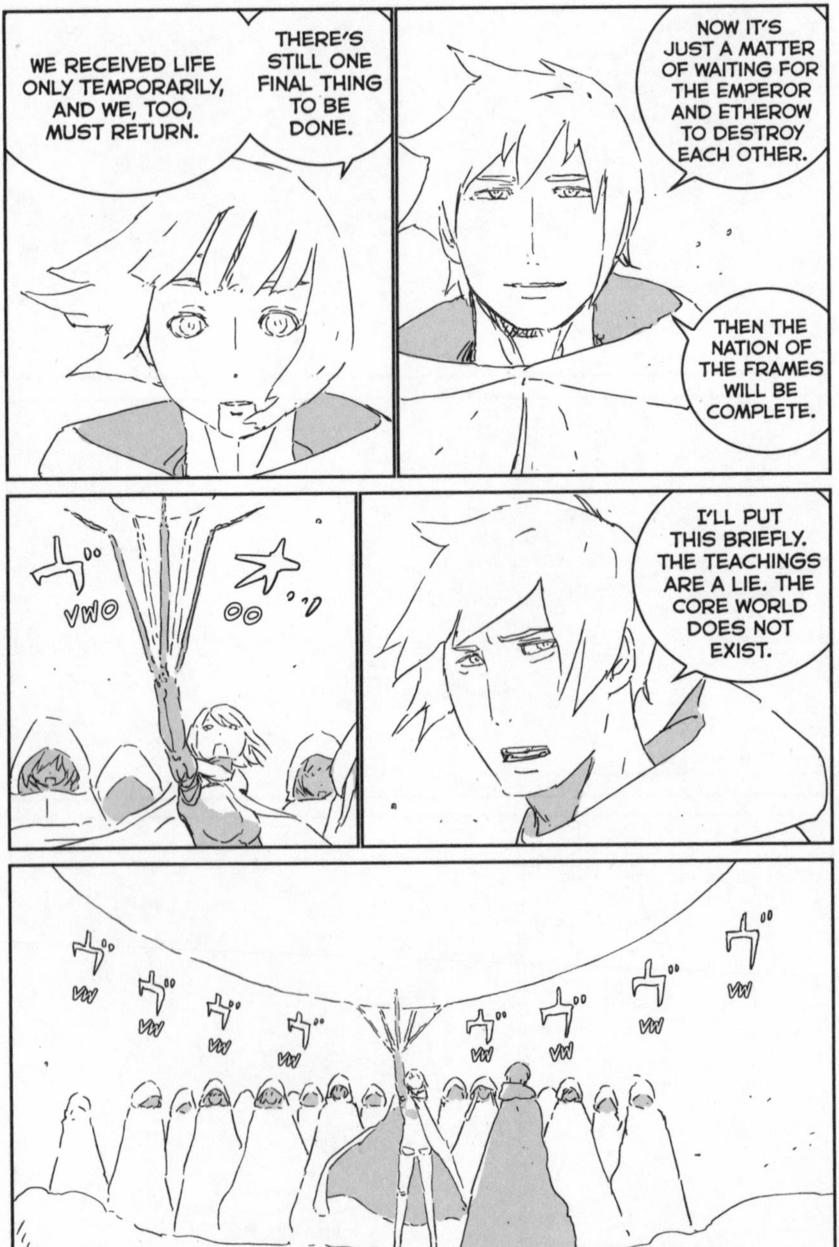

NOW IT'S JUST A MATTER OF WAITING FOR THE EMPEROR AND ETHEROW TO DESTROY EACH OTHER.
THEN THE NATION OF THE FRAMES WILL BE COMPLETE.
THERE'S STILL ONE FINAL THING TO BE DONE.
WE RECEIVED LIFE ONLY TEMPORARILY, AND WE, TOO, MUST RETURN.
I'LL PUT THIS BRIEFLY. THE TEACHINGS ARE A LIE. THE CORE WORLD DOES NOT EXIST.
OO
VWO
VW
VW
VW
VW
VW
VW
VW
VW

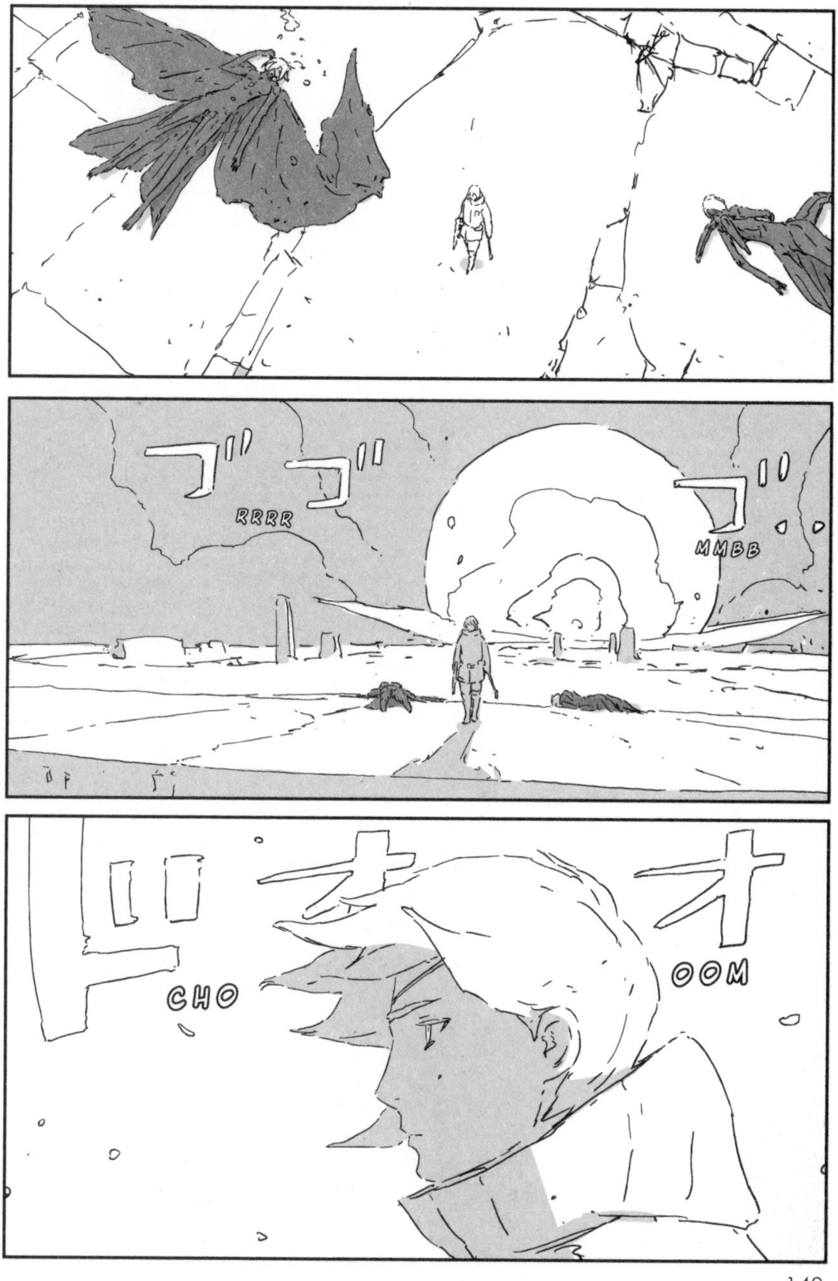
ゴゴ
RRRR
ゴ
MMBB
ドオオ
CHO
OOM

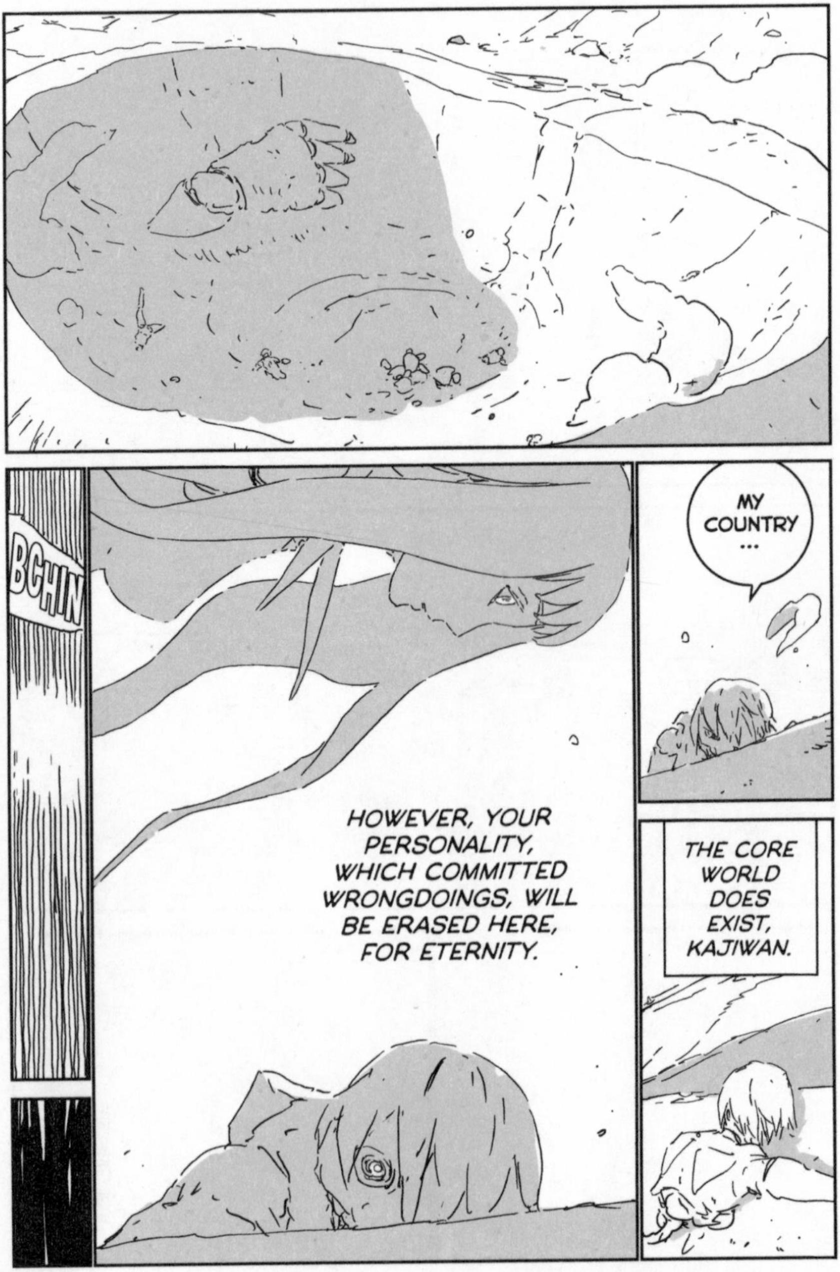
MY COUNTRY ...
THE CORE WORLD DOES EXIST, KAJIWAN.
HOWEVER, YOUR PERSONALITY, WHICH COMMITTED WRONGDOINGS, WILL BE ERASED HERE, FOR ETERNITY.
BCHIN

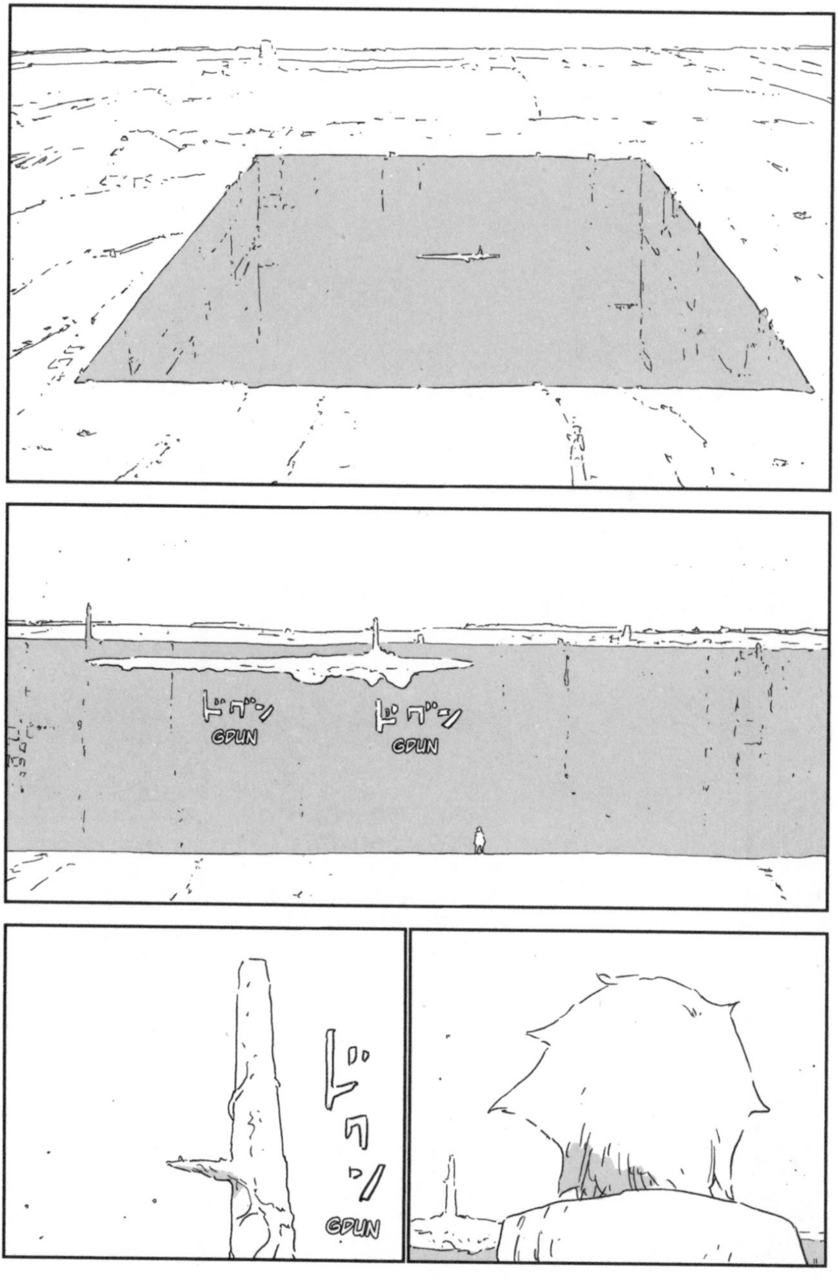
ドグン
GDUN
ドグン
GDUN
ドクン
GDUN

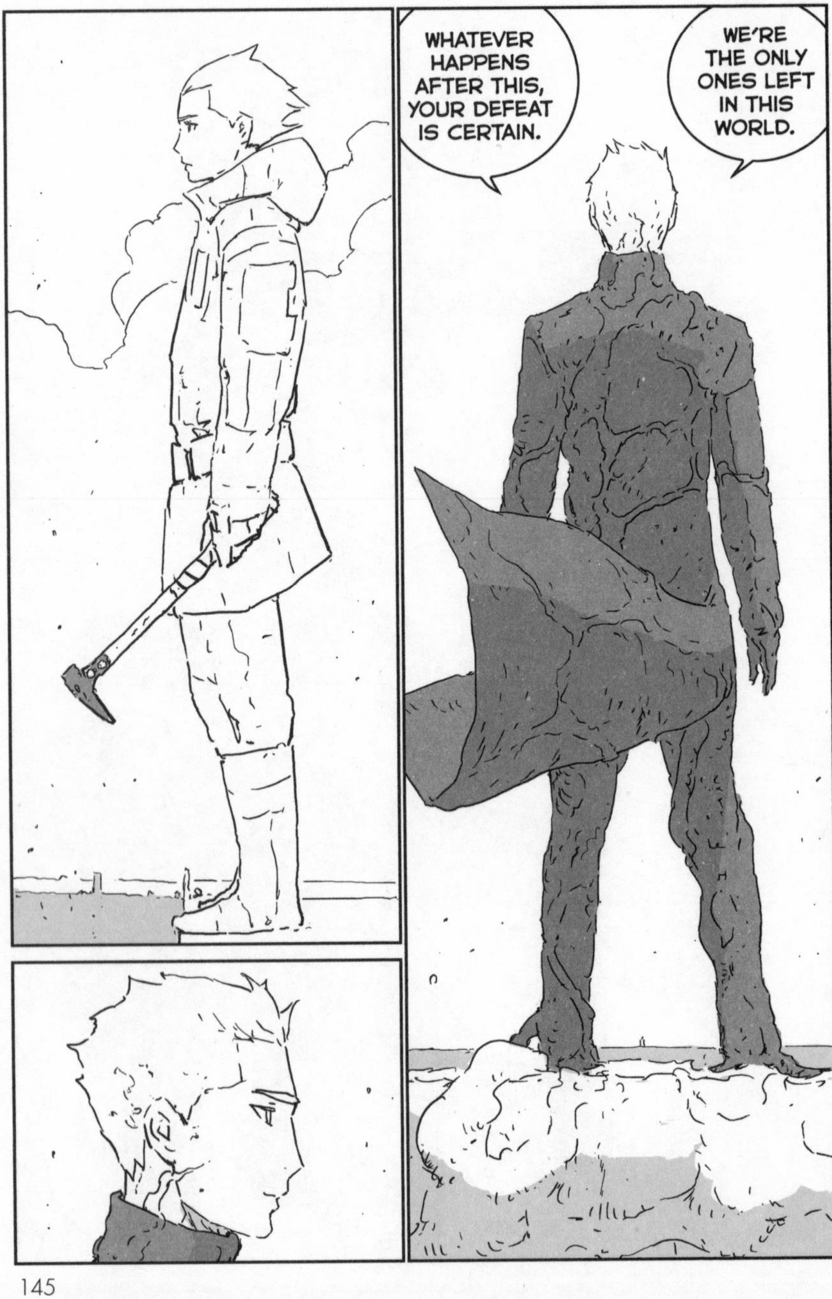
WE'RE THE ONLY ONES LEFT IN THIS WORLD.
WHATEVER HAPPENS AFTER THIS, YOUR DEFEAT IS CERTAIN.

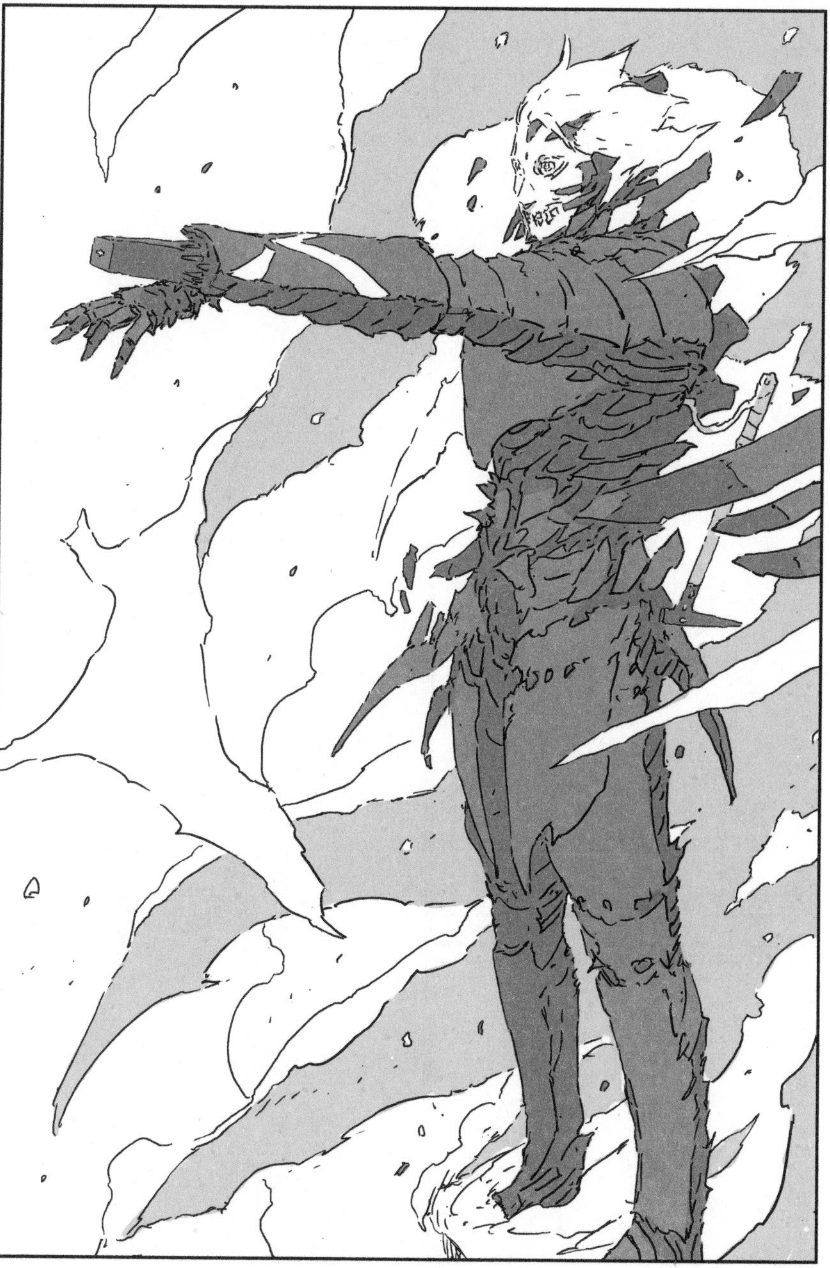

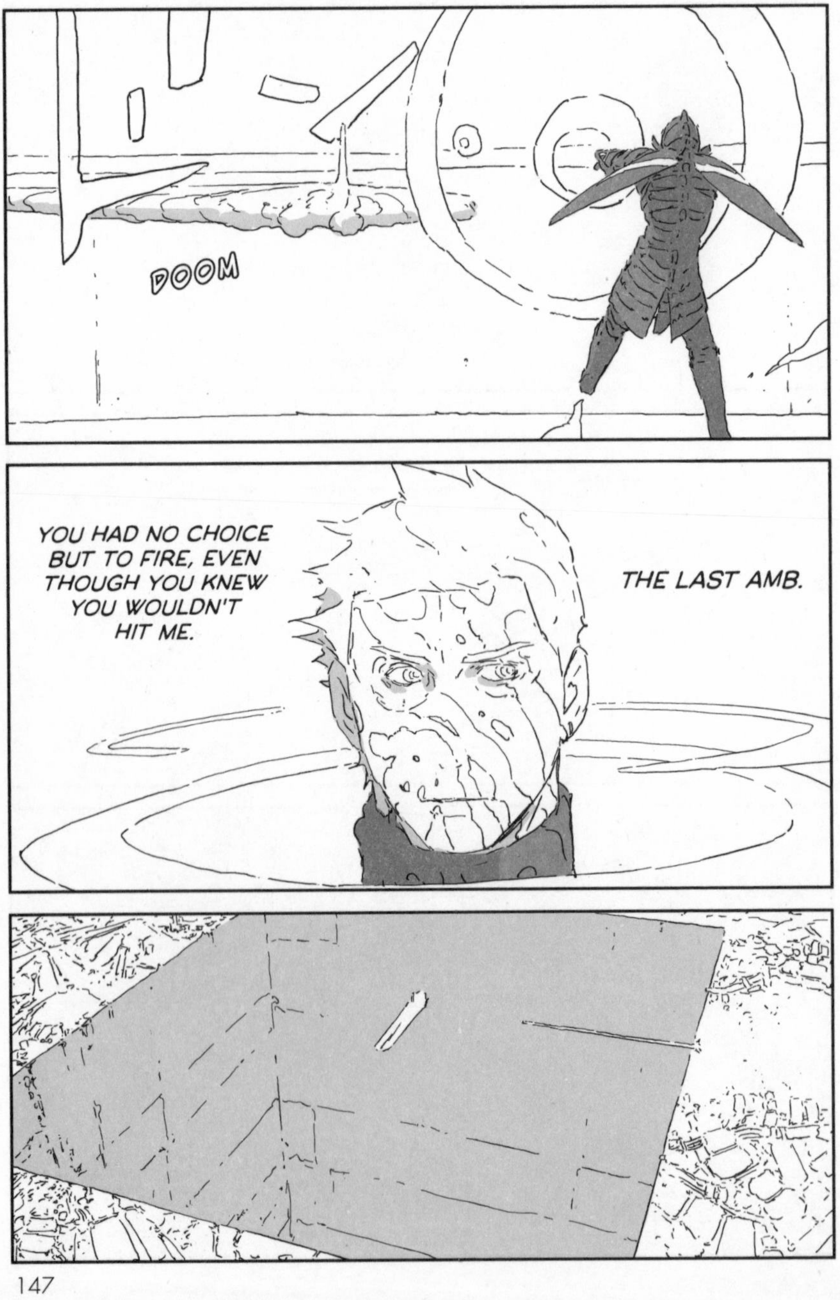
DOOM
THE LAST AMB.
YOU HAD NO CHOICE BUT TO FIRE, EVEN THOUGH YOU KNEW YOU WOULDN'T HIT ME.

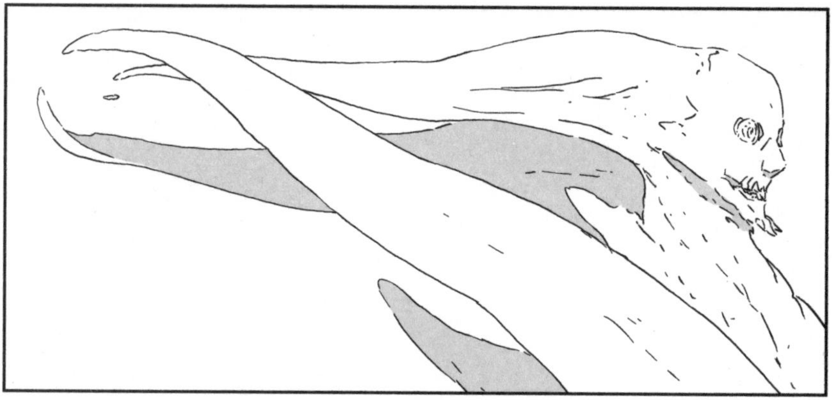
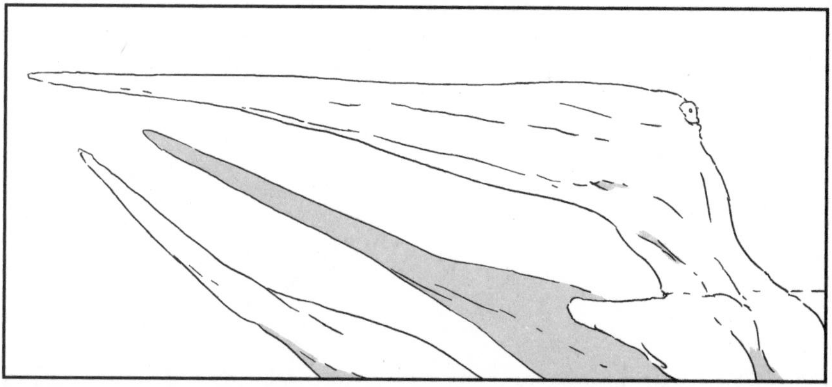
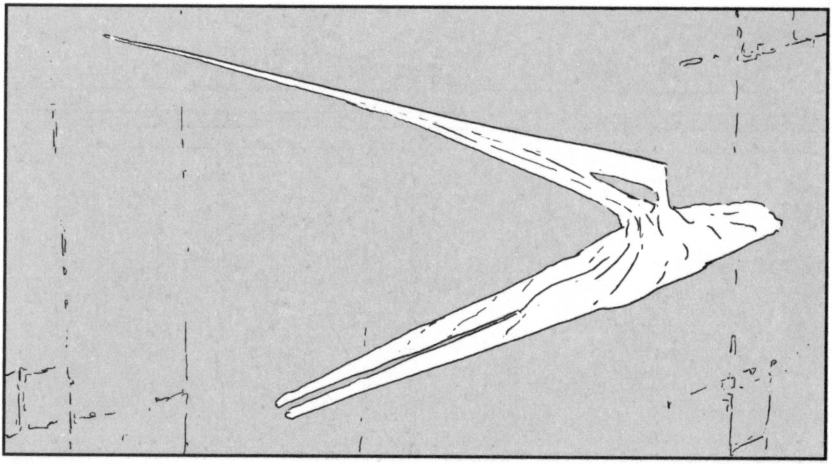

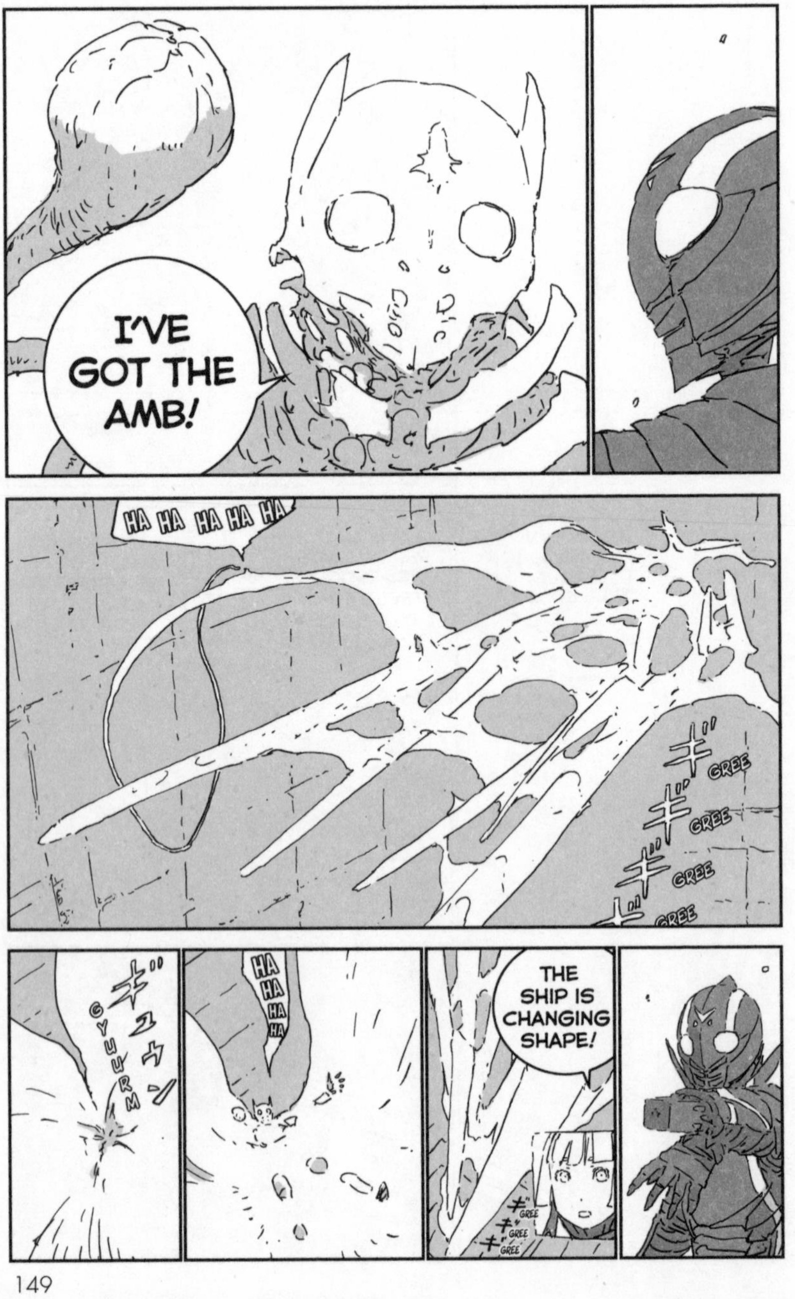
I'VE GOT THE AMB!
HA HA HA HA HA
GREE
GREE
GREE
GREE
THE SHIP IS CHANGING SHAPE!
GREE
GREE
GREE
HA HA HA HA
GYUURM

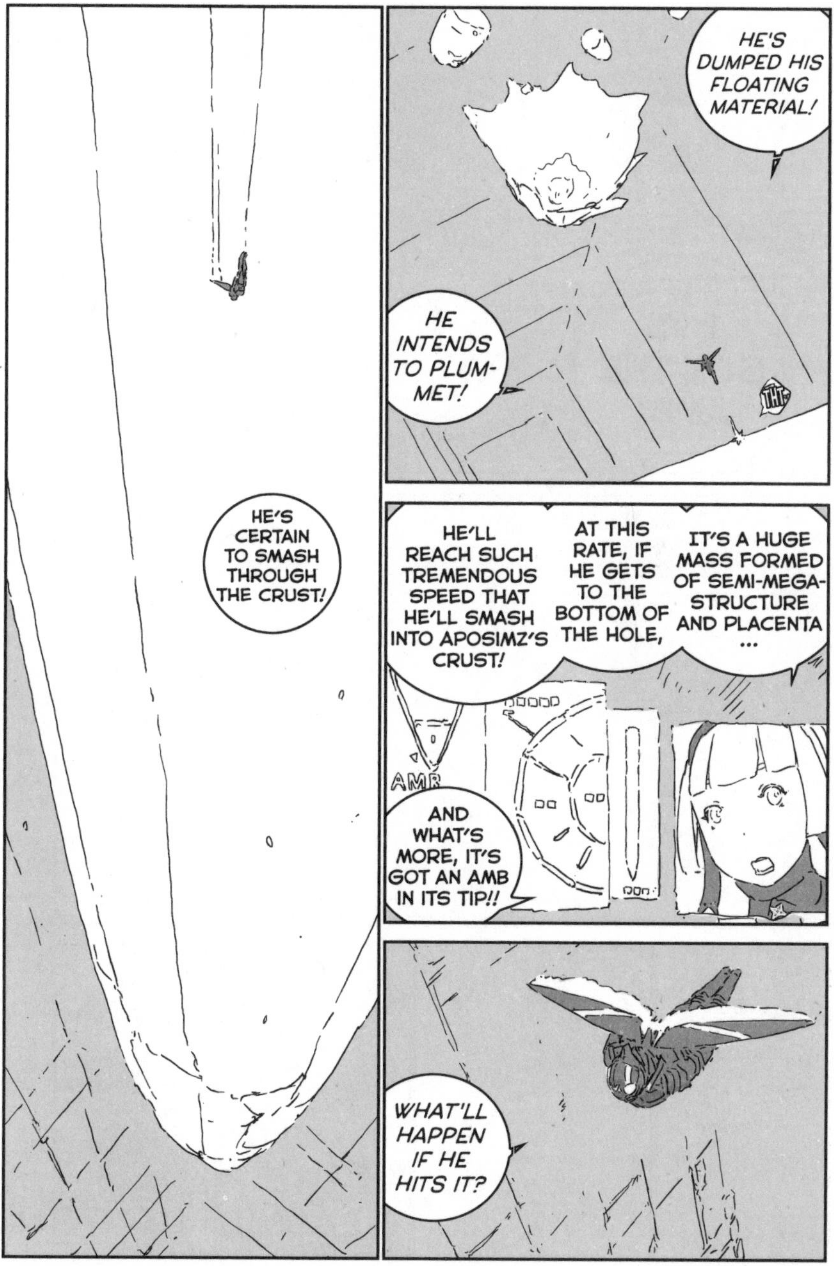
HE'S DUMPED HIS FLOATING MATERIAL!
HE INTENDS TO PLUM-MET!
THT
IT'S A HUGE MASS FORMED OF SEMI-MEGA-STRUCTURE AND PLACENTA ...
AT THIS RATE, IF HE GETS TO THE BOTTOM OF THE HOLE,
HE'LL REACH SUCH TREMENDOUS SPEED THAT HE'LL SMASH INTO APOSIMZ'S CRUST!
AND WHAT'S MORE, IT'S GOT AN AMB IN ITS TIP!!
WHAT'LL HAPPEN IF HE HITS IT?
HE'S CERTAIN TO SMASH THROUGH THE CRUST!

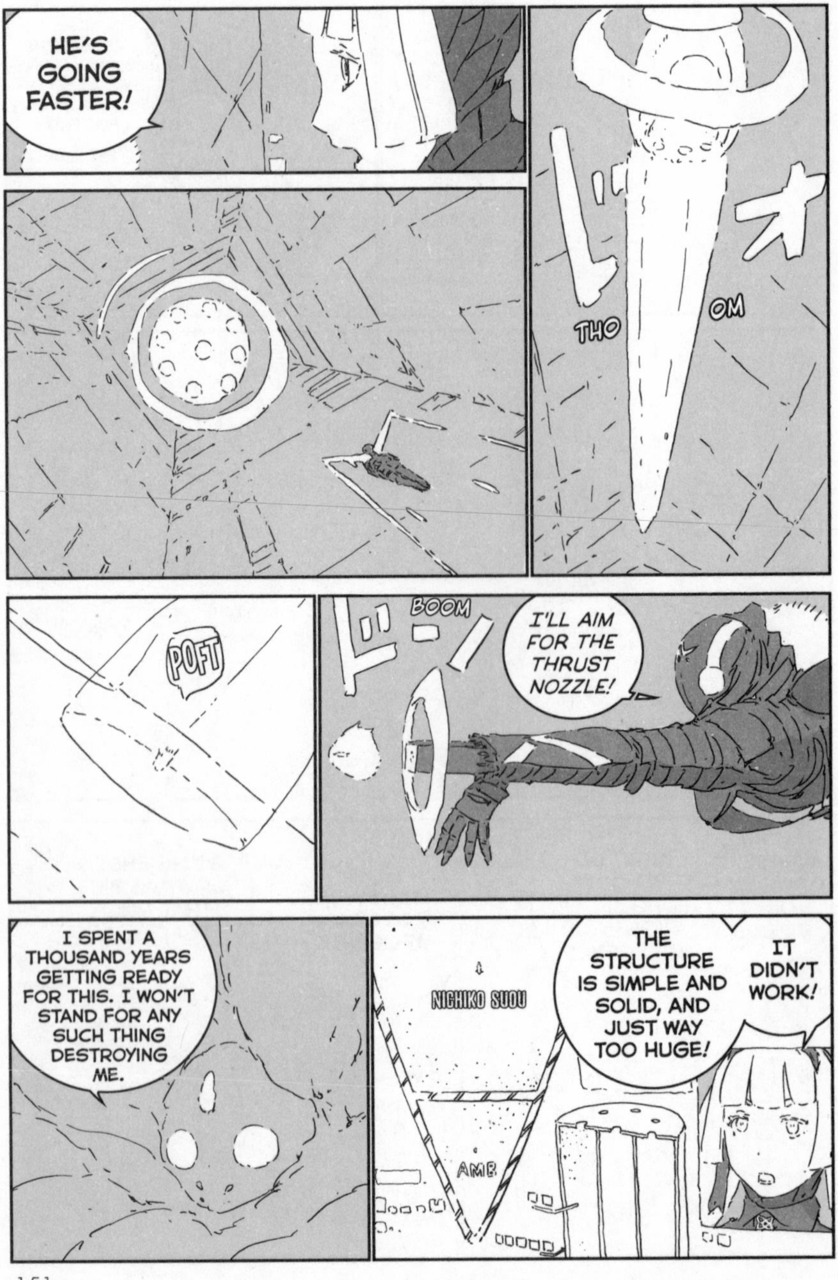
THO
OM
HE'S GOING FASTER!
BOOM
I'LL AIM FOR THE THRUST NOZZLE!
POFT
IT DIDN'T WORK!
THE STRUCTURE IS SIMPLE AND SOLID, AND JUST WAY TOO HUGE!
NICHIKO SUOU
AMB
I SPENT A THOUSAND YEARS GETTING READY FOR THIS. I WON'T STAND FOR ANY SUCH THING DESTROYING ME.

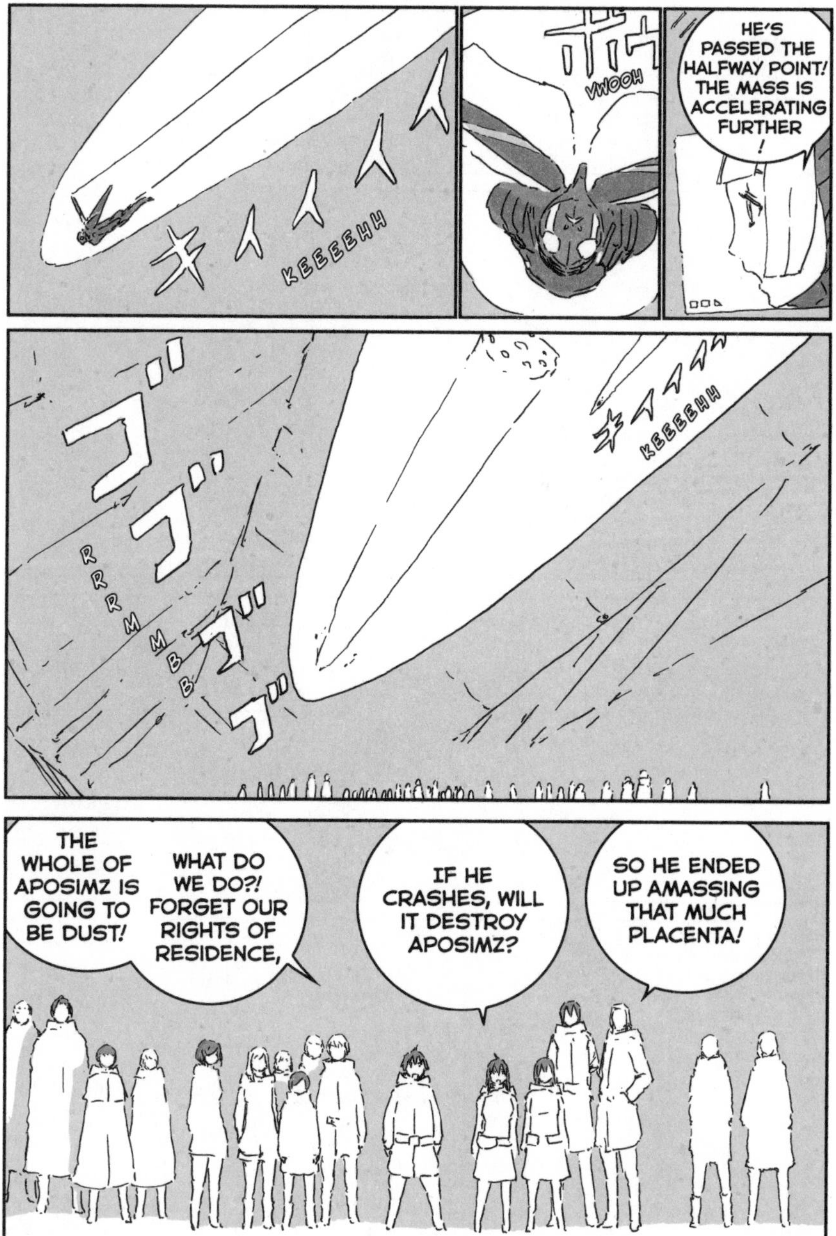
HE'S PASSED THE HALFWAY POINT! THE MASS IS ACCELERATING FURTHER!
VWOOH
KEEEEHH
KEEEEHH
RRRMMBB
SO HE ENDED UP AMASSING THAT MUCH PLACENTA!
IF HE CRASHES, WILL IT DESTROY APOSIMZ?
WHAT DO WE DO?! FORGET OUR RIGHTS OF RESIDENCE,
THE WHOLE OF APOSIMZ IS GOING TO BE DUST!

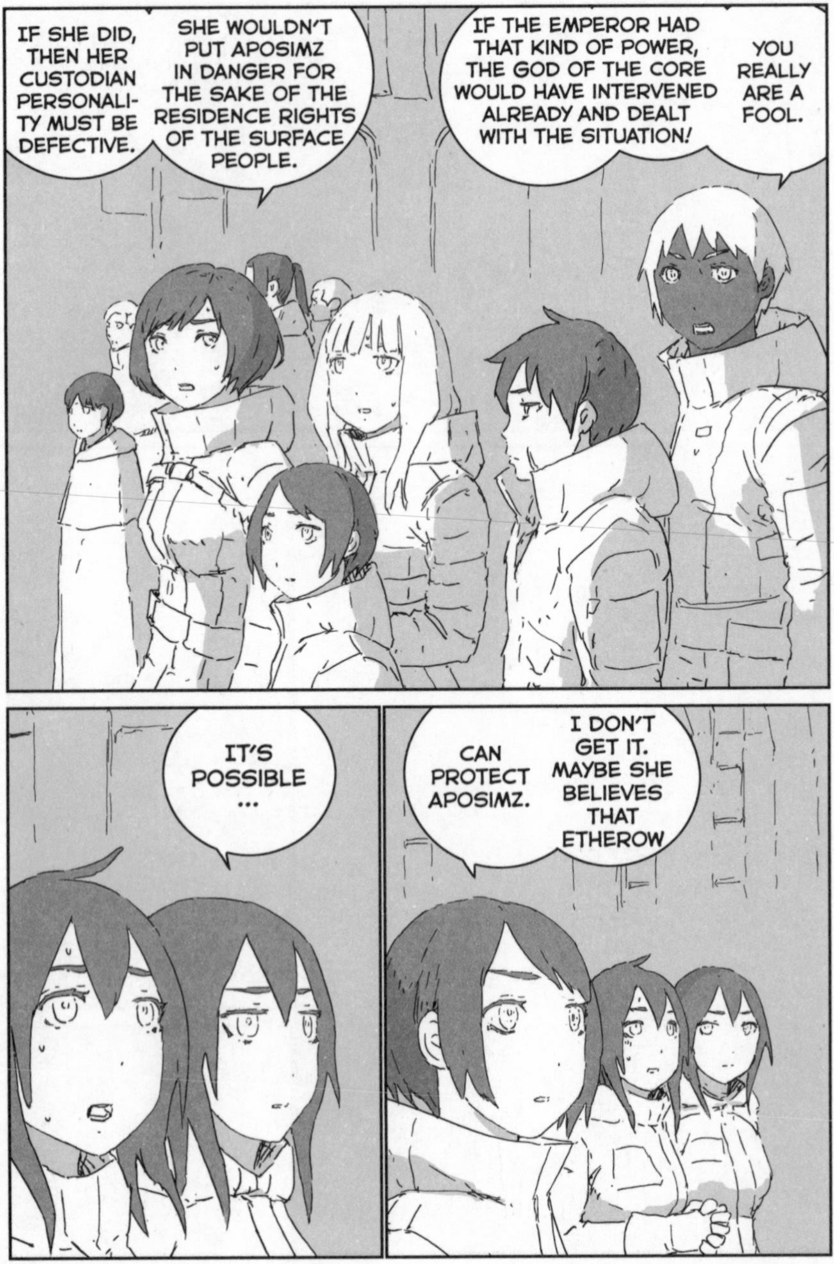

YOU REALLY ARE A FOOL.
IF THE EMPEROR HAD THAT KIND OF POWER, THE GOD OF THE CORE WOULD HAVE INTERVENED ALREADY AND DEALT WITH THE SITUATION!
SHE WOULDN'T PUT APOSIMZ IN DANGER FOR THE SAKE OF THE RESIDENCE RIGHTS OF THE SURFACE PEOPLE.
IF SHE DID, THEN HER CUSTODIAN PERSONALI-TY MUST BE DEFECTIVE.
I DON'T GET IT. MAYBE SHE BELIEVES THAT ETHEROW
CAN PROTECT APOSIMZ.
IT'S POSSIBLE ...

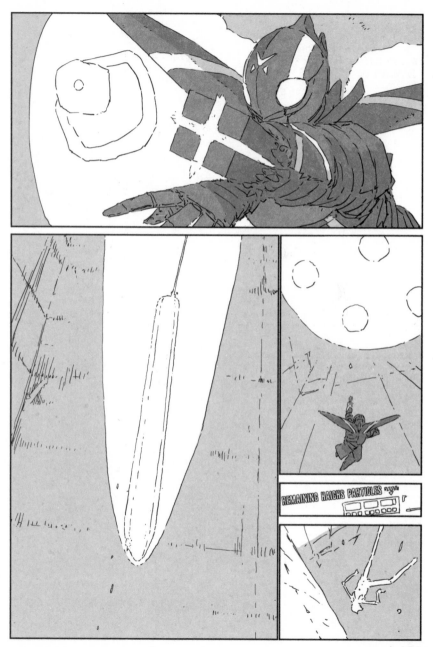

REMAINING HAICHS PARTICLES *rush*

154

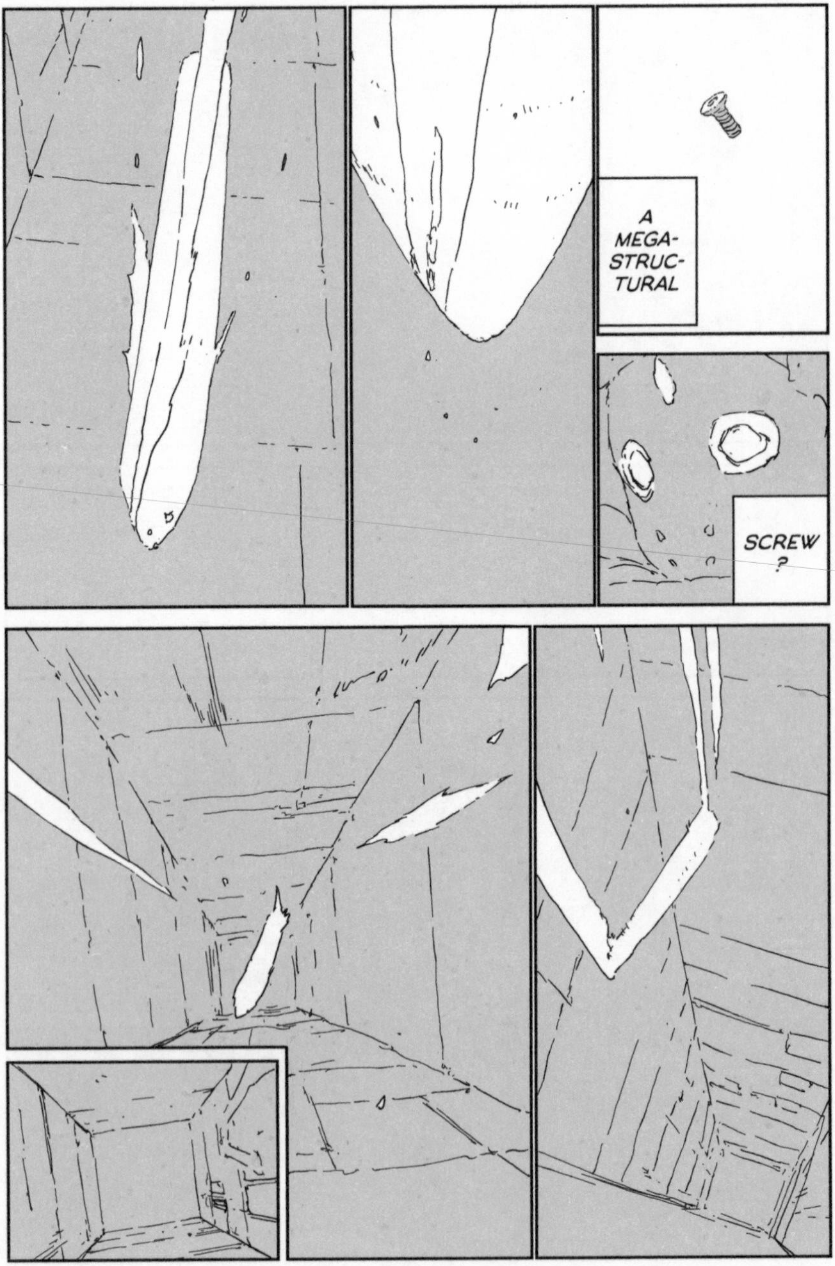
A MEGA-STRUCTURAL
SCREW ?

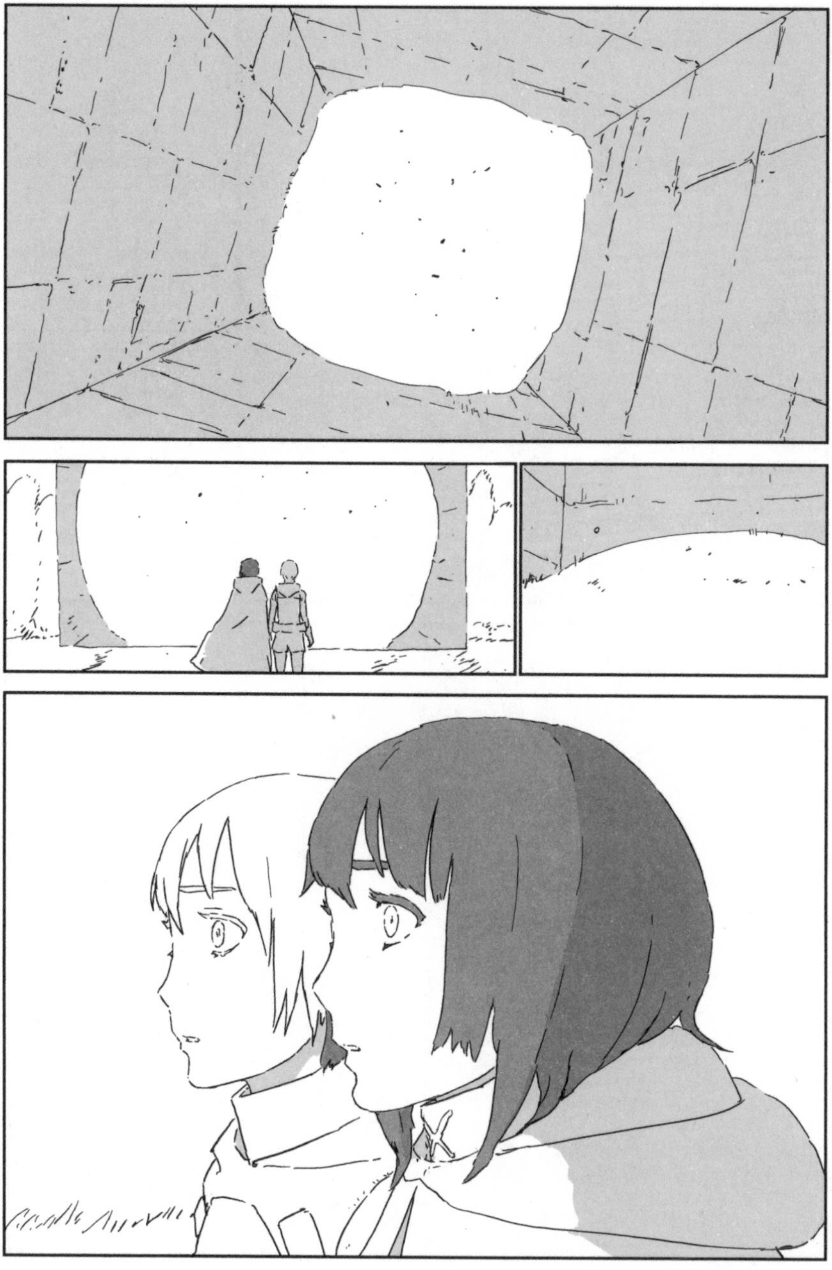

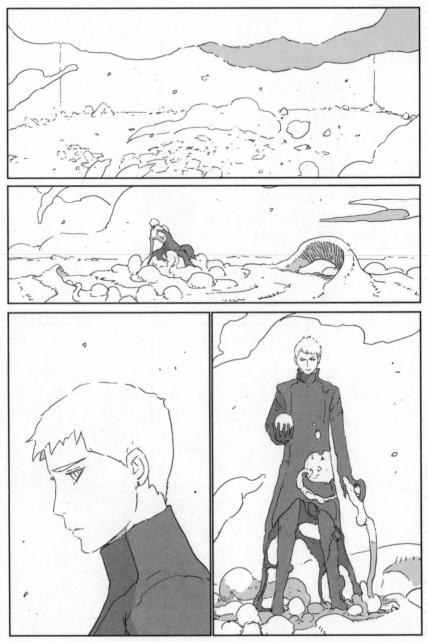

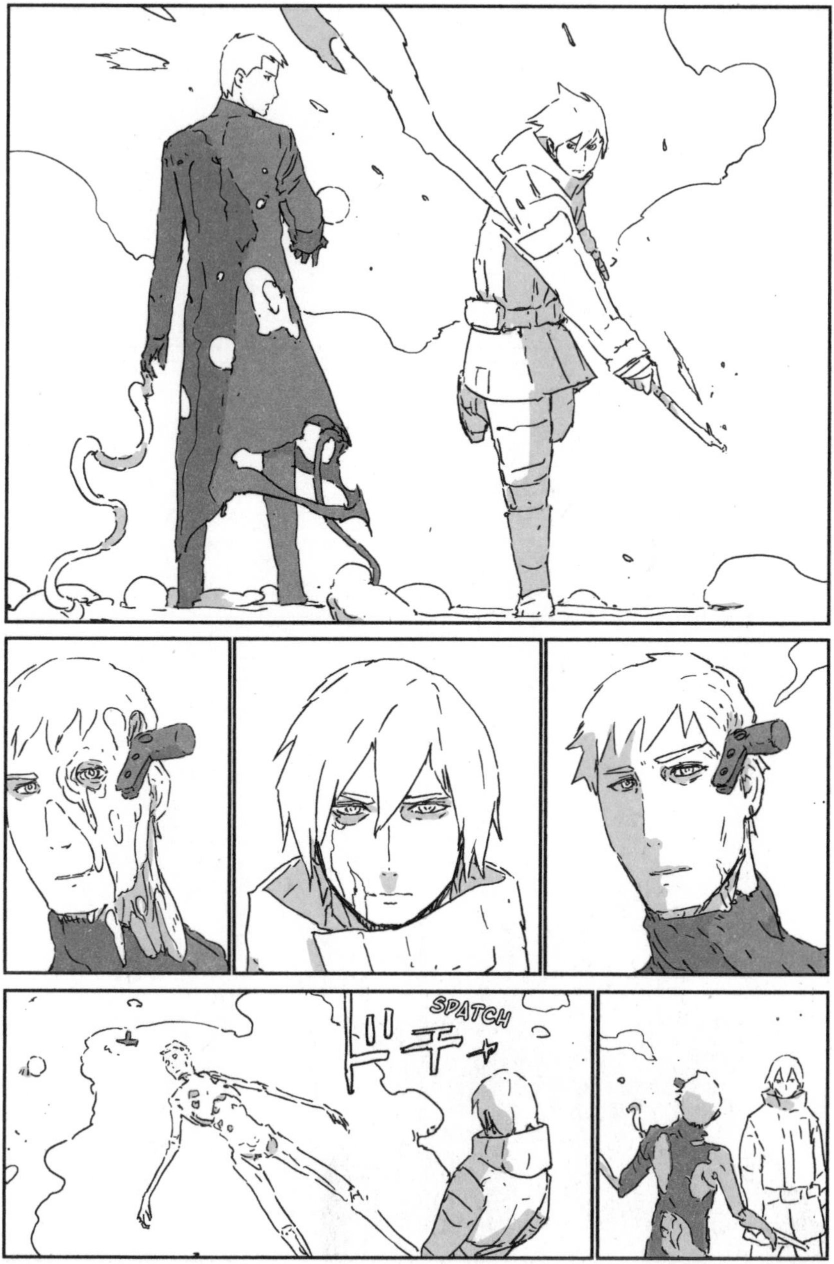
SPATCH
ピチャ

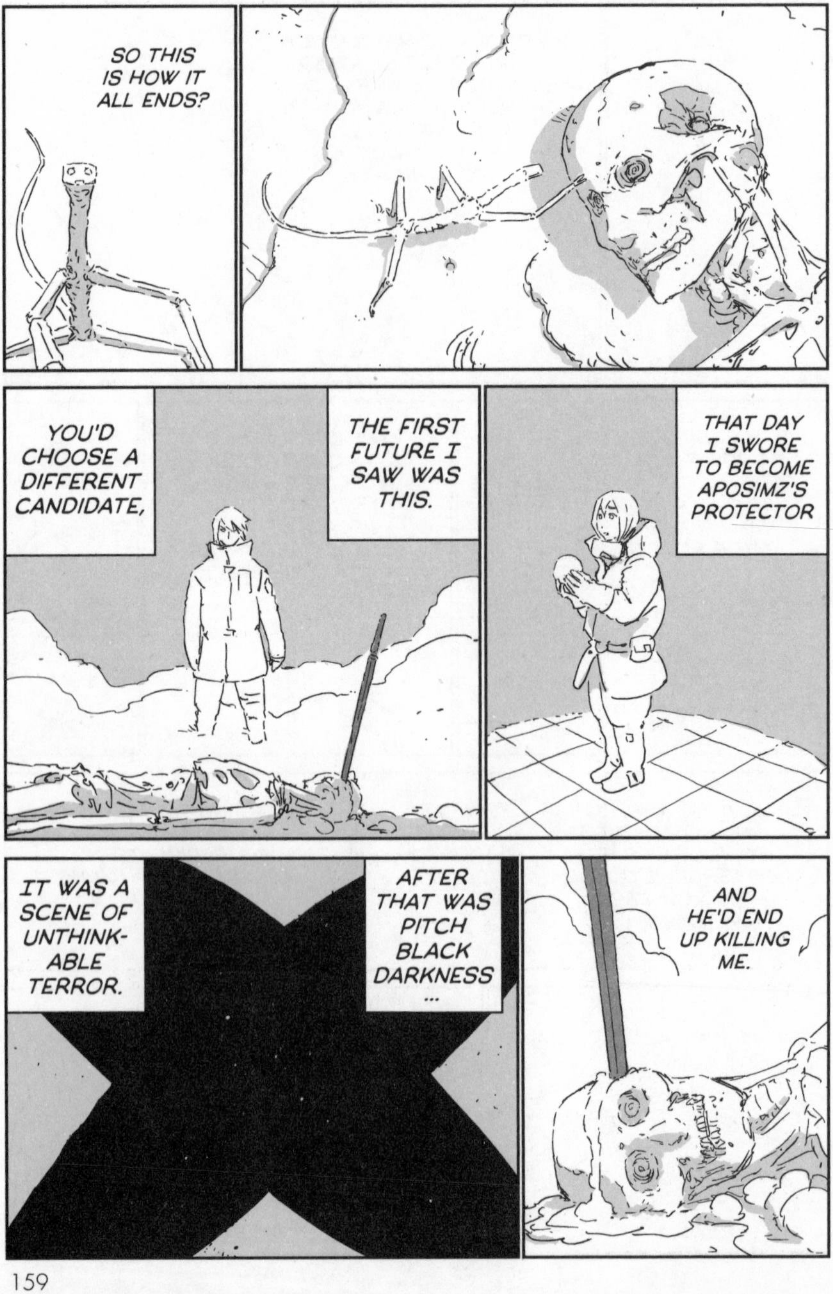
SO THIS IS HOW IT ALL ENDS?
THAT DAY I SWORE TO BECOME APOSIMZ'S PROTECTOR
THE FIRST FUTURE I SAW WAS THIS.
YOU'D CHOOSE A DIFFERENT CANDIDATE,
AND HE'D END UP KILLING ME.
AFTER THAT WAS PITCH BLACK DARKNESS ...
IT WAS A SCENE OF UNTHINK-ABLE TERROR.

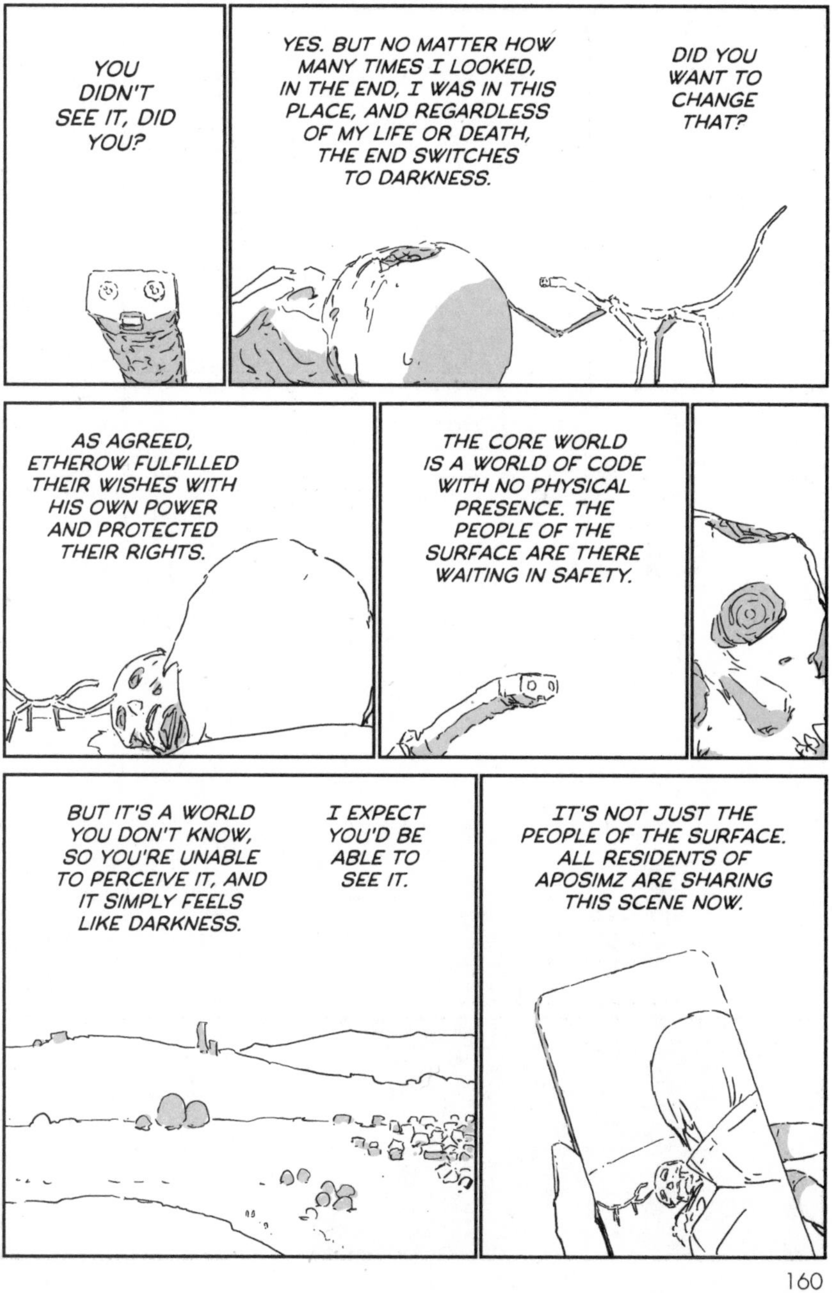
DID YOU WANT TO CHANGE THAT?
YES. BUT NO MATTER HOW MANY TIMES I LOOKED, IN THE END, I WAS IN THIS PLACE, AND REGARDLESS OF MY LIFE OR DEATH, THE END SWITCHES TO DARKNESS.
YOU DIDN'T SEE IT, DID YOU?
THE CORE WORLD IS A WORLD OF CODE WITH NO PHYSICAL PRESENCE. THE PEOPLE OF THE SURFACE ARE THERE WAITING IN SAFETY.
AS AGREED, ETHEROW FULFILLED THEIR WISHES WITH HIS OWN POWER AND PROTECTED THEIR RIGHTS.
IT'S NOT JUST THE PEOPLE OF THE SURFACE. ALL RESIDENTS OF APOSIMZ ARE SHARING THIS SCENE NOW.
I EXPECT YOU'D BE ABLE TO SEE IT.
BUT IT'S A WORLD YOU DON'T KNOW, SO YOU'RE UNABLE TO PERCEIVE IT, AND IT SIMPLY FEELS LIKE DARKNESS.

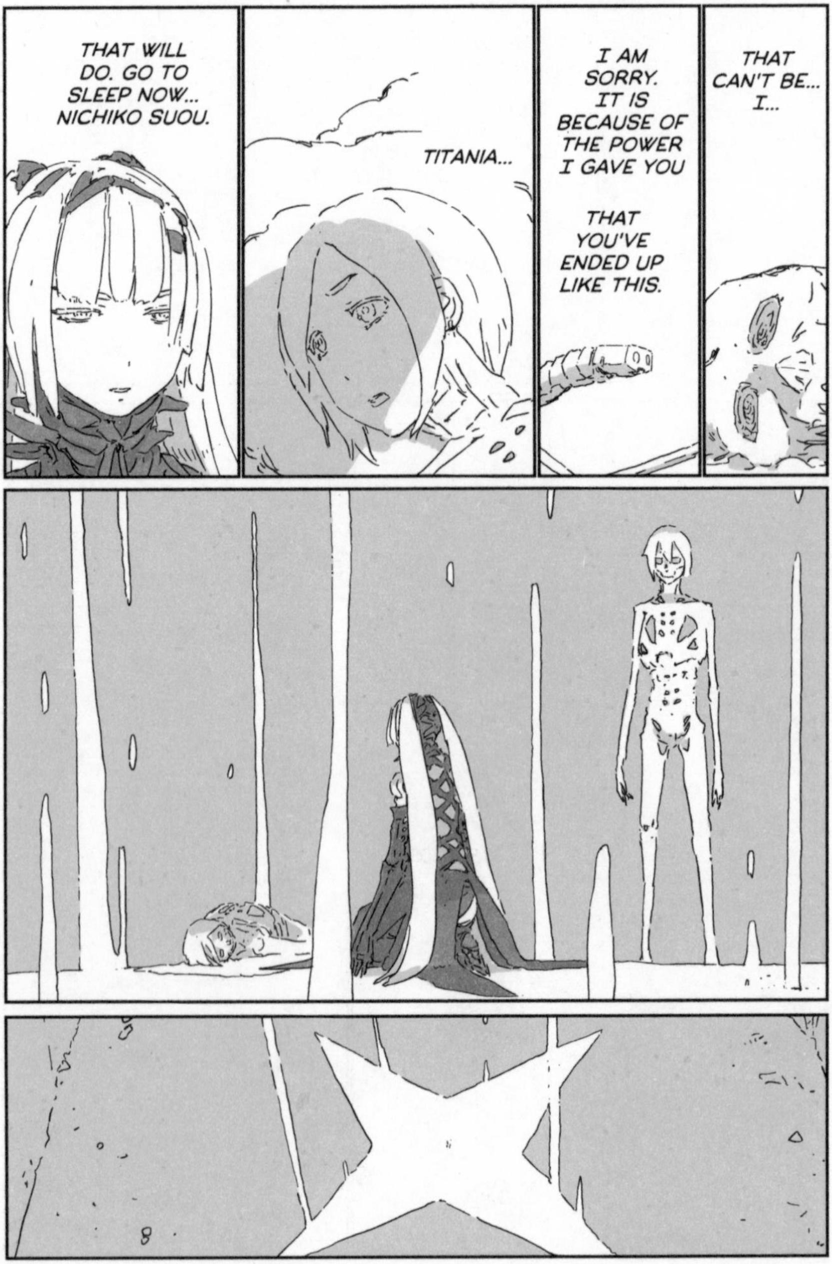
THAT CAN'T BE... I...
I AM SORRY. IT IS BECAUSE OF THE POWER I GAVE YOU
THAT YOU'VE ENDED UP LIKE THIS.
TITANIA...
THAT WILL DO. GO TO SLEEP NOW... NICHIKO SUOU.

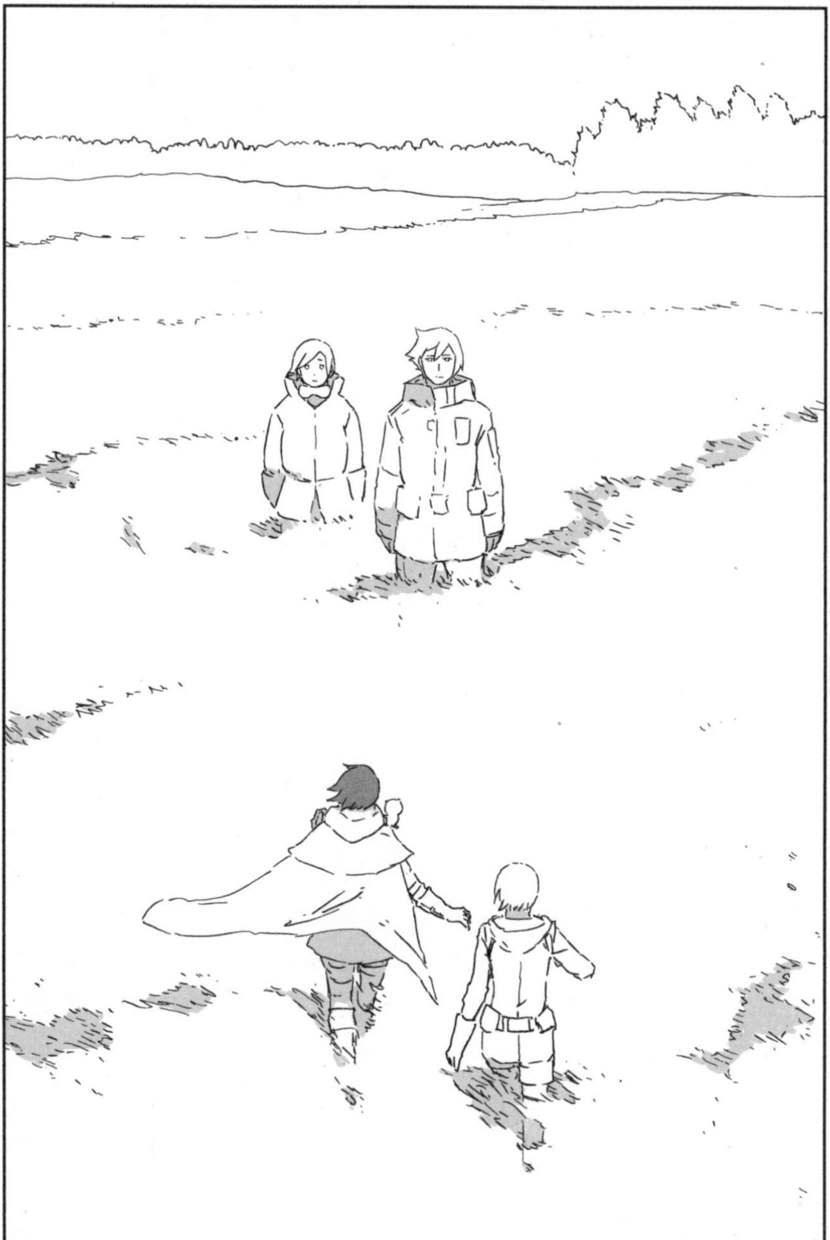

APOSIMZ
END

‖‖ ‖ ‖‖‖‖‖‖ ‖‖ ‖ ‖ ‖ ‖‖‖‖‖‖‖‖‖‖‖‖‖‖ ‖‖

W9-BIR-933

APOSIMZ volume 9

A Vertical Comics Edition

Translation: Kumar Sivasubramanian
Production: Grace Lu
             Shirley Fang
             Darren Smith

Copyright © 2021 Tsutomu Nihei. All rights reserved.
First published in Japan in 2021 by Kodansha, Ltd., Tokyo
Publication for this English edition arranged through Kodansha, Ltd., Tokyo
English language version produced by Vertical Comics,
an imprint of Kodansha USA Publishing, LLC

Translation provided by Vertical Comics, 2022
Published by Kodansha USA Publishing, LLC, New York

Originally published in Japanese as *APOSIMZ 9* by Kodansha, Ltd.
APOSIMZ first serialized in *Monthly Shonen Sirius*, Kodansha, Ltd., 2017-2021

This is a work of fiction.

ISBN: 978-1-64729-100-6

Printed in Canada

First Edition

Kodansha USA Publishing, LLC
451 Park Avenue South
7th Floor
New York, NY 10016
www.kodansha.us

Vertical books are distributed through Penguin-Random House Publisher Services.